The Powers of Music

Plate 1. From George Bickham's *The Musical Entertainer* (London, 1740)

The Powers of Music

AESTHETIC THEORY AND THE INVENTION OF OPERA

Ruth Katz

WITH A NEW INTRODUCTION BY THE AUTHOR

Transaction Publishers
New Brunswick (U.S.A.) and London (U.K.)

Library of Congress Catalog Number: 94-1960
ISBN: 1-56000-747-8
Printed in the United States of America

Library of Congress Cataloging-in-Publication Data

Katz, Ruth, 1927-
    [Divining the powers of music]
    The powers of music: aesthetic theory and the invention of opera/Ruth Katz; with a new introduction by the author.
    p.   cm.
    Originally published: Divining the powers of music: aesthetic theory and the origins of opera. New York: Pendragon Press, c1986, in: Aesthetics in music series.
    Includes bibliographical references and index.
    ISBN 1-56000-747-8
    1. Music—Philosophy and aesthetics. 2. Opera. 3. Opera—Italy. I. Title.
ML3858.K32   1994
782.1'09—dc20   94-1960
                                                      CIP

Contents

Introduction to the
Transaction Edition

This essay in cultural history conceives the institution of opera as a "laboratory" for continual exploration of the hidden powers that lurk in the interaction between words and music. Its origins in Renaissance Italy are traced to the belief of the Humanists that the magical properties of music could be harnessed; to the transition from polyphony to monody that gave musical expression to individualism; to the melodramatic propensity of Italian culture reflected in its literary and theatrical arts; and, more immediately, to the Florentine salon of burghers, aristocrats, scientists, and artists whose agenda included the challenge to rediscover how the ancient Greeks succeeded in heightening the rhetorical power of words by allying them with music.

This introduction to the Transaction edition provides an opportunity to dwell on three afterthoughts on these ideas. The first has to do with the perception that there has been a major change in the academic climate for this kind of analysis. The second relates to my present concern with the Eighteenth century expansion of the Florentine comparison of the attributes of the arts, from which music emerges as the purest of all, for being freest of external reference. Finally, I would like to reconsider my impression that opera was on the wane. I wish to take note of opera's apparent revival—perhaps because of its referentiality, that is, because it may be satisfying a renewed interest in the ostensibly outmoded expectation that music should make sense and bear meaning.

The Reframing of Cultural History

Not so long ago, academic historians of culture had to ask their colleagues' indulgence, so to speak, in order to invoke extrinsic factors for the explanation of stylistic change, generic innovation, and new cultural institutions. They considered themselves "at risk" of being labeled popularizers, Marxists, or eclectics lacking in scientific rigor, for stepping outside their disciplines to search for the economic and social forces, value orientations, or institutional arrangements that had bearing upon the problem they had chosen for study. Even the isolation of a "problem" was considered problematic by disciplinary purists whose focus was on a given "period," or on the progression of "precursors" that led to the blossoming, and then the decline, of a given style or genre. Unaware that biological models of determinism and Hegelian teleology are often implicit in evolutionary studies, efforts to grapple with problems of causality were also frowned upon.

Nowadays, the climate for work of this kind has changed considerably. Most importantly, contextual analysis is "in." Scholars are rewarded for searching wherever their problem takes them, and for equipping themselves as best they can to traverse disciplinary boundaries. It is acceptable now to piece together those fragments that create a coherent picture of a social or cultural institution, where the emphasis is not on time as simple chronology but on time and place as contexts for structuring events and relating them to each other.

This is a more sociological approach to history that searches for explanation as much as for description, for causal connections that are not simply proximate ones. It is an approach that directs us to make "tiger leaps" into linear history (to use Benjamin's phrase), in order to compare related cultural manifestations irrespective of time and place, while allowing, nevertheless, for the assessment of differences in time and place.

My re-analysis of the workings of the Florentine Camerata is an example of this kind of "leap." The interactions among the members, the competitiveness over being "first," the relations with outsiders who shared similar interests, virtually beg to be compared with the structurally analogous networks norms, invisible colleges, and paradigm shifts that characterize the early institutionalization of science. While groups like the

Camerata were occupied with questions, preferences, and experiments on the ordering of symbols, other circles were similarly occupied with the ordering of matter. Both sets of groups were alike demographically and intellectually, and both were guided in their pursuits by basic agreements on problems and methods, so much so that I venture that modern aesthetic theory emerged from the same sort of social and intellectual context—and, indeed, in the same period—that brought about the scientific revolution.

But there is an important difference between the two institutions. Whereas matter is a given (even if its description is not), nothing about a symbol is given. In their quest for the answer to "What are the powers of music?" the Camerata, in their "laboratory," began a process of *creating* the very thing they were looking for. There is nothing "out there" as far as music is concerned, even though the Camerata did not know this. They were inventing a system of symbols and investing it with meaning.

Had this project been undertaken today, it would resonate well with some of the work that is catalogued as the sociology of culture, cultural studies, and popular culture. Indeed, if the study of popular culture refers to the "beliefs and practices, and the objects through which they are organized, that are widely shared among a population," (Mukerji and Schudson, 1991), then the emergence of opera in Italy falls squarely in this domain. As Leo Braudy (1993) notes in his introduction to the new opera, *Marilyn*, "the American dream of opera as an exclusive high culture realm is a prejudice based primarily on language differences. In Italy, of course, opera is popular culture. Any Ligurian farmer or Milanese mechanic can quote his favorites at length just as in Greece, audiences can weep at *Hecuba* as if it had happened yesterday."

The view presented here resonates also with the search for critical events or cultural performances in cultural studies (Turner, 1992; Grossberg et al., 1992), symbolic anthropology (Singer, 1984; Geertz, 1973; and V. Turner, 1974), as well as "the new historicism" (Veeser, 1989). As cultural performance, opera told Italians who they were, no less than cockfighting or carnival inform Indonesians and Brazilians about themselves. Opera provided not only music and libretto but the sensuality, the acting out, the lyricism, the spectacle, the immediate gratification which spelled Italian, both in public and in private. Another Leo, the great philologist Spitzer (1944), makes this point in the remarkable book that traces the etymology of the word *Stimmung*: "the masses in most countries . . . can no longer imagine (as however the Italian peasant can still do, who, when he sings, sings always an aria) a level of existence on which man spends his life in song."

Although I can hardly complain about how this study was received, were it undertaken in the 1990s—rather than in the 1960s when I began, or the 1980s when it was published—I would have felt better supported both inside and outside my discipline of musicology.

That does not mean that I would have been less self-conscious about what I was doing. The contrary is more likely. Given the persistent call of present-day cultural studies for theoretical and methodological reflexivity (perhaps because there is so little theory and method in evidence), I would have been more attentive, for example, to the status of questions about contingency and causality, to the question of what is "popular" within a culture, to the validity of distinctions between high and popular culture, and to the pitfalls of interdisciplinarity, notwithstanding its indispensability.

In addressing this work to fellow musicologists in the first place, I could take their familiarity with the "text" for granted. Addressing non-musicologists calls for more explicit exposition of the basic "texts," not just the social institutions and value orientations in which they reside. To a certain extent, I have done this in my analysis of the contemporary forms of music and theater and of the ways in which each of them tried to wed words to music. Starting over again, however, I would have elaborated on the aesthetics of these genres, not just because it would better fit the new audience for cultural studies, but because I had the opportunity of gleaning some of the prodigious knowledge of the late Carl Dahlhaus during the several years we worked together on our overview of the philosophy of music (Katz and Dahlhaus, 1987-1992). While there is room, obviously, for many more trees, I still believe in the forest I have planted.

Comparing the Arts:
The Eighteenth-Century Sequel

In the meantime, there is also more forest. The Seventeenth-century deliberations over the attributes of words and music and the ways in which they fit together to make meaning have taken me into the Eighteenth century where these issues were both continued and transformed. I am interested in the second half of the Eighteenth century, when the Seventeenth-century preoccupation with meaning was gradually being supplanted by the twin realizations that meaning in music is not inherent but acquired, and, more important, that music "makes sense" even when it is devoid of meaning.

These far-reaching conclusions—which point still further towards the emergence of modern art and contribute retrospectively towards modern theories of cognition—are foretold in scores of Eighteenth-century treatises that are occupied with the comparative study of the properties of poetry, painting, and music. In the course of this theorizing, the status of music was elevated from the art that is least able to cope with referentiality on its own to the art that is unencumbered by referentiality, and hence the purest—that is, the most abstract—of them all.

Although my own interest focuses as much on the consequences of these deliberations as on the deliberations themselves, it is important, in either case, to understand how two hundred years of music, and of theorizing about music and the arts, led up to them. A place to begin is in the early chapters of this book that report on the Renaissance quest for the lost formulae of the Greeks who allegedly knew how to use music to heighten the power of words. The members of the Camerata were concerned over the trivialization of both words and music in the music of their time. They protested that the words were lost; that they were being used ornamentally to embroider, not to persuade, indeed, hardly even to signify. The music, they said, had no powers; it tantalized the ears as mere entertainment. In their quest, whether as true or feigned archaeologists, they identified new declamatory forms for effective song-speech, and new formulae for relating words to music, from which opera emerged. This was not rediscovery, however, but invention. In their explorations and experiments, these Italians began, willy nilly, to associate certain kinds of words to certain musical forms, and gradually to craft a semantics of musical expression.

Over a period then, the systematic marriage of words to music branded meaning into the music, and the music, in turn, gave specificity to the words. This expressive coinage was so well established by the middle of the Eighteenth century that, ironically, words were no longer deemed necessary! This had consequences for instrumental music. While there were works of instrumental music theretofore, this was the period when instrumental music flourished on a large scale, having come into its own. Thus, prerequisite to the discovery that musical form and content are inseparable and that musical coherence depends on no external referent were the developments in music itself. In other words, Eighteenth-century thinkers did not unveil something that was there all the while but unnoticed; rather, their discoveries depended on what was created in the interim. The late Eighteenth century could address the Florentine agenda anew only because of the music that the Florentines and others had set into motion. The emergence of instrumental music was one such step, signifying that music could stand alone, because it was thought capable of bearing its own semantic load.

At the same time, superimposed musical schemes were seen to be giving way, more and more, to musical forms that emerged from within. These forms grew from simple to complex structures, from single lines to complex relationships among them. The developments that took place in musical theory from the time of the unifying thorough bass to the emergence of functional harmony made it possible to perceive that music had its own referential system albeit a probabilistic one, that is, its own tonal grammar. Relations hierarchy and functions characterize the inner logic of this system, guiding the unfolding of music in ways that "make sense" syntactically, if not semantically. The functional aspects of the system also called attention to expectations, as one of the crucial factors that guide the listening to music.

Developments in instrumental music in the late Eighteenth century went even further in simulating dramatic tension and relaxation, in telling and retelling "stories" and the like—all without benefit of words or allusions to words. As purely dynamic structure, free of the specific and the particular, instrumental music seemed to compete favorably with the semantic and contextual constraints of verbal rhetoric. Late Eighteenth-century theorists and their successors could then say that music affects us by concentrating on purely musical events such as attention, connection, and relation. The "unfolding" of music was conceived as a process of relating "empty signs" to each other in intricate, cohesive, and coherent ways. Referentiality was now internally oriented, not directed outside.

A parallel thread runs through the history of thinking about the other arts. In the latter part of the Seventeenth century, the arts were gradually disconnected from science. Although still united by the shared orientation to active "doing," philosophers in the Eighteenth century relegated the Fine Arts to the "lower cognitive faculty" (Baumgarten, 1735) and discussed them collectively as well as comparatively. Compared with science, the arts were considered lacking in adequate conceptualization, characterized rather by fusion and continuity, while aspiring, like science, to clarity and coherence, that is, to the aesthetic notions of order and unity. The principle of "sufficient reason," was applied equally to the arts as to science, although regularity in the arts is said to be achieved through associations or resemblances.

Liberating the creative process from the presumed logic and rigor of normative science, these scholars focused attention on artistic processes of combining and recombining perceptions and symbols. Artists were given license to engage in the construction of symbol systems that have no necessary referent in any external reality. The thinking about creativity in these terms led to the crystallization, in the Eighteenth century, of that branch of philosophy we call aesthetics and, with it, the realization that art is better conceived as constructed within itself rather than as a set of relationships to the "outside." The thrust of the transformation from the late Sixteenth century through the Eighteenth is best expressed as a paradigmatic shift from the conception of art as mimesis—imitation of nature—to a conception of art as world-making. Art resides in the making, they concluded.

It is apparent how readily these two strands converged, the one that first separated music from words and then separated sense from meaning, and the other that saw invention rather than imitation in the work of all of the arts. It is easy to see how music triumphed in this process of reorientation. Compared with the other arts, music was chosen to exemplify the new aesthetic tendency because it was thought to possess its own self-referential system. If at the beginning of the Eighteenth century it was still held that music did not qualify as an independent art because of its "empty signs" it was precisely this quality to which the other arts would later aspire. Music is now thought to possess, or, rather to be possessed by meanings, although the process of associating specific, expressive meanings or affects to particular musical configurations is a convoluted one. It is better to think of music as creating, rather than disclosing, that which supposedly inheres within it, and more so through its syntactic and self-referential structure than semantically or by external reference.

The liberation of the arts from referentiality, in which music took the lead, may be said to have signalled the birth of modern art. Moreover, a significant contribution to the cognitive turn in epistemology may be discerned in the separation of "sense"—that is, syntactic and self-referential structure—from semantic and extrinsic "meaning," and the realization that art—especially music—could be decoded without meaning. Of course, syntactics, no less than semantics, needs an interpretive community, and a "contract" between consumers and producers. The theoretical role played by these Eighteenth-century deliberations to current theorizing about cognition is the subject of the book on which I am presently engaged together with my colleague, Ruth Hacohen.

Referentiality and the Revival of Opera

The processes described above may have gone too far. The valuation of structure over subject matter, of construction over reference, of abstraction over representation was lost on a lot of people. One of Bourdieu's measures of "distinction" is between those who see landscapes in the "landscapes" on their walls and those who see only shapes and their interrelations.

Even more people are lost to modern music. Indeed, one often wonders whether modern music itself has not lost its syntactic, let alone semantic, sense. Even if structure is all, it must be understood. No less than representations, as has just been said, structure and its invention must be perceived and consensually decoded. The composer as well as the artist cannot hope to communicate, if that is their intention, if they invent structures which audiences fail to comprehend.

I had thought that opera was declining in popularity. Not so long ago, it seemed to me that opera was going nowhere. There appeared to be an absence of new works in significant number and an unacceptable obfuscation of the melodic line. I also sensed a renewed unwillingness to accept the convention of people speaking to each other in song, in melodramatic gesticulation, and in a foreign tongue to boot. I thought, too, that the hierarchical arrangements of most opera houses were alienating.

I believe now that I was wrong. New opera houses are being built and subsidized, with more egalitarian audiences in mind. The subtitles that have made opera successful on television and video have been introduced in the halls. Directors of theater and film have responded to invitations to reinterpret the classics of opera, and stage more modern works. The multimedium—the *Gesamtkunstwerk*—seems to be back in fashion, and the audiences look and sound enthusiastic, as if they had discovered something new.

On a deeper level, there is room to suggest that the revival of opera may also express a rejection of the modern, and perhaps even a thirsting for referentiality. The refurbished opera may be attractive, in other words, because it offers a return not only to sense but to meaning, to words and music encapsulated in musical forms that speak languages we understand, syntactically and semantically.

Ruth Katz
September, 1993

References

Baumgarten, Alexander (1735/1954), *Reflections on Poetry*, tr. and ed. K. Aschenbrenner and W.B. Holther, Berkeley: University of California Press.

Benjamin, Walter (1968), "Theses on the Philosophy of History," ed. Hannah Arendt, *Illuminations*, New York: Harcourt and Brace.

Braudy, Leo (1993), "An Operatic Heroine for Our Time," *New York Times*, September 12, 1993, p. 45.

Geertz, Clifford (1973), *The Interpretation of Cultures*, New York: Basic Books.

Grossberg, Larry, et al., eds. (1992), *Cultural Studies*, New York: Routledge.

Katz, Ruth and Carl Dahlhaus, eds. (1987/1992), *Contemplating Music*, vols. 1-4, Stuyvesant, NY: Pendragon Press.

Mukerji, Chandra and Michael Schudson (1991), *Rethinking Popular Culture*, Berkeley: University of California Press.

Singer, Milton (1984), *Man's Glassy Essence: Explorations in Semiotic Anthropology*, Bloomington: Indiana University Press.

Spitzer, Leo (1944/1963), *Classical and Christian Ideas of World Harmony*, Baltimore: Johns Hopkins University Press.

Turner, Graeme (1992), *British Cultural Studies: An Introduction*, Boston: Unwin Hyman.

Turner, Victor (1974), *Drama, Fields, and Metaphors*, Ithaca: Cornell University Press.

Veeser, H. Aram (1989), *The New Historicism*, London: Routledge.

Preface

I have long felt—even during the heyday of C.P. Snow's "Two Worlds"—that 'problem-solving' in the sciences, as it is called nowadays, has its analogue in the arts. This book represents my attempt to interpret a moment in the history of music that coincides not only in spirit but in time, with the scientific revolution in the West.

To be sure, the idea that the several domains of culture are interconnected was never entirely abandoned. That the application of human intelligence in all its domains is governed by overriding directives that prevail at given times and places is echoed in phrases like 'climate of opinion', 'Weltanschauung' and Zeitgeist. But the vagueness and evasiveness that tend to accompany such phrases have more often than not come under attack, less for their underlying premises than for their too-casual application.

Indeed, the danger of dilettantism hovers over the interdisciplinary regimen implied by such conceptualizations. It is no wonder, therefore, that in musicology, as elsewhere, serious scholarship has avoided such temptations, preferring to play it safe. Moreover, the rapid growth of knowledge over the last decades made specialization, even within a given discipline, not only 'safe' but necessary.

In retrospect, however, it appears that this very specialization opened the back door, as it were, to a renewed interest in interdisciplinary work. The shift from discipline to subject matter challenges traditional boundaries of investigation and reaches out to other fields. This long-awaited legitimation of interdisciplinarity is not a resurrection of the old phrases and their vague premises but rather the rigorous and responsible application to one's own domain of the knowledge and tools of 'other' domains.

Looking back, it seems to me that those of us who were fortunate enough to have been at Columbia during the Lang-Hertzmann period got a good start in this respect. Lang never lost sight of the fact that music was part of a larger whole, while Hertzmann did not let us get away with it, insisting, as he did, on detail and accuracy. I am grateful to them all the more now, as I have come to know the field better and to watch it grow. I hope that their joint influence is apparent in the present work. Even the briefest mention of those Columbia days must also pay homage to that blessed seminar on early opera given by Pirrotta on his first visit to the United States. All of us who participated had our eyes opened, and have remained indebted and grateful to Pirrotta, the scholar and the man, ever since.

The list of people whom I would like to thank is evident in my bibliography. Without their diligent work, I could not have undertaken the kind of synthesis attempted here. One name not in the bibliography is Elihu Katz, my husband, whose advice I enlisted in matters of sociology and communication. I should also like to acknowledge that parts of Chapter One appeared in *Israel Studies of Musicology,* vol. 3, and parts of Chapter Two in the Hebrew journal, *Molad.* A version of Chapter Three appeared in the *Journal of the History of Ideas.*

I hope the book will be read for what it tries to do, not for what it does not. It does not try to unveil new 'facts' about the early history of opera, but rather to offer a new 'look' at them. After all, in the Age of Information, the problem is not one of information but of interpretation and evaluation.

Jerusalem
August 1985

List of Illustrations

Chapter One
Explaining the Origins of Opera

What Needs Explaining?

Like all attempts at historical explanation, this one is imposed in retrospect, using conceptual tools of the present to reinterpret, and to better understand, the past. The problem in this case is to explain the rise of opera as a new musical institution, and the explanation attempted here views opera as emerging from the venerable preoccupation with defining the powers of music, as this preoccupation found expression, and became institutionalized, in Italy of the late Renaissance. Thus, the explanation proposed here weaves together two different strands: an aesthetic strand—with roots in philosophy, magic and ideology—in which the Humanists lead us back to the Greeks and forward to the aesthetic theorists of the Florentine salons; and a socio-cultural strand in which the waning of religion, the ascent of science, the strengthening of the middle classes and the lyrical culture of the Italians are all brought to bear. If the rise of opera may be related to the effort to explore the limits of words and music, the subsequent history of opera may be written as a contribution to this ongoing discussion. Indeed, the composers and spiritual godfathers of the earliest operas pioneered in the search for solutions to the problem of juxtaposing the elements of a music drama, and the search appears to be unending.

Even from these few lines of introduction, it is obvious that what follows is an interdisciplinary exercise. For one who does not claim expertise in all the relevant disciplines, the act of explanation, at least in this case, cannot be to unveil new evidence, but rather to draw together relevant materials that have already been reported, extracting each from its honored place in its own disciplinary forum. This kind of exercise can succeed only to the extent that the experts whom one calls upon, and introduces to each other, are well chosen and carefully suited. This book will draw heavily on the musicology of Pirrotta and Palisca, on the

1

history of ideas of Walker, Yates, Kristeller, Spitzer and Trinkaus, on the philosophy of Goodman, and on the histories of art and literature of Hauser, Gombrich, D'Ancona and Symonds, to mention but a few. It will also invoke concepts current in the sociology of art and science. For example, the notion of cultural "code," now in vogue, serves well to identify the choices and biases that give cultures their continuity and distinctiveness, and it will be applied here to Italy. In the same way, the notion of "social circle" will help describe the network of interpersonal relationships in which the new art form was conceived, experimented with and diffused.

Introducing another current concept, it will be shown that the crystallization of problems and their solutions in art is analogous to the development of a "paradigm" in science.[1] And as Gombrich and others have suggested, it will become clear that style represents a kind of collective problem-solving by a group of artists.[2] In turn, such agreed-on solutions, or styles—as Crane suggests— are inherent in "invisible colleges" or social circles of colleagues whose informal networks of communication nurture the paradigm and fructify it.[3]

Those familiar with the history of opera will immediately recognize the relevance of these concepts to the Camerata, the group of Florentine intellectuals whose name is so closely associated with the genesis of the new medium. Behaving almost like a "circle" of scientists, they focused—as part of their varied activities—on a problem (how to make language attached to music audible); they agreed on a methodical approach to its solution (adapting music to words or words to music: the direction was in dispute); and they agreed on the types of phenomena to be manipulated and observed (the power of music "to move the

[1]The term is used here with full awareness of the ambiguities that have accompanied its widespread recent use. Indeed, Kuhn himself has recently discerned several different meanings attributable to the concept, electing to emphasize shared puzzle-solving techniques as the most useful definition. Others use the concept to refer to a new way of seeing things, a "cognitive event." Expounding Kuhn's thesis, Mulkay defines paradigm as "a series of related assumptions—theoretical, methodological and empirical—which are generally accepted by those working in a particular area, while suggesting that "cognitive and technical norms" would serve the purpose better. We prefer the term paradigm partly because it encompasses some of the very ambiguities in the subject treated here and partly to emphasize the usefulness—already noted by Kuhn and Crane—of viewing creativity in art as analogous, in many ways, to creativity in science. See Thomas S. Kuhn, *The Structure of Scientific Revolutions*,

passions of the mind"). These are Kuhn's terms for describing the directives in a paradigm: identification of problem, methods and phenomena to be observed. "Without these," says Crane, "a group of scientists would be unable to produce findings that are interrelated and cumulative." Moreover, it is suggested that "the concept of style that represents the end result of a period of innovation is analogous to theory in the sciences."[4]

This sampling will give an inkling, perhaps, of the kind of analysis undertaken here. Sociologists and cultural historians may find it congenial; some musicologists, perhaps, may not. The perils of such speculative analysis, however stimulating or persuasive, constrain most historians of music—with a few notable exceptions—to confine themselves to the rigorous exegesis of manuscripts and scores. The risk of reaching debatable conclusions is thereby minimized, and more important, the music itself—the first order of business and the most important single source for the study of style and stylistic change—is given the attention it deserves.

The Risk of Explanation

Yet somebody has to take the risk, and not just for the fun of it. For the fact is that historical explanation in the arts cannot be complete without looking outside the works of art themselves. Unquestionably, the prerequisite to historical explanation in music is the availability of a representative corpus of the relevant musical materials, and their careful structural analysis. But this analysis requires a "Theory," and the theory resides in a larger cultural and social context. The integration of these three—the music, the theory and the context— is called for.

This will sound obvious to some, and heretical to others.

Chicago: The University of Chicago Press, second edition, 1970, p. 161; Diana Crane, *Invisible Colleges: Diffusion of Knowledge in Scientific Communities*, Chicago & London: The University of Chicago Press, 1972, p. 29; M.K. Mulkay, *The Social Process in Innovation*, London: The Anchor Press, 1972, pp. 31-32.
[2]See E.H. Gombrich, "The Renaissance Conception of Artistic Progress and its Consequences" in *Norm & Form*, London & New York: Phaidon, 1966, pp. 1-10.
[3]Crane, *op. cit.*; Also see Harrison C. White & Cynthia A. White, *Canvases and Careers: Institutional Change in the French Painting World*, New York & London: John Wiley & Sons, 1965.
[4]Crane, *op. cit.*, pp. 136-7; Also see Kuhn, *op. cit.*, pp. 160-73; 208-9.

But the fact is that attempts have been made to perform musical "analysis" even in the absence of the actual musical materials themselves. Much more frequent is the attempt to analyze musical materials without making explicit the theory that guides the analysis. Even more rarely does one encounter an effort at a systematic introduction of the sort of contextual analysis attempted here. It is already evident in what has been said that historical theories of music must look outside—to culture, to philosophy, to the other arts; even to society, politics and economy—to help explain the meaning of music. A particular set of social and economic conditions do not prescribe specific artistic forms, but a certain form, once given, can often be related to the social and cultural reality from which it emerged. The transition from the minuet to the waltz, for example, may be shown to reflect the socioeconomic changes that took place at the turn of the eighteenth century, even if the forms of the minuet and waltz cannot be derived from knowledge of the socioeconomic changes alone.[5]

In arguing the case for music, theory and context as prerequisite elements for musicological analysis, it is interesting to point to examples where the absence of one of the elements is particularly problematic. Most dramatic of all, perhaps, is musicological analysis without an adequate body of representative music. The case of the analysis of Greek music will illustrate how, in the absence of a representative body of musical examples, neither the many verbal treatises that have been handed down to us nor the vast knowledge we possess of the culture of ancient Greece is sufficient to establish an unequivocal image of the music of that culture or of its influence on subsequent development in the West. For example, the concept of a scale is supposed to have come from the Greeks into the music of the Middle Ages. Thus, the Pythagorean tradition of harmonics, based on the principle of expressing intervals by ratios—indeed, the entire doctrine of expressing the universe in numbers—has commanded a respectable place in the theory of music in the West. Nevertheless, tuning notwithstanding, such mathematical thinking did not strongly manifest itself in the practice of music as an art. Even the question to what extent it affected the art of

[5]See Ruth Katz, "The Egalitarian Waltz" in *Comparative Studies in Society and History*, vol. XV, 1973, pp. 368-77.
[6]Isobel Henderson, "Ancient Greek Music," *The New Oxford History of Music*, London: Oxford University Press, 1957, vol. I, p. 342.

music in ancient Greece is still an open one. Because of the inconclusiveness of the evidence, some have gone so far as to claim that when ancient theorists measured musical intervals, whether by ratios or by units, they had no practical purpose in mind.[6] According to this claim, the tradition of harmonics was a "self-propelled" science interested in the nature of the universe rather than in music as art, aiming at a theoretically satisfying scale conceived as a structural element in the cosmos.[7] Indeed, it seems undeniable that this harmonic science was part of a cosmological doctrine that embraced an idea of music not necessarily related to its actual aural qualities. As in many other ancient cultures, the Greeks attributed magical powers largely to the "unheard" part of music, rather than to the part that was heard.

Even disregarding such extreme claims, however, it can be argued that Greek music should not be conceived of in terms of continuous scales, bearing in mind that only the tuning of the perfect fourth was invariable and only the notes connected with it were fixed.[8] The others were mobile. The tonoi, which are often described as transpositions of the harmoniae, were actually keys whose development into an organized system was intricate and not altogether clear.[9] They have been discussed in terms of pitch nevertheless, ignoring the question of whether such a possibility existed in the absence of absolute standards of pitch.

Thus, in spite of the goodly number of theoretical documents available, little is known with certainty about the musical practices of the ancient Greeks. From a historiographical point of view, it is interesting to consider why historians, for decades, have preferred to emphasize the contribution of Greece to our musical heritage over that of, say, Southwest Asia. The reason seems to lie with the historian's preference for the evidence of the treatises, and of the few compositions inscribed on stone and papyrus, over the few instruments and the melodic material preserved by oral tradition.[10] Such preference, to be sure, implies a

[7]*Ibid.*, p. 341.
[8]Two disjunct tetrachords, each enclosed by an invariable fourth, create two interlocking invariable fifths and an invariable octave. The basic structural unit, however, is the fourth.
[9]See the discussion on this subject in Gustave Reese, *Music in the Middle Ages*, New York: Norton, 1940, pp. 28-44.
[10]This situation has long since been rectified in modern musicology by eminent scholars like Peter Wagner, Egon Wellesz, Curt Sachs, Robert Lachmann, A.Z. Idelsohn and Eric Werner to mention but a few.

"theory" regarding historical conjecture whereby (1) written documents are favored over oral tradition, and (2) the amount of material available commands greater attention than the information that is manifestly missing. That this methodology does not necessarily lead to more persuasive conjectures hardly need be said. Conjectures, however effected, are subject to a test of "fitness" based on preceding and subsequent developments. Just as oral tradition must be judged in terms of its "prediction" of the past, so written documents must prove their relatedness to a future, both aiming at intelligibility in terms of the present.

Although it may seem obvious that practical musical materials are indispensable for musicological analysis, this digression into the music of the Greeks shows that it is not so obvious. Even less so is the obverse: that musical materials alone are insufficient for musicological research.

It might suffice to examine the music alone were it possible to establish that music follows laws that are not susceptible to historical change, and that its development is completely determined by certain specific musical dictates. If such were the case, nothing but music would be necessary for the study of music history; in fact, one could even predict its future development thereby.

The history of music adequately shows that such circumscribing laws cannot be established and that music is free to develop in different directions at any given moment. If it does pursue one course rather than another at a given time and place, this is due largely to the intervention of non-musical factors. Even theories like those of Sachs, for example, in which styles are seen as developing in cycles from static to dynamic, coolness to warmth, essence to appearance, etc., are not based on immanent development, and do not refer primarily to the material and working techniques of the artist. Rather, they emphasize the artist's social habitat, which in turn affects his feelings and attitudes.[11]

Of course, like that of other arts, the history of music must reckon with the development of the craft, whose cumulative advances can sometimes be viewed as autonomous. Nevertheless, the fact that music history finds it necessary to differentiate

[11]Curt Sachs, *The Commonwealth of Art: Styles in the Fine Arts, Music and the Dance*, New York: Norton, 1946.

among composers—both individuals and groups—who possess the same means implies that there is more to the history of music than the development of such means. Indeed, the means themselves do not altogether escape being affected by the conditions of life. Styles are characterized both by what is said and how, and the two are intertwined. The direction taken by music at a given time, therefore, needs to be explained. Merely to pinpoint a course of development through the description of structure and technique as they change over time—a possibility in itself questionable—would establish facts without revealing their historic evolution, not to speak of their artistic significance. For what we hear largely depends on what we expect to hear.

In order to obtain a picture of the evolution of music, it is necessary to explain how alternate developments that were at the disposal of music at a given moment were eliminated. The curbing of alternatives in the development of musical expression results from interplay among many expressions, musical and non-musical. The same principle applies to the individual composer. He is confined to alternatives which are part of his social, psychological (and technical) reality. His choice bears witness to an untold story, which the historian endeavors to make explicit.

The choice among alternatives should not be confused with the debate over whether style can be defined in such terms. The emergence of a "free" style challenging a "strict" style, the choice between *prima* or *seconda pratica* in the early part of the seventeenth century or, for that matter, the possibility of their coexistence can be discussed in terms of screening processes, but the styles themselves cannot be so defined. The view that style should be treated as a complexity that resists reduction to a literal formula is well taken.[12] In fact, styles of music are created and perceived without being able to specify their necessary and sufficient conditions.[13] Their uniqueness cannot be explained in terms of composers' conscious choices among alternatives. Only knowledge of the origin of the music, however attained, can tell us how it is to be listened to, and provide a base for the discovery of "non-obvious ways" in which one composition may be said to differ from, or to resemble, others.[14] While discrimination

[12]Nelson Goodman, "The Status of Style," *Critical Inquiry*, vol. I, 1975, p. 799.
[13]*Ibid.*, p. 811. This is precisely what makes for the difficulty of "programming" a given style for the computer.
[14]*Ibid.*, p. 810.

among styles is fundamental to the comprehension of music, such discrimination is not affected by music alone.

As with the analysis of style, so with the aesthetic evaluation of musical tradition: it is not only enhanced by placing it in its respective context, but altogether depends upon it. There are no absolute aesthetic principles that can serve as yardsticks for evaluation. All aesthetic principles are derived from works in which they have already been realized, satisfying historically conditioned requirements. An aesthetic evaluation depends above all on a familiarity with the aesthetic outlooks of both the producer and the consumer of the music. For what once ranked as absolute beauty—in the broad sense, including desirability—strikes us as style when it is followed by a new concept of beauty.[15] Aesthetics, as Goodman points out, is a byproduct of the perception of style. Accordingly, history and criticism do not differ on subject matter but in exchanging ends for means. Whereas the historian uses style for purposes of identification of a work, the critic uses identification as a step towards discerning the particular properties of the work.[16] In sum, although it increases the degree of uncertainty, consideration of the broader cultural aspects that affect the development of music is not optional but obligatory.

The History of Music and the Philosophy of History

Historians of music have always agreed that there is a relationship between music and the other cultural expressions of a given time and place. Moreover, they have acknowledged that such expressions are organically related to the modes of life and thought of the cultures from which they stem. Yet, for all that, most historical investigations of music, with a few notable exceptions, pay only fleeting attention to the cultural environment. Those that do branch out into other areas of culture in their attempt to comprehend the historical and stylistic development of music seem mostly to juxtapose the cultural phenomena which they sense to be related rather than to *explain* the relation-

[15]"A style is not merely an idiom or mannerism; it becomes these only when, ceasing to be a conquest, it settles down into a convention." André Malraux, *The Voices of Silence*, trans. Stuart Gilbert, New York: Doubleday and Company, 1953, p. 318.
[16]Goodman, *op. cit.*, p. 810.

ships among them. While such procedures do, at times, yield sensitive observations, they fail, by choice or default, to interpret what has happened. To point out that a given phase in the development of music is accompanied by a parallel development in the plastic arts does not explain the musical development, but rather challenges chance as an adequate explanation. The nature of the relationship, however, remains unexplained. Moreover, it often implies a commitment to a highly questionable theory about the existence of a "primal intangible spirit" on which parallel manifestations are supposed to converge.

An explanation of the relationships among the cultural phenomena of a given period and the way they affect each other presupposes an arrangement of the relevant phenomena in a logical sequence revealing the functions of the relationships. Much that can be said in advancing an explanation depends on such an arrangement, no less in music than in other fields. The "risks" of such arrangement-making are obvious. Most historical events have multiple determinants, and causal relationships are not easily established in history. They are speculative, at best, although what appears as accidental today may be seen tomorrow as causally determined. Even so they would not possess the inevitability of a logical deduction, but would rather be logically contingent. Causality cannot be subjected to simple verification or falsification, since that branch of knowledge which records and explains, explains and records, partakes in the creation of the historical event itself.

Still, historians do search for causal explanations. Without the explanation of the causes and origins of events, history becomes indistinguishable from chronicle. An event is historically significant only when one knows why it is relevant. Historians rearrange their materials continually, seeking better and more orderly arrangements as they acquire new facts and ideas. Such arrangements and classifications depend upon an ordering of materials according to some presupposition about the "goal" of the development, which in itself must be confirmed and corrected again and again. History is not in search of laws; it is largely in search of *meaning*. Historical analysis, therefore, is interpretative by definition, and the meaning of events is perpetually open to revision.

The conjectural nature of the study of history is compounded by the fact that events have been selectively recorded, and as such reveal prejudice of one kind or another. Indeed, history at its purest—music history not excepted—is a conceptually structured selection of detail importing signification. Even the use of different metaphors is itself indicative of historical preference. The predilection of the historian regarding historical dialectics has, more often than not, affected his perception of the direction taken by historical motion "away from" or "towards" what he considers to be the "normative" state.[17] The "emergence" of the sonata, "crystallization" of the suite, "breakdown" of tonality, etc. all imply the organization of details into patterns of comparability and contrast suggestive of norm, continuity and change in the historical process. Strict chronologies portraying the development of music in the West are inconceivable. Even theories of progressive development, though they are based on patterns of cumulative advance, are faced with the problem of directionality. They are mostly challenged by historical "interruptions" which have to be accounted for, even if they are construed in terms of contingent progress.

It could be argued that seeing historical direction in the context of "mixed" schemes of time[18] need not necessarily reflect philosophies or theories of history but may result from transient, albeit persuasive, connection, whereby history is shaped and reshaped to reveal comprehensible meaning. In the historical account, the only constant factor, it seems, are the rules of the game, which require that when a historian makes a claim that he be able to justify it.[19]

Justifications notwithstanding, the philosophy of history has amply shown how the past is invariably construed according to patterns reflecting prior ideas and commitments, whether or not these are readily apparent. "Ideas lurk behind ideas,"

[17]See Randolph Stern, "Meaning Levels in the Theme of Historical Decline," *History and Theory: Studies in the Philosophy of History*, 1975, vol. XIV, pp. 3-31.
[18]Nisbet suggests that the tenacious use of organic analogies—growth, age, youth—in Western historical thought reveals a preference for seeing historical direction in the context of "mixed" schemes of time—cyclical, spiral, undulating, etc. See Robert A. Nisbet, *Social Change and History: Aspects of the Western Theory of Development*, New York & London: Oxford University Press, 1969, pp. 211-23.
[19]For a discussion on this point see Elazar Weinryb, "The Justification of a Causal Thesis: An Analysis of the Controversies over the Theses of Pirenne, Turner, and Weber," *History & Theory*, vol. IV, 1966, pp. 33-5.

claims Walsh, adding significance or uncovering assumptions.[20]

Not all ideas are equally durable or valid, nor do they contribute equally to historical understanding. The search for better judgment and more effective explanations is a continuous one and fundamental to historical discourse. Phenomena as such, observes Danto, are not conceived of as self-explanatory; they become explanations through descriptions.[21] Such descriptions must do justice to the facts that serve as evidence, but in a way which makes past events intelligible "in terms of present-day experience." Discussing the causation of ideas, Walsh endeavored to show how objective situations have no automatic effect on thought. Instead, men conceive their situations and shape their ideas against a given backgroud of assumptions. "Social conditions," argues Walsh, "are constituted by social facts together with social attitudes, which are themselves ideas awaiting embodiment in action." It is the task of the historian to consider what people "reveal" or "let slip," as well as what they say explicitly.[22] In other words, at all times such considerations are not a prerogative but a must.

The digressions of these last pages deals with some by no means settled issues in the philosophy of history. More than merely contributing to the advancement of the arguments, these aim to make explicit the premises from which the pages that follow procced. Historians of music, in general, have not often joined in such methodological discussion, and that is regrettable. Theoretical and methodological premises deserve to be spelled out as much in connection with the detailed collection of facts that preoccupies the musicologist as with the kind of synthesis attempted here. Indeed, the author has pleaded elsewhere for a more precise definition of the elementary units of musicological analysis,[23] and there is no contradiction between the two. In both cases, meaningful units of analysis are required

[20]W.H. Walsh, "The Causation of Ideas," *History and Theory*, 1975, vol. XIV, p. 190.
[21]Arthur C. Danto, *Analytical Philosophy of History*, Cambridge, 1965, p. 218.
[22]Walsh, *op. cit.*, pp. 192-8.
[23]See Dalia Cohen and Ruth Katz, "Remarks Concerning the Use of the Melograph in Ethnomusicological Studies," *Yuval*, 1968, Vol. I, pp. 155-68. Especially pp. 158-59; Also see Cohen-Katz, "Quantitative Analysis of Monophonic Music: Towards a More Precise Definition of Style," *Orbis Musicae*, 1973-75, vol. II, pp. 83-96.

for the marshalling of evidence, and rules for relating the evidence need to be made explicit. In both cases the ultimate goal is to give meaning to musicological analysis.

For those taking the "risk," it may be comforting to remember that the examination of music itself—let alone music which is no longer part of a living musical tradition—generates hypotheses about the intentions of the artist. The stylistic peculiarities of a piece of music, a composer or a period are exterior representations, at least in part, of specific solutions to the technical problems engendered by the intentions of the creator.[24]

Aesthetic Theory and the Origins of Opera: Some Problems and Proposed Explanations

In reopening the questions surrounding the early history of opera, one of the purposes of this book is to examine the definition of the properties of music arising thereby. A second, and related, purpose is to enlarge the social and intellectual context in which the early history of opera has been set. The object of this is not enlargement for its own sake; it is not simply to describe the broader economic, political, religious, intellectual and, above all, artistic currents that accompanied the rise of opera. Rather, the object is to try to connect these contextual factors more explicitly than has been done hitherto, and thus to enhance understanding of how a confluence of particular factors in Italy at the end of the sixteenth century gave impetus to the musical institution called opera, as it drew upon and contributed to the renewed concern with the peculiar powers of music.

Much has been written about the beginnings of opera. Many facts have already been recorded. Attention has been

[24]The question of the relevance of the artist's outlook and intention in the judgement of the work of art is by no means a closed issue. The so-called intentional or extrinsic approaches to art have been considered a "fallacy" by those for whom the comprehension and evaluation of the work of art is only measured against something outside the creator and the world for which it was created. The counter-arguments are held not only by Freudians and Marxists, for whom they "logically" fit into given systems of thought, but many others who are neither committed to a specific psychological theory nor to a particular theory of history. The views supporting the relevance of historical, sociological and ideational data for the understanding and evaluation of art are more widely held, and on the whole more convincingly expounded, than those which repudiate them.

given not only to the earliest examples of the new medium but also to its immediate precursors.[25] The musical development that made opera possible has likewise been traced, centering, as it does, around the establishment of accompanied monody. Nor has aesthetic theory been overlooked; the musico-aesthetic movement of which opera was a part had its origins not among the experimenters with early opera but in the writings of sixteenth-century theorists.

It would seem, at first glance, that the emergence of the new medium may have been adequately explained and enhancement of understanding adequately served. Yet closer examination of the available historical accounts raises questions that have either not been treated at all or have not yet been answered satisfactorily.

As a sweeping generalization, it might be said that in attempting to explain the rise of opera, historians of music have placed their emphasis on the major constituent elements comprising the opera, and in particular, on the stages of their development immediately preceding its rise. With some notable exceptions such as, for example, the work of Pirrotta, the factors underlying these stages of development are not often brought to bear. Emphasis is placed primarily on historical facts concerning the theatre and music, as well as on the unveiling and examination of examples of early operas and the variety of other theatrical presentations containing music. Since the boundaries of these investigations are determined by the components of the medium itself, they largely prescribe the trends to be discovered. To "explain" by pointing out that, prior to opera, one encounters musical and dramatic forms that have elements similar to opera is begging the question anew. It is for this reason that a theory concerning the rise of opera that also takes cognizance of factors extrinsic to the medium itself is justified. Though social conditions and prevailing ideas cannot simply be equated with artistic characteristics, and manifest themselves only through a chain of intermediaries, a music history that goes beyond formal

[25]Some of the major works in this area are: Allessandro D'Ancona, *Origini del teatro italiano*, 2 vols., 2nd ed., Torino, 1891; Arnaldo Bonaventura, *Saggio storico sul teatro musicale italiano*, Livorno, 1913; Romain Rolland, *Some Musicians of Former Days*, trans. Mary Blaiklock, New York, 1915; Angelo Solerti, *Le origini del melodrama*, Torino, 1903, and *Gli albori del melodrama*, Milan, 1905, vol. I; and more recently Nino Pirrotta's indispensible work, *Li due Orfei: da Poliziano a Monteverdi*, Torino, 1969.

analysis of the musical material itself must relate the work of art to both the disposition of the artist and the aspirations of the society to which he belongs. And if this is true for an individual musical work, it is true *a fortiori* for a musical institution.

Thus it is clear, for example, that the development of music in the sixteenth century was not primarily affected by the development of the theater or vice versa, but that the development of both was symptomatic of other factors affecting music and theater alike. The union of the two became possible because music and theater drew closer to each other in spirit. What were the factors affecting them both?

Likewise, the people associated with the early operatic experiments—the Camerata, in particular—are accorded a position more honorable than that of experimenters, although it has been amply proven that their musico-aesthetic theories had been stated in one form or another earlier in the century.[26] What then earns the group its (deserved) image? What was unique about either the group or its writings? And why did its musico-aesthetic theories, expounded earlier, find acceptance only then? What factors made this possible?

In attempting to address these questions, the pages that follow will argue that the institution of opera may be thought of as the embodiment of a statement about the nature and power of music. It is a declaration about the import of music, pointing to that which music can do best. The intensive effort to animate the text through music created a strain to define the properties of each.

In fact, many of the musical forms of the same period may be characterized as partaking in a search for the answer to the question, "What is music?" Accompanied monody, the cantata and the opera all engaged in the search. This process led, ultimately, to the shaping of a language of music, which, while divorced from text, contained decodable meaning, as exemplified—at its climax—in the *Affektenlehre* of the mid-eighteenth century.

---

[26]Already Rolland has the following to say: "The history of opera has been recounted a good many times during the last few years. But the error that historians have fallen into up to the present has been in believing, or in allowing others to believe, that this distinctive form of art sprang in full battle array from the heads of a few inventors. Creations of this kind are rare in history . . .

More than the other musical expressions of its time, how-ever, opera is quintessentially the search for an answer to ques-tions about the nature and powers of music. The opera, there-fore, is a child of its times: it is the embodiment of the aesthetic preoccupations of those who gave it birth. Even those who ar-gue that the birth was unplanned will agree.

The reader is now asked to consider that the aesthetic ques-tions put to the arts by the intellectuals of the Florentine acade-mies are actually counterparts of scientific concerns. To ask "What is music?" for example, is not different than to ask "What is matter?" (Parenthetically, it might be noted that the study of music as sound did, indeed, move eventually to the scientific field of acoustics.)

This parallelism, of course, relates to the fact that the rise of science and the renaissance of aesthetic theory in the arts coin-cided in time. The scientific revolution of the seventeenth cen-tury addressed itself to fundamental questions concerning the makeup—properties and order—of the world, questions which until that time had been officially relegated to the domain of religion. To be sure, these questions have been an integral part of philosophical inquiry at all times, but in the Middle Ages reli-gious institutions had preempted them, in the minds of all but a very few. Even if science began to make inroads into the intellec-tual domain of the Church, it could not supersede the experien-tial function of religion. The expressive and experiential contin-ued to flourish inside the Church. But the arts also assumed an increasingly important role outside the Church, as a source of emotional experience alongside the intellectual role of science. Certain writers, even modern ones, have gone so far as to equate the spiritual status of music with that of religion, given the long and close association between the two, the emotive powers as-cribed to music, and ultimately its relationship to the "prime movers" of the universe. Influenced by Weber, Western music is seen as a kind of bridge between the religious/expressive and the rational/cognitive elements in our civilization, given the ra-

---

The thing we call a creation is often nothing but a re-creation; and in the present discussion one may pertinently ask if that opera, which the Florentines believed in all good faith they created, was not in existence, except for some slight differences, long before their time." R. Rolland, *ibid.*, pp. 25-6.

tionalistic basis in which the emotive power of Western music is anchored.[27]

In other words, aesthetic and scientific questions were closely analogous at the time of the emergence of opera. Indeed, they were being discussed by some of the same people in some of the same salons and academies. Or, as Panofsky puts it, "Is it not possible that the whole idea of clean-cut separation between artistic and scientific activity must be reexamined when we deal with the Renaissance? Is it not possible that at this stage of European history, a science . . . which was just beginning to turn 'experimental,' and an art whose practical procedures had thus far, by and large, not sought support in a systematic theory and which just was beginning to claim a position among the 'Artes Liberales' by doing precisely this—that such a science and such an art advanced, as it were, on a united front? Should we not give the allegedly less productive sciences some credit for the results achieved by the admittedly flourishing arts, and, more important, consider some of the achievements of the arts to be vital contributions to the process of the sciences? In short, should we not realize that the Renaissance was a period of *decompartmentalization*: a period which broke down the barriers that had kept things in order—but also apart—during the Middle Ages?"[28]

If the Middle Ages dealt with the identification of some basic musical parameters and problems of their notation, and the Renaissance dealt primarily with laws of composition and structure, the late Renaissance and early baroque—together with the new science—asked questions about the essence of music and the processes through which it communicates and influences. This professed return to the concerns of antiquity evoked issues that were never completely dropped—implied as they are in *musica reservata*, and in earlier attempts to make music expressive of

[27]See, for example, H.G. Koenigsberger's interesting article, "Music and Religion in Modern European History," in *The Diversity of History: Essays in Honour of Sir Herbert Butterfield*, H. Elliot and H.G. Koenigsberger, eds., Cornell University Press, Ithaca, New York, 1970, p. 35-78.

[28]Erwin Panofsky, "Artist, Scientist, Genius: Notes on the 'Renaissance-Dämmerung'," in *The Renaissance: Six Essays*, New York: Harper & Row, 1962, pp. 127-8. Also see Marie Boar, *The Scientific Renaissance 1450-1630*, London: 1962, esp. Chap. VIII, "The Organization and Reorganization of Science," Joseph Ben-David, "The Scientific Role: The Conditions of its Establishment in

its text. Towards the end of the sixteenth century, however, these issues reach a point of crystallization in musical theory and become a central focus of debate.

The chapters that follow will elaborate on the analogy between the aesthetics of music and scientific theory and method. The notion that opera, as a medium, is an ongoing "laboratory" to test the nature and boundaries of musical powers will be discussed in Chapter Two. The modern origin of this concern, perhaps, is in the continuous "experiments" on the influence of music on the mind and the passions as practiced by the Humanists; Chapter Four will build on the writings that have analyzed these theories.

Chapter Three examines the nature of the "social circles" in which these ideas were debated toward the end of the sixteenth century, and the analogy—indeed, the overlap—between groups like the Camerata and others of its kind, which were concerned with the sciences and the arts. This group will be shown to have been working with a kind of "paradigm" of the sort that guides scientists in their work, and which led, in this case, to experiments in the paradigmatic form later to be called opera.

Chapters Four, Five and Six place this group and its Humanistic predecessors in the cultural and social context from which it emerged, examining the idiosyncrasies of the Italian "spirit," the social and economic changes affecting the character of creativity in the late Renaissance, and developments in the other arts. Chapter Seven deals with the "exhaustion" of the paradigm and the disintegration of the union between individual expression and shared meaning.

Europe," in George Basalla, ed., *The Rise of Modern Science: External or Internal Factors*, Lexington, Massachusetts: 1968, pp. 47-54; Martha Ornstein, *The Role of Scientific Societies in the Seventeenth Century*, New York: 1975, Part II; and Frances A. Yates, *The French Academies of the Sixteenth Century*, London: 1947, Chaps. III and XII. On the relationship of art and science, see Georgio di Santillana, "The Role of Art in the Scientific Renaissance" in Marshall Clagett, ed., *Critical Problems in the History of Science*, Madison, Wisconsin: 1968, pp. 47-54, and D.P. Walker, *Studies in Musical Science in the Late Renaissance*, London: 1978.

Chapter Two

Opera as a Laboratory for Defining the Powers of Music

It is customary to reduce the manifold views on the nature of opera to four basic approaches which correspond roughly to its historical development. The Classicist and Neo-Classicist approaches, which predominated in the Seventeenth and Eighteenth centuries, viewed music as subservient to the text. The Romantic approach, which reversed the roles of words and music, predominated in the first half of the Nineteenth century. The "perfect union approach," stressing equality, flourished in the second half of the same century and was followed by the "separate but equal" approach of the Twentieth century.[1] More important than a characterization of the development of opera, this classification scheme reflects a spirit of experimentation within the medium, exhausting, as it were, its four logical possibilities.

These combinations—and the more subtle variations that emerge when one takes account of the other arts that are also partners in the opera—existed from the start, as the following chapter on the Camerata will show. In a sense, these experiments in the juxtaposition of the several arts constitute a laboratory for the exploration of their nature and their combinatorial rules. The history of opera, and of opera theory and criticism, can almost be written as a scientific enterprise aimed at charting the domain of each of the arts, but more particularly the domain and powers of music.

Of course, one must look to practice more than to theory. Opinions stating a preference for one approach over the other in different periods and places are not really conclusive. In practice, the importance assigned to each of the two major components of the *Gesamtkunstwerk* is far from simple-minded. Regardless of their professed beliefs, the composer and librettist of an opera, must confront the same problem: how to forge a success-

[1]See Ulrich Weisstein, ed., *The Essence of Opera*, Glencoe: The Free Press, 1964, pp. 5-6.

ful relationship between text and music. At such moments, theory often gives way. The juxtaposition of the arts leads to new relationships, which are not simply the sum of the artistic parts.

Ironically, some of the most instructive ideas about the marriage of words and music come from those who are critical of the very legitimacy of opera. Opera as an art form has been subject to criticism almost from its very inception. While it is true that all the arts have their adversaries as well as their devotees, it is unlikely that any other art form has been challenged so often over its right to exist. The reasons vary, depending on time, place and the particular critic. While their variety is of interest, even more interesting is what there is to learn about the medium from the struggle to find persuasive reasons to discredit it. For these critics were not boors: many knew opera well, and made a sincere effort to understand it. Even Saint Evremond, Addison and Voltaire, whose rejections of opera as a medium have become classic, can be shown to have had more understanding for the medium than many a supporter. Whether one accepts or rejects their opinions, their arguments give insight into the inherent features of opera and why those features lend themselves so readily to controversy.

St. Evremond, for example, who accepted the essence of opera least of all—for in opera "all of life's activities are set to music"[2]—nevertheless understood that in the union of poetry and music each element has its own function and the two do not merely duplicate each other. He attributes great expressive power to music, the power to convey emotions and passions.[3] What he objects to is the "indiscriminate" use of music, where words alone would be appropriate. He rejects opera because of this irrationality and believes that for opera to be successful the composer must be subordinate to the poet.[4] In other words, music should only be employed where it serves the function for which it is best suited. The division of labor between music and words is not as simple as is implied by St. Evremond; nevertheless it is a basic idea and finds its counterpart in the stand taken

[2]St. Evremond, *Oeuvres*, III, p. 172. St. Evremond talks about the "through composed" Italian opera. It is clear that he considers the dramatic element the most important one in opera. This is why he would like to substitute the spoken word for the recitative.
[3]*Ibid.*, p. 173.
[4]*Ibid.*, p. 174.

by Mozart, who expected the poet to be subordinate to the composer. In fact, any collaboration between poet and composer is successful only when the aesthetic function of each is clearly understood by both.

Addison, like St. Evremond, attacks the "absurdities" of opera, which he considers an insult to the intellect. He believed that music, architecture and painting should not only follow their own artistic dictates but, like poetry and rhetoric, talk to the mind and appeal to the tastes. Rather than people being compelled to adjust to art, art should adjust itself to people. Anyone with "healthy ears," says Addison, can judge whether a given passion is expressed in suitable tones, or whether a melody sounds pleasant or not.[5] It would seem at first that Addison does not believe that taste rests on cultivation, norms, etc., and that "judging" whether a given passion is expressed in "suitable" tones depends on some kind of socialization. Yet, at another point, criticizing the transplantation of Italian opera to England, he talks about the relativity of musical taste, claiming that music is of a "relative nature" and that which is understood or appeals to one nation may be foreign to another.[6] This observation is insightful, even if it seems "obvious" to us now. It is an important observation to bear in mind when national characteristics of opera, or for that matter, its historical development, are analyzed. Insightful as he may be, Addison nevertheless fought the conventions of opera, the conventions of the lyric stage that reflect the predilections of the people that gave birth to it. And, though he thought in relative terms, he looked for "absolutes" in this medium. This dichotomy in Addison's thinking is noteworthy as it is quite characteristic of a number of opera critics and reformers who were engaged in a search for "final" solutions to the "problem" of opera.[7]

Voltaire, a great admirer of Addison, referred to the music drama as "le beau monstre de l'opéra." He too, despite his ridicule and cynicism, reveals a basic understanding of the medium

[5]Georgy Calmus, "Drei satirisch-kritische Aufsätze von Addison über die italienische Oper in England (London, 1710)," *Sammelbände der Internationalen Musikgesellschaft*, vol. IX, p. 140.

[6]*Ibid.*, p. 138.

[7]It is interesting that Addison himself wrote a libretto, "Rosamund," in 1707, as an attempt to write an English opera on Italian model. The music was written by Clayton. The whole was a big failure. In 1733, the libretto was set to new music written by Dr. Arne and was reportedly a success.

he attacks. In the introduction to his *Oedipus* he takes issue with M. de la Motte, defending the three unities of tragedy against de la Motte's attempt to prove that one can do without them.[8] De la Motte's argument was based on the fact that this had been successfully done in opera. De la Motte's argument, says Voltaire, "is as absurd, as to endeavor to correct a regular government by the example of anarchy."[9] He continues,

> The opera is a spectacle as whimsical and absurd as grand and magnificent, where the eye and ear receive more satisfaction than the mind; where its subjection to music makes the most ridiculous faults even necessary; where we are forced to sing ballads at the destruction of a city, and dance round a tombstone; where we are presented with the palaces of Pluto and the sun, gods, demons, magicians, signs and wonders, monsters, palaces built and pulled down in the twinkling of an eye. We suffer these extravagances, and are even fond of them, because we are in a land of fairies; and provided we have but fine fights, good dancing and music, with a few interesting scenes, we are very well satisfied. It would be ridiculous to require the unities of time, place, and action in Alcestes, as to introduce dance and devils in Cinna or Rodogune. Notwithstanding, however, that operas may dispense with these rules, those are still the best where they are least violated: in many, if I am not mistaken, they are re-established, so necessary and natural are they, and conducing so effectually to interest the spectator; how then can M. de la Motte reproach our nation with levity, for condemning in one entertainment the very things which we approve of in another? Every man must see the absurdity of it. I expect, and with reason, more perfection in a tragedy than in opera; because at a tragedy my attention is not divided; it is not on a saraband or a minuet that my pleasure depends, my mind is to be filled, my soul is to be delighted . . . [10]

From the above it is clear that Voltaire is referring to French opera, with which he is most familiar. He is not willing to put opera on a par with tragedy. He expects less of opera than he does of tragedy, because opera neither "fills" his mind nor does

---

[8]M. de la Motte wrote in 1726 two versions of Oedipus, one in verse, the other in prose. Neither was successful. The first was played four times and the latter never.
[9]Rev. Mr. Franklin, trans., *The Dramatic Works of M. de Voltaire*, Dublin: R. Marchbank, 1772, vol. XXI, p. 11.
[10]*Ibid.*, pp. 11-12.

it "delight" his soul. He does not expect opera to be logical because it presents a "land of fairies." Voltaire's attitude toward the operatic genre is very much like Dryden's, which places this art form in a secondary position in the hierarchy of artistic expression.[11] Yet, while he does not endorse opera fully, to say the least, he accepts its conventions. He understands that each artistic medium has its own rules and that the one should not be judged by the rules of the other. That this was understood by an Algarotti or a Beaumarchais, full endorsers of the medium, is not surprising. Coming from Voltaire, however, such a realization carries the weight of unbiased judgment, precisely because he is negatively biased. This understanding—that opera should not be judged by the rules governing the spoken stage—is of major importance in attempting to understand opera and its history.

Having become identified as outright rejecters of opera, St. Evremond, Addison and Voltaire display more understanding of the medium than one has learned to expect. Perhaps the insights they do reveal have been better formulated by others. The fact remains, however, that St. Evremond differentiates between the separate functions of music and words; Addison perceives the basic relativity of musical expression; Voltaire realizes that a medium has its own conventions and must be judged in terms of its own rules. All these elements are basic to any analysis of opera and its history. Two of these ideas—those of conventions and functionality—pertain to the medium itself. The third idea—that of musical expression—extends beyond the limits of opera, but is a basic assumption underlying this book. Opera, as will be said repeatedly, is a story of people telling each other what they feel. The success of such communication, we maintain, depends on the "musical socialization" of the listeners' emotions. The shared language which is required for this purpose is bound by time and place.

Before parting from these critics, note that all three (and many others) are disturbed by the "irrationality" of opera. Yet there was a time (indeed, it was during the lifetime of Voltaire) when opera enjoyed the status of one of the most rational of artistic expressions. Ironically, this was in the so-called Age of Reason. The advocates of Reason limited art to the imitation of

---

[11]See Dryden's "Preface to 'Albion and Albanius,' an Opera," in Weisstein, *ibid.*, p. 36.

nature and usurped the artist's power to create. These men strongly believed that the "laws of nature" are available to the experience of all men and, since all are governed by the same laws, they do not have to create laws but merely to unveil them. Such a world outlook made an unambiguous codification of emotions not only feasible but logical, and in turn served as the underlying rationale for the *Affektenlehre*. The doctrine of affections is in fact an aesthetic theory, according to which the chief aim of music is to portray certain typical emotions. The laws of nature being definite and within the grasp of individual thinkers, precision, clarity and concrete meaning were considered indispensable to true communication. Instrumental music, therefore, was somewhat frowned upon. Although considered capable of expressing a definite idea, image, scene, etc., it was not believed to have full expressive potential.[12]

In *Der Vollkommene Capellmeister*, the best source for the theory of affections, Mattheson asserts that texts in vocal music are the "portrayals" (Beschreibungen) of the affections. Instrumental music, like vocal music, must do justice to the affections by trying to be intelligible "so dass die Instrumente, mittelst des Klanges, gleichsam einer redenden und verständlichen Vortrag machen."[13] Music received its fullest expression, accordingly, only when allied to words (in one form or another, including rhetoric), which provide, so to speak, the "labels" which help to clarify whatever ambiguity was left. "Die Gefühls theorie" says Sondheimer, "bevorzught die von Worten begleiteten Musik . . . weil der Gefühlsausdruck durch die Wortebegleitung viel bestimmter und feststellbarer ist als der reinen Instrumentalmusik. Daher steht um achzenten Jahrhundert insbesonders die Oper die sum hörbaren noch den sichtbaren Gefühlsausdruck hinzugestellt im Vordergrund des Interesses . . . "[14] Indeed, opera reigned supreme in the Age of Reason.

It is quite apparent that the attitude toward opera, like the attitude toward any other cultural expression, was never divorced from the general world outlook and aesthetic concepts of

---

[12]See A.R. Oliver, *The Encyclopaedists as Critics of Music*, chapter V ("Instrumental Music"), New York: Columbia University Press, 1947.

[13]Johann Mattheson, *Der Volkommene Capellmeister*, Hamburg: Christian Herald, 1739, p. 127.

[14]R.J. Sondheimer, *Die Theorie der Symphonie*, Leipzig: Breitkopf und Härtel, 1925.

those who tried to understand and judge it. This could have been the case even if, hypothetically, opera had never undergone changes. Of course, the changes themselves incorporated and reflected the various attitudes; they resulted in part from "improvements" and in turn gave rise to new sets of criticism.

Singing: The Convention of Opera

Pro or con, it is evident that the debate over opera centers on the convention that it is sung. Paul Bekker calls this the "fixed axis" of opera. The dramatic, the musical, the decorative, etc. are temporal characteristics, marking the "manifestation that is opera and the changes in its form." But singing is the essence of opera, and the only answer as well to Bekker's question "whether opera has within itself an element that distinguishes it from all other art forms . . . [or whether] it is only a sort of half-developed drama, shunted off into a wrong path . . . remarkable only because so many man of genius have concerned themselves with it?"[15]

All art rests on convention, a convention being a tacit agreement to take something for granted, however bizarre, and accord it legitimacy at a given time and place. To the extent that the conventions of an art form are not taken for granted, criticism arises and is directed at the medium itself. While painting has not been attacked for lacking relief, sculpture for lacking color, or pantomime for being mute, opera has been challenged for using song as its natural speech.[16] Opera was not singled out accidentally, however; the reason lies in the simple fact that its "fixed axis" cannot easily be taken for granted. If Beaumarchais asks of the singers to speak more "naturally," reminding them that "to sing means simply to speak more forcefully," he is conceding thereby that singing does indeed pose problems.[17] It is not easily reconciled with the other elements in opera. To handle the complexities with skill, to avoid reminding the spectators that they

---

[15]Paul Bekker, *The Changing Opera*, trans. by Arthur Mendel, New York: Norton and Company, 1935, pp. 25-9.
[16]For a good discussion of the above, see Brander Matthews, "The Conventions of the Music-Drama," *Musical Quarterly*, vol. V, 1919, pp. 155-63.
[17]See his "Preface to 'Farare'" in Weisstein, *op. cit.*, p. 151.

are partners to an agreement, is the challenge of opera.[18] To understand how this challenge may be met successfully, and the various solutions that have been attempted, one must first understand the characteristics and functions of all the participant elements in opera and the interrelationships among them.

Two approaches characterize the work of scholars who have tried to "solve" this problem. One is anchored in aesthetics. Its starting point is the analysis of the ways in which music and drama nourish each other, and the conditions under which their interaction is most likely of success. A glimmer of this approach is revealed in the debates of the critics and defenders of opera, but a more systematic discussion will be attempted later in this chapter.

The other approach is more historical and sociological. Arguing that the survival of opera, in the beginning just as now, was based on its acceptance by audiences, this approach seeks to locate the precursors of the convention of combining sung words and deeds in Italian theater. It argues that the opera must have built on audience experience applying music to certain kinds of dramatic or poetic characters and scenes.

Both approaches, of course, reflect the basic experimental problem of how, and when, to unite music and words. Both approaches reflect the experience of those who have actually tried, in their "laboratories," to do so.

By far the most interesting historical work on this subject— and the most insightful of generalizations—comes from the writings of Nino Pirrotta, who discusses the kinds of dramatic situations that provide rather obvious "pretext" for singing. Thus, Pirrotta suggests some of the implicit and explicit constraints that music places on the writing of dialogue and action if they are to be joined with music and song.

The audiences for Italian theater were already accustomed to the appearance of singers and dancers for several decades prior to the first operas. The song-like speech of classical drama was also something to which audiences had become accustomed. The gods of pastoral drama were useful in having license

[18]Lessing believed that the dramatist must avoid everything that reminds the spectators of their illusion, because the illusion is gone as soon as they are reminded of it. Oskar Bie, talking about the opera, makes use of this very idea and says that opera is "ein Traum, der niemals ganz Leben werden kann, weil er unwirklich wird, wenn er seine Illusionen verliert." See *Die Opera*, Berlin: S. Fischer Verlag, 1913, p. 9.

to speak differently from ordinary mortals, "in harmonies sur-
passing that of ordinary speech." The earliest operas took classical themes, more for this reason, says Pirrotta, than from a desire for more profound philosophic connection with the
ancients. Moreover, Apollo and Orfeo and other musical figures
are presented as protagonists in early opera in order to justify
the use of singing. The use of a musical protagonist preempts
criticism of the unrealism of sung speech. Indeed, the dramatic
pastoral and the tragi-comedies were already employing this device, and it is from these forms that the first libretti emerged.[19]
Moreover, there is a great intimacy between the characters of the
pastorals and the muses. Citing Guarini, Pirrotta argues that this
"poetic status and familiarity with music" was further pretext
for their sung speech. In a similar way, says Pirrotta, "sung prologues had also been an admissable choice at least since the beginning of the 16th century."[20]

The singing of realistic characters aroused resistance. Gods,
shepherds, magicians, madmen, comedians fared much better,
Pirrotta asserts. They had a "right to sing." For this reason, says
Pirrotta, certain real heroic figures were de-historicized and virtually deified in the theater, to take advantage of the musical
license that such mythological status provided.

Opera might not have survived at all, according to Pirrotta,
if it were not for politics. Despite the inventiveness of librettists
and composers, the innovation of speech song was resisted, and
audiences did not take easily to the new convention, especially
when realistic characters were involved. In Rome, however,
where the *commedia dell'arte* was suppressed, opera was supported by the Barberinis and given a chance to compete against
spoken theater.[21] The comic opera—the *commedia per musica*—was
the favorite form, not least because comedy also provided an
easier, and already familiar, setting for song. The fast-moving
plot, says Pirrotta, demanded textual clarity, which in turn induced certain musical innovations—a certain form of the recitative, for example—to keep up with the words.[22]

---

[19]Nino Pirrotta, "Early Opera and Aria" in *New Looks of Italian Opera, Essays in Honor of Donald J. Grout*, William Austin, ed., Ithaca, New York: Cornell University Press, 1968, pp. 80-81.
[20]*Ibid.*, p. 88.
[21]*Ibid.*, pp. 90-97.
[22]*Ibid.*, p. 97.

Like comedians, other deviant characters earned a natural right to song. Thus, magicians were a favorite in operatic history—especially in the Seventeenth century—because of their musical incantations; madmen because of their right to burst out or to converse to and about themselves. Related to madness, Pirrotta adds whimsically, are delusions of grandeur of all kinds, as well as perversions, stuttering, gluttony, imitations of others, etc. All these had legitimate recourse to singing.[23] One can continue this kind of analysis. Thus, religion would be another good example. The repertoire of opera is full of church scenes in which liturgy, prayer and ritual are naturally sung. Religion is intrinsically allied with music; hence the many operas in which religious rites are given a central place on the stage.

But the need for "pretexts" for singing continually underlines the fundamental problem opera confronts: namely, the problem of marrying words and music and the resistance that this encounters in the music drama. Hence the extensive theorizing about the aesthetics of opera, and the persistent efforts to define the power and the limits of words and music, which have accompanied the empirical efforts of composers to find solutions. Often enough, composers and librettists themselves have entered the aesthetic debate.

On the Limits of the Arts

It has been claimed that no solution is possible, i.e., that the problems of opera result from the fact that it is a union of arts whose laws of structure and form conflict. In line with this, some writers have attributed different dimensions to the different arts. The dimension of time is attributed to music because "music is always changing; it progresses, it changes the state of mind and emotion of the audience." The dimension of "length" is attributed to painting since scenery is a static art whose influence on the spectator "remains constant," and so on.[24]

Without enumerating the other dimensions, it is quite clear, even from the two examples, that assigning different dimensions in this oversimplified fashion to the component arts of op-

---

[23]*Ibid.*, pp. 100-106.
[24]See Geraldine P. Dilla, "Music-Drama: An Art Form in Four Dimensions," *Musical Quarterly*, vol. X, 1924, p. 494.

era does not necessarily indicate conflict. While it is true that music unfolds in time, it is quite arguable whether it continuously "changes the state of mind and emotion of the audience." Such an assertion denies the ability of music to create a communicative whole. Indeed, it is the "changes" themselves and their relationships to each other which create a "state of mind" or an "emotion." Aristoxenus already seems to have realized that listening to music presupposes an intellectual activity whereby impressions are collected and built up in one's memory. "Musical cognition," he says, "implies the simultaneous cognition of a permanent and of a changeable element."[25] In more recent times, since Hanslick's assertion that sound and motion ("tönend bewegte Formen") constitute the essence of music[26]— of that "illusion begotten by sound"—aestheticians have viewed musical duration as the passage of life experienced as "expectations becoming now." Such passage is measurable only in terms of sensibilities, tensions and emotions and differs from scientific time in measure as well as in structure.[27] Without any further elaboration on the concept of time with regard to music, it seems quite clear that the dimension of time does not necessarily conflict with that of length.

The same assertion can be made from the point of view of "length." From a psychological analysis of the process of perceiving painting or scenery, one can argue that time is operative here, too. As Goodman says, a painting can grow on its beholder, or he can tire of it in time. Art invites a continuous process of search. Moreover, within this dimensional frame of reference, one should have relatively little trouble wedding poetry to music, since both qualify as temporal.

This is not to say that there are no differences among the arts; it is to illustrate, rather, that it is not so easy to pin down their differences and make them stick. Even so, there is a case to be made—as we shall see—for the relevance of more sophisticated versions of the same kind of dimensions just enumerated.

---

[25] Aristoxenus, from the "Harmonic Elements" in Oliver Strunk, ed., *Source Readings in Music History*, New York: Norton, 1950, p. 27.
[26] Edward Hanslick, *The Beautiful in Music* (1854), trans. by Gustav Cohen, New York: The Liberal Arts Press, 1957, p. 48.
[27] See Susanne K. Langer, *Feeling and Form*, New York: Charles Scribner's Sons, 1953, pp. 109-116; 150. Also see Leonard B. Meyer, *Emotion and Meaning in Music*, Chicago: The University of Chicago Press, 1956, pp. 23-32.

Nor is this to say that the arts are, or should be, saying the same thing in the same way, albeit with different sensuous materials,[28] in order not to conflict. The opposite may well be true. Each of the arts, after its fashion, (1) may indeed be constrained to do and say different things, and (2) these different things, moreover, may complement each other rather than conflict. The first of these points is the essence of Lessing's famous argument; the second leads us to Wagner's.

Comparing poetry and sculpture, Lessing concluded that the nature of each of these dictates its subject matter, or more correctly, limits the subject matter to that which the particular art is most qualified to handle. Lessing took issue with Winkelmann, who saw only different artistic conceptions as seperating Virgil's Laocoön and the Greek sculpture. According to Winkelmann the two artists might well have done the same thing, each in his own way, but simply chose to do it differently. The different conceptions, he believed, are expressed in the fact that Virgil makes Laocoön give a terrible cry of pain, whereas the Greek master endeavored to communicate restraint in Laocoön's face. Attacking Winkelmann's basic assumption, Lessing claimed that "the reasons for the moderation observed by the sculptor of the Laocoön in the expression of bodily pain shows them to lie wholly in the peculiar object of his art and its necessary limitations."[29] He goes on to explain:

> When Virgil's Laocoön screams, who stops to think that a scream necessitates an open mouth, and that an open mouth is ugly? . . . Further, nothing obliges the poet to concentrate his picture into a single moment . . . Every change, which would require from the painter a separate picture, costs him but a single touch; a touch, perhaps which taken by itself, might offend the imagination, but which, anticipated, as it has been by what preceded and softened and atoned for by what follows, loses its individual effect in the

[28]"It is a mistake of much popular criticism to regard poetry, music and painting . . . as but translations into different languages of one and the same fixed quantity of imaginative thought supplemented by certain technical qualities . . . .A clear apprehension of the opposite principle—that the sensuous material of each art brings with it a special phase of beauty untranslatable into the forms of any other, an order of impressions distinct in kind—is the beginning of all true aesthetic criticism." From Walter Pater, "The School of Giorgione," in *The Renaissance,* New York: Modern Library, p. 107.

[2]Gotthold Ephraim Lessing, *Laocoön: An Essay Upon the Limits of Painting and Poetry,* trans. by Ellen Frothingham, New York: The Noonday Press, 1957, p. 20.

admirable result of the whole. Thus were it really unbecoming in a man to cry out in the extremity of bodily pain, how can this momentary weakness lower in our estimation a character whose virtues have previously won our regard? Virgil's Laocoön cries; but this screaming Laocoön is the same we know and love as the most far-seeing of patriots and the tenderest of fathers. We do not attribute the cry to his character, but solely to his intolerable sufferings . . . Who blames the poet, then? Rather must we acknowledge that he was right in introducing the cry, as the sculptor was in omitting it.[30]

Lessing, too, is obviously concerned with the different dimensions with which poetry and sculpture deal, seeing poetry as a temporal art and sculpture as a spatial art. However, his major point is not that the arts have different dimensions, but rather that as a result, they differ in their choice of subject matter which itself is limited by their natures.[31]

Lessing's thesis about the limits of the arts should not be confused with the theories expounded by Wagner in his "Art Work of the Future," though some historians have been guilty of that.[32] Wagner does talk about the limits of the various arts, but he is concerned with the limits of their development. He believed that the separate arts had already reached their limits—in Greek sculpture, Florentine and Venetian painting, Shakespeare's poetry and Beethoven's music. Having reached its utmost limits, each demanded to be joined to a sister art because "man as artist can be fully satisfied only in the union of all the art varieties in the collective art work; in every individualization of his artistic capacities he is unfree, not wholly that which he can be; in the collective art work he is free, wholly that which he can be."[33] This is the theory that led Wagner to his *Gesamtkunstwerk* (not that he was the first to conceive of the idea).

Although his emphasis is entirely different from Lessing's, Wagner's theory inevitably leads him to a definition of the subject matter of the individual arts. This, of course, follows from

[30]*Ibid.*, pp. 20-21.
[31]For a stimulating discussion of the nature of the individual arts, see W.A. Ambros, *The Boundaries of Music and Poetry*, trans. by J.H. Cornell, New York: G. Schirmer, 1893, pp. 13-22. Although the book dates as far back as 1856, it contains valuable insights by one of the greatest music historians of all time.
[32]See Dilla, *op. cit.*; also see Erich Valentin, "Dichtung und Oper: eine Untersuchung des Stilproblems der Oper", *Archiv für Musik-forschung*, vol. III, 1938.
[33]Richard Wagner, from *Das Kunstwerk der Zukunft*, in Strunk, *op. cit.*, p. 900.

his attempt to apply his own theory of the "limits" of the arts in the creation of the music-drama. The shortcoming of Wagner's theory, then, is not that he fails to define the individual arts and, heaven knows, not that he overlooks the uniqueness of a *Gesamtkunstwerk* in which all the arts must be concerned with the attainment of its dramatic aim, but rather that he does not anticipate the changes in the character of each of the individual arts that result from their union. Examining opera as a medium, it is the mutual interaction of the arts that requires close consideration.[34]

What, then, does happen to Poetry and Music when they are wed in the opera? What is revealed of the power of music? Hesseltine tries to sum it up by suggesting that "music may come to the rescue of drama at the point where words and actions begin to fail in subtlety of expression." Rather than simply echoing St. Evremond's prescription that the use of music be limited to those places where it serves as the best vehicle of expression, the present argument calls for marrying music to the kind of drama that "aspires toward the condition of music." Where drama strives beyond the representational toward the symbolic, says Hesseltine, there "lies the true sphere of opera."[35] Or as Susanne Langer says, "anything that can enter into the vital symbolism of music belongs to music, and whatever cannot do this has no traffic with music at all."[36]

There is a seeming contradiction here. In defining the kind of drama that aspires towards the "condition of music," it appears that music is able to say *more* than words and action, and yet, it cannot say *that* which words and actions can say. Obviously, this seeming contradiction is a useful one: due to its "symbolic" nature, music cannot be definite in its representation, but it can convey directly that which language can only describe. "Quando il poeta vuole che la visione generi uno stato d'animo evidente, ne la parola ne gli artifizi scenici sono sufficienti per esprimerlo resulta un vuoto che solo la musica puo' riempire . . . "[37]

---

[34]Because of the importance of the interrelationship between the arts in opera, it is more correct to call it a fusion of arts rather than a union of arts. The term "wholeness" of opera is vague in this respect, and lends itself to a number of interpretations.

[35]Philip Heseltine, "The Scope of Opera," *Music and Letters*, vol. I, 1920, p. 230.

[36]Langer, *op.cit.*, p. 152.

Music, then, best conveys a "disposition," what Tommasini here calls "uno stato d'animo." Music acts synthetically; it gathers up the predominant elements described and analyzed by verbal and scenic images to express them in their totality.[38] Thus, the problem of the interaction between words and music is not due to the fact that both appeal to the same sense, as many have pointed out,[39] but more exactly because they use the same sense differently. While both unfold in time, the difference is in duration of use: music takes more time—real time not to be confused with musical time—than words. While it is true that poetry and music appeal to the same sense, and that both are temporal arts, poetry in its continuous movement presents a succession of images, whereas music requires expansion to communicate any single "disposition." Thus in the fusion of the two, music does not come to the "rescue of drama," but it dictates the character of the latter. It limits the role of poetry to the function of suggesting and arousing the musical idea. This is what Tommasini means in his statement: "Quando Gluck nella prefazione dell'Alceste dice che la musica deve essere quasi serva della poesia, dimentica d'aggiungere: de quella tal poesia che a sua volta eserva umilissima della musica."[40] The above could equally apply to Wagner. Despite his theories, music remained the determining factor in his works. In fact, Wagner's use of the orchestra rather than the voice is a logical continuation of this idea.

The peculiar relationship between music and poetry, then, is one in which music makes demands of poetry and action rather than vice versa. Music can "come to the rescue" of certain literary works much more effectively than of others. Castelnuovo-Tedesco speaks of setting music to poems that have an "expressive core"; and he too speaks of a "state of soul" (stato d'animo). Not too many words, he pleads; "a certain margin should be left for the music." Intimacy and restraint in the text are preferable to intricacy or embroidery or sonority. The

---

[37]Vincenzo Tommasini, "Del drama lirico," *Rivista Musicale Italiana*, vol. XXXIX, 1932, p. 76.

[38]For an excellent discussion of this point, see Guido M. Gatti, "Gabriele D'Annunzio and the Italian Opera Composers," *Musical Quarterly*, vol. X, 1924. See also Ralph M. Eaton, "Music or Poetry," *Musical Quarterly*, vol. IX, 1923, and Ambrose, *op. cit.*, pp. 52-3.

[39]See, for example, Harold Child, "Some Thoughts on Opera Libretto," *Music and Letters*, vol. II, 1921.

[40]Tommasini, *op. cit.*, p. 83.

key to the poem is to be found in its "expressive core," he says, and having found the key, the composer can give it new form "through 'symbolic' musical means." The composer confesses that he has always felt the urge "to unite music to poetic texts that arouse interest and emotion, to interpret them and at the same time to set them forth in lyric expression, to stamp them with the authentic and therefore undetachable seal of melody, to give utterance to the music that is latent within them, and, in doing so, to discover their real source in the emotions that brought them into being."[41]

It follows that a poem can be "too completely developed and closed" from the point of view of its compatibility with music. As is well known, many composers have shrunk from setting Goethe's poems because they were too complete. Poems that fit music "imply as much as they speak." Here is Tommasini's "vuoto"—the void into which music flows to fulfill the potentialities of the words, to complete and summarize them. "A song conceived poetically," says Langer, "sounds not as the poem sounds, but as the poem *feels* . . . "[42]

Elaborating, Langer speaks of "a principle of assimilation, whereby one art swallows the products of another." This principle, she says, not only describes the (legitimate) relationship of music to poetry, "but resolves the entire controversy about pure and impure music, the virtues and vices of program music, the condemnation of opera as 'hybrid'."[43] Langer argues strongly against those who distinguish between a pure music of form and a "dramatic music," which, subservient to words, simply underlines or stimulates correlative feelings. Music can assimilate drama, she insists, not only words. "Dramatic actions," like the 'poetic core,' "become motivating centers of feeling, of musical ideas . . ."[44]

This conception, which guided some of the greatest of opera composers, reflects centuries of experimentation with the relationship of words and music, as well as the other components of opera. It illustrates the sense in which opera has been a laboratory for defining the powers of music not only in the actual

[41]Mario Castelnuovo-Tedesco, "Problems of a Song-Writer," *Musical Quarterly*, vol. XXX, 1944, p. 102.
[42]Langer, *op. cit.*, p. 159.
[43]*Ibid.*, p. 157.
[44]*Ibid.*, p. 158.

practice of composers and librettists, or in the chequered story of their collaborations, but also in the subsequent work of scholars who have derived their aesthetic generalizations about the arts from the experience of their interrelations, and their limits, in the empirical history of the music-drama.

It is easy to see, moreover, how the idea of music "swallowing" words in the opera, or in the poem set to music, leads repeatedly to the misunderstanding that the words, or the action, are less important. Composers are as much to blame as librettists. Accepting the idea that music reigned supreme, many a composer has treated the words as nonsense and shifted them around to his convenience, omitting or adding words as he pleased. For their part, librettists often made no attempt to write sense into their words. This was particularly likely in those compositions where aria and recitative were clearly differentiated, the former summing up the emotions and the latter the actions.[45] Viewed cynically or seriously, it is clear that operatic atrocities resulting from the misuse of a basic understanding of the medium are endless.[46]

It can be shown how in the course of operatic history it is primarily the "misuse" of correct "understanding" that led to ideas of reform. It can also be shown that the medium was not necessarily misunderstood in periods where the influence of the poet was very strong, which was the case, roughly speaking, in the first two centuries of operatic activity. There are whole periods which can be designated by the name of a poet rather than that of a composer. All it denotes is that the opera was conceived by the poet as an aesthetic whole, regarding both poetry and music. While significant, it does not by any means imply the subservience of music to poetry. In fact, it is the Metastasian kind of opera, and the unanticipated abuses of it, which provoked Marcello's satire *Il Teatro alla moda* and led to efforts at reform, attempting to inject renewed dramatic vigor into opera. It is interesting to note that composers (Jomelli, Traëtta, Gluck) were prominent in bringing about the change, though they were not the only ones responsible for it. The relative importance of

[45]See Edward J. Dent, "A Best-Seller in Opera," *Music and Letters*, vol. XXII, 1941.
[46]See Louis G. Elison, "Atrocities and Humor of Opera," *Musical Quarterly*, vol. VI, 1920. Also see H.G. Sear, "Operatic Mortality," *Music and Letters*, vol. XXI, 1935.

composer, poet, artist, machinist, etc. and the status bestowed upon each varied in the course of operatic history depending on time and place. Though sociologically and historically interesting, taken by itself, such variation does not necessarily imply a shift in the understanding of the role of music in the music drama.

In an effort to generalize from the problems encountered by actual composers and librettists in their experiments with opera, certain musicologists have provided real insight into the ways in which words and music constrain each other. Pirrotta's analysis has already been cited. Pirandello-like, he argues that in early music drama it was the song that set out in search of its hero rather than the hero who set out in search of his song.

Discussing the difficulties of adapting D'Annunzio's tragedies by Italian composers, Gatti provides empirical support for the argument that simplicity of plot, structure, character and emotions are essential if the music is to say all that it can say. He, too, stresses the incompatibility of verbosity and verbal ornamentation and the inspiration of musical emotion. The characters, he says, must remain in their "simplest expression," the drama in the "stark nudity of its contrasting elements."[47] Minute self-description or intricate introspection on the part of the characters "interferes with and annuls the power of music, which, with a single beat, can illumine the very depths of the soul, and bring us into intimate psychological contact with what is behind the veil."[48] Even if Gatti allows himself to be carried away by his own poetry of "the single beat" (to make a musical point takes much more than that), his message is clear: that libretti, and the other operatic arts, must allow themselves to be fulfilled by music. "The music drama," he says, "should be, above all, action: it should show the motives underlying the impulses of the characters taking part in the action, and define their mutual attitudes, following their movements and seeking to condense in fewest words the revelations of the emotional motives inspiring them."[49]

---

[47]What Gatti calls "simplest expression," Wagner called pure human nature, "das Reinmenschliche." Wagner admired Shakespeare because of the pure human nature of his characters, which reflects the common ground of all human emotions. This he recognized as the essentially musical element in drama.
[48]Gatti, *op. cit.*, pp. 268-69.
[49]*Ibid.*

This is not the place to enumerate the many fine studies that provide valuable insights into the workings of the music-drama. The above represents a sort of consensus, unencumbered by the stress placed on a single point or points by individual scholars.

Why Does Music Have These Powers?

In the process of actual experimentation with the wedding of music and drama, and in the works of those who have attempted to record, analyze and debate these experiments, the differences among the arts become clearer. The powers of music become more apparent with each successive attempt to define, empirically or theoretically, what music adds to the telling of a story. In the previous sections of this chapter, the focus of attention was on the power of music to sum up a "disposition" or "state of soul" and the kinds of words that give this power its fullest play.

In the present section, we turn to the question "Why?" *Why* does music have these powers? What is it about the nature of music that makes it different from words, and why is music able to say something more and less than words? Two sorts of answers deserve attention.

The more classical of the two builds on the argument that music and the emotions are profoundly related, in a way which words and emotions are not. Indeed, current studies of brain physiology and cognitive psychology suggest that music and pictures are processed on the right side of the brain, which specializes more in emotional matters. Susanne Langer argued that music and emotions are isomorphic. While rationality, ultimately, arises from the elaboration of feelings, its archetypal locus is in the verbal discourse in which cognition predominates. Discourse, and discursive language, are poor models for the more "primitive forms of feeling," says Langer. These, rather, are institutionalized in art that gives form to "the unlogicized aspects of mental life" and formulates "the rhythmic continuity of our selfhood."[50]

Of all the arts, music follows the pattern of life itself as it is felt and directly known, argues Langer. "The tonal structure we

[50]Susanne K. Langer. "The Art Symbol and the Symbol in Art" in her *Problems of Art*, New York: Charles Scribner's Sons, 1957, pp. 125-33.

call 'music' bears a close logical similarily to the forms of human feeling—forms of growth and of attenuation, flowing and stowing, conflict and resolution, speed, arrest, terrific excitement, calm or subtle activation and dreamy lapses—not joy and sorrow perhaps, but the poignancy of either and both—the greatness and brevity and eternal passing of everything vitally felt. Such is the pattern, or logical form, of sentience; and the pattern of music is that same form worked out in pure measured sound and silence." Langer concludes this passage with the assertion that "music is a tonal analogue of emotive life."[51]

Leonard Meyer develops this theme further, but anchors his argument in a tighter psychological theory of affect, taking greater care to insist that the close relationship between music and the emotions is, nevertheless, something learned. Nor is it only "referential meaning" that is learned, according to Meyer. Even the "absolutists" who maintain that the meaning of a piece of music inheres in the relationships set forth in the work itself need recourse to the idea of learning. A musical event is important not because it refers to anything outside itself, but because it refers to, and creates expectations of, the next musical event.

Drawing on psychological theory, Meyer teaches that emotion is aroused when the tendency to respond is arrested or inhibited. Expectations in music, when perceived, are like other expectations, and frustration of the tendency to respond in music is like other inhibited tendencies—except that it is an altogether intrinsic part of music. Arguing that the self-same musical stimulus activates and inhibits tendencies and provides meaningful and relevant resolutions, Meyer's argument recalls Langer's effort to find correspondence between the primeval flow of human emotion and the patterns of music. While Langer, too, insists on the connection between rational cognition and basic affects, Meyer finds even less room for their separation. How music is experienced is a function of the technical level on which it is analyzed, whether rational, formal or intuitive. But basically the same processes that give rise to cognition give rise to affect, and "affective experience is just as dependent upon intelligent cognition as conscious intellection," thinking and feeling are "not polar opposites, but . . . different manifes-

---

[51]Langer, *Feeling and Form, op. cit.*, p. 27.

tations of a single psychological process."[52]

However much they may differ, both Langer and Meyer find a strong connection between music and emotion. For Langer, the connection is isomorphic but the art symbol—including music—is an objectification of feelings presented for contemplation. Thus, both Langer and Meyer connect emotion and cognition.

Goodman makes them identical; he denies that aesthetic experience is different from cognitive experience. While Langer reserves for art the special realm of providing frames for primitive forms of feeling, "the difference between art and science," says Goodman, "is not that between feeling and fact, intuition and inference . . . sensation and cerebration . . . or truth and beauty, but rather a difference in domination of certain specific characteristics of symbols." Goodman thus goes even further than Langer or Meyer in not wanting to disassociate art from other symbol systems, all of which, ultimately, function in "the creation and comprehension of our worlds."[54]

Thus, Goodman's answer to the question of "why" music says both more and less than words (although he would never phrase the question in this way) is based on the analysis of different symbol systems and the ways in which they operate in perceptions and actions, whether in the arts or the sciences. Music and words are products of two different kinds of symbol systems, and Goodman's approach makes room for interesting speculations on what happens when words and music come together, as in opera.

Western music, for Goodman, is an example—indeed, the prime example—of a notational system that answers to five definitional requirements. Two of the requirements are syntactic, and three of them semantic. Briefly, the symbol scheme of every notational system is notational. It consists of characters ("inscriptions," "marks," "utterances") the essential feature of which is an "abstraction class of character indifference among inscription," i.e., each inscription of a character is a true copy of the character and no mark may belong to more than one character. The syntactic requirements of a notational system are that

[52]Meyer, *op. cit.*, p. 39.
[53]Nelson Goodman, *Languages of Art*, New York: The Bobbs-Merrill Company, 1968, p. 264.
[54]*Ibid.*, p. 265.

the characters be disjoined and finitely differentiated. Disjointness is assured by a classification that counts every difference as
a difference of character. Finite differentiation is assured by a
scheme of clearly differentiated inscriptions, so that if two characters have an inscription in common, it must be theoretically
possible to determine to which of the two characters the inscription belongs.

Symbol systems consist of symbol schemes "correlated
with a field of reference." A symbol, however, may or may not
denote that which it refers to. A mark is ambiguous if it has
different "compliants" at different times, even if it is an inscription of a single character. If "scores" are to be correlated with
performances, whatever is denoted by a symbol must comply
with it. The three semantic requirements upon notational systems are thus: unambiguity, disjointness and finite differentiation. Unambiguity pertains to an invariance in compliance relationships; disjointness stipulates that "no two characters have
any compliant in common"; and finite differentiation assures
the theoretical possibility to determine that a given object does
not comply with the first or the second of two characters which
have different compliance classes if that object does not comply
with both.

The above five requirements are not optional, but a must, if
a symbol system is to function as a notational system.[55] Standard
musical notation is a prime example of a notational system.
"Identity of work and of score," says Goodman, "is retained in
any series of steps, each of them either from compliant performance to score-inscription to true copy. This is ensured by the
fact, and only by the fact, that the language in which a score is
written must be notational—must satisfy the five stated requirements."[56] In short, performances of music are not an instance of
a musical work, but the end products of the work as defined by
its notation.

This does not mean that performances do not differ, or may
not differ, from each other. In fact, they do because all the aspects that affect the quality of performances are not notational,
only those that affect the identity of the work are. Developing a
notational system like that of music means having arrived at "a
real definition of the notion of a musical work," says Good-

[55]*Ibid.*, p. 156.
[56]*Ibid.*, p. 178.

man.[57] A painting, by contrast, is its own beginning and end, lacking a notated "score," as it were, from which and into which it can be reproduced.

This is not the place to develop Goodman's theory about "autographic" and "allographic" arts and why the first cannot be transformed into the second. The point stressed here is the definitiveness of musical works, and also that none of the natural languages is a notational system. Discursive languages meet the syntactic requirements but not the semantic ones. It follows that utterances are not the end products of a literary work in the way that performances are the end products of a musical work. Although a literary work may be articulate and "exemplify" or "express" what is articulate, it nevertheless requires "search" in order "to determine precisely what is exemplified or expressed."[58] This is due to the fact that literature is only syntactically articulate but semantically "dense." By definition, then, language leaves something "unsaid" while music says it all, or all it can say. Or as Goodman would have it: "While under a discursive language one complete object or event complying with a character does not uniquely determine character or compliance class," projection from sample to compliance class in music is uniquely determined, "the decisions have already been taken in adopting the system."[59]

Despite the fact that scores define musical works, the exemplification or expression of anything beyond the score constitutes reference in a semantically dense system. Representation is relative to different symbol systems, and a scheme is representational only insofar as it is dense. Unambiguity together with syntactic and semantic disjointness and differentiation are properties required of notational systems, but these requirements are negative and generally "designed to preclude otherwise inevitable trouble, not to ensure a vocabulary or grammar adequate for a given subject matter."[60]

Expression, according to Goodman, is no different from exemplification, representation and description insofar as they are types of reference. Resemblance is not necessary for reference

---

[57]*ibid.*, p. 197. Of course, Goodman refers to the standard musical notation of the West.
[58]*Ibid.*, p. 240.
[59]*Ibid.*, pp. 202-3.
[60]*Ibid.*, p. 154.

and almost anything may stand for anything else. Denotation, not imitation, is the core of representation. While expression, like representation, is a species of denotation, it is invariably related to exemplification, and exemplification, in turn, is a mode of symbolization based on labeling. A certain piece, or genre, of music, for example, may be labeled sad. That which expresses sadness is metaphorically sad—actually sad, but not literally so— by virtue of "transferred application of some label coextensive with sad."[61] What is expressed is thus "possessed"; the symbol takes on an acquired property. "Establishment of the referential relationship," says Goodman, "is a matter of singling out certain properties for attention, of selecting association with certain other objects. Verbal discourse is not least among the many factors that aid in founding and nurturing such association."[62]

There is more to Goodman than in the above oversimplified presentation of some of his ideas. However, even from the little said here it emerges that the interaction between music and words involves a relationship between a fully articulate symbol system and a symbol system that is only syntactically articulate while semantically "dense." The former leaves no room for ambiguity; the latter provides the reference. It is in this sense that music provides an unambiguous statement to that which it cannot even name; once it is linked with a label, it can provide a unique definition.

It may be argued, then, that the "denser" the discursive language the more it is able to benefit from an association with music for the purpose of elucidation. Conversely, the less ambiguous the utterance is, the more the recourse to music may prove inefficacious or even alienating. If mood, disposition and the like are thought to be best expressed by music it is because music is capable of pinning down, incontestably, so to speak, that which is most ambiguous in discursive language. Here is St. Evremond's or Gatti's prescription for the union of the two arts, and herein lies a clue to Schopenhauer's view of music as an art which men are "content to understand directly" but renounce all claim "to an abstract conception of this direct understanding itself."[63] Schopenhauer recognized the fact that his explanation of the "inner nature of music" and its "imitative relation to the

[61]*Ibid.*, p. p. 85.
[62]*Ibid.*, p. 88.
[63]Arthur Schopenhauer, *The World as Will and Idea*, p. 282.

world" assumes and establishes a relation between "music as idea" to that which "from its nature can never be idea." Music, therefore, has to be regarded "as the copy of an original which can never itself be directly presented as idea."[64] According to Schopenhauer, music, like the other arts, is a "way of *viewing* things independent of the principle of sufficient reason," but it is "by no means like the other arts the copy of the Ideas, but the copy of the will itself whose objectivity the Ideas are."[65] The effect of music is more powerful and penetrating than that of the other arts because "they speak only of shadows, but it speaks of the thing itself."[66]

Of course, Schopenhauer and Goodman are worlds apart, but the latter may assist in demystifying the former. Music, among the arts, is charged by many aestheticians with the expression of feelings, with the "stato d'animo." Yet words are needed to label these feeling-states. By inference from Goodman, we see how music clarifies feelings once they have been named, and thus, how opera—in combining music with the other arts—is the supreme communicator of feelings. Over and over, we shall say that opera is the medium through which people tell each other how they feel. At least until it becomes a cliché—a frozen metaphor, in Goodman's term—music determines precisely that which is exemplified or expressed; it eliminates the need for all further search.

The Ever-Changing Balance: Concluding Remarks

But still the search goes on. Since there is no limit to the ambiguity of words seeking expression in the precision of music, and since no musical work—by definition—is like any other musical work, there can be no limit to the unique combinations of text and song and no end to the search for the ideal marriage. The go-betweens, obviously, are kept very busy.

The search goes on also because the conceptions of the powers of each of the media are continually changing—typically without benefit of the awareness that all representation is rooted in social agreements. Conventions become worn, ideologies are

[64]*Ibid.*
[65]*Ibid.*, p. 283.
[66]*Ibid.*

MVSICK.

Although the Cannon, and the Churlish Drum
Haue strooke the Quire mute, and the Organs Dumb:
Yet Musicks Art with Ayre and String, and Voyce
Makes glad the Sad, and Sorrow to Reioyce.

Plate 2.   Music. An engraving by P. Lambert (1612-1682) depicting music. The accompanying verse speaks of the "powers of music"

retired, paradigms are exhausted and new formulae arise to take their place.

This may be an opportunity also to state briefly that music—for the reasons discussed above—is well suited for what may be called the "socialization of sentiments" and consequently also for their reinforcement or arousal. Repeated association between a particular kind of music and a particular reference may endow the music with reference without having to be explicit about it. The history of opera is replete with musical formulae that may be viewed as examples of "referential music." In fact, the *Affektenlehre* of the Eighteenth century, according to which the chief aim of music was to portray certain typical emotions, may be viewed largely in terms of the socialization of sentiments by music. Elaborate formulae entered into the process of musical composition as explicit statements. Ostensibly, the "powers" of music are enhanced thereby and the communicative potency of music made salient; but we know from the discussion of Goodman that pushing music in the direction of language and labelling ultimately detracts from the uniqueness of its powers. If the theory of affections causes puzzlement at times, the way some music is used in the cinema leaves little doubt that musical socialization really works.

Thus, the taste and world-outlook of the audience, itself perpetually changing in composition, also affect the union of words and music. This is particularly true for the early centuries when opera was, by and large, commissioned for a definite place and occasion. The picture does change somewhat with the change in the original purpose of operatic production, when in place of writing for a single festive occasion one finds the "urge to secure musical stage works for all time, and if possible for all nations."[67] Naturally, with such a purpose in mind the artist is less likely to experience the dictates of the taste of the audience. He does not address himself to a large group, but rather to a very limited one, under the delusion that the cultivated taste and knowledge of his audience override the boundaries of time and place.[68]

[67]See Alfred Einstein, "The Mortality of Opera," in *Music and Letters*, vol. XXII, 1941.
[68]This attitude is partially the product of the theory of "Art for Art's Sake," which isolates art from all relation to practical life and leads to the belief that "the dignity and value of Art is somehow enhanced by divorcing it from all

While the claim to permanence is most characteristic of the romantic period, it is germane to all reform movements, regardless of time. Gluck no less than Wagner believed that he created a species of opera that could claim international success and permanence. Being the object of much criticism, it is readily understood why opera had more than its share of reform seekers, people who attempted to "solve" the "problems" of opera once and for all. This holds true even for a Beaumarchais and a Hofmannsthal, despite their admitted great insight into the operatic medium. Opera, says Goldschmidt, is a "niederschlag einer nie stillstehenden Geistesbewegung. Mit dem Fühlen und Denken der Gebildeten auf das innigste verknüpft, müssten sie und werden sie in Zukunft selbst die intimsten Schwankungen des psychischen Lebens eines Volkes wiederspiegeln. Und das muss sich naturgemäss nicht nur in der Beziehung von Wort und Ton, sondern in den Qualitäten der Musik selbst und in ihren Formen äussern. Es war ein fast unbegreiflicher Irrtum Wagners, wenn er meinte, in seinem Musik-drama eine Formel Gefunden zu haben, die den Schaffenden aller Zeiten die Werkstatt der Opern eröffnete."[69] Goldschmidt is undoubtedly right even without having to add that opera is and always was a costly affair. As such it was invariably "linked" in one form or another with an audience that sponsored its production. This point was recently reiterated in a paper by Bianconi and Walker who claim that Seventeenth century opera, for example, was first and foremost an instrument and demonstration of political authority.[70] Whether

---

practical considerations and . . . that any work or performance which can be shown to have a utilitarian purpose or end must be considered not a genuine work of art." See Felix Clay, "The Origin of the Aesthetic Emotion," in *Sammelbände der Internationalen Musikgesellschaft*, vol. IX, p. 283.

[69]Hugo Goldschmidt, "Die Reform der Italienischen Oper des 18 Jahrhunderts", *III Kongress der Internationalen Musikgesellschaft*, 1909, p. 197. Wagner was by no means the only one who explicitly talked about "the opera of the future." Men like Algarotti, Diderot, and Herder, to mention only a few, were just as guilty of such a misconception. Also see Martin Ehrenhaus, *Die Operndichtung der deutschen Romantik*, doctoral dissertation, University of Breslau, 1911. Ehrenhaus' study serves as a good example showing opera as being a "Niederschlag einer Geistesbewegung." Ehrehaus is primarily concerned with the relationship between German romantic opera and German romanticism as a whole and its literary movements in particular.

[70]Lorenzo Bianconi and Thomas Walker, "Production, Consumption and Political Function of 17th Century Opera," a paper read at the 12th Congress of the IMS, 1977.

their thesis is correct or not does not change the fastness of their premise, namely that the full understanding of what takes place on the stage requires the projection of limelights onto relevant off-stage "scenes."

Inevitable, continuous change is not the exclusive property of opera, to be sure. It is, paradoxically, the only constant factor in any cultural expression. If it is overlooked at times, this is due to the fact that the creative genius is bound by his own moment in history, which is invariably the last stage of development with which he is familiar. Dealing with the "essence" of things causes even greater oversights. It creates the illusion that one's analysis shares the same "essential" qualities and is free to ignore contextual factors. The fact remains, however, that the utterances of librettists and composers as well as the assertions of aestheticians can be fully understood only in their historical context just as the theory of music may be said to reflect the aesthetics and practices of the music of the day at every stage of its development. Nevertheless, there are always some people who expect current music theory to be the guide and analytic tool for all of music.

It would be wrong to assume, however, from what has been said, that every change means something new. It invariably implies something different (from what is) but not necessarily new. The "something different" can be new, partially new, or even familiar from an earlier stage of development. But it can never be the same, because its original context has changed. Thus, though opera and its aesthetics have been changing continuously, its history reveals points of recurrence. These can be detected only partially in the art works themselves; they are primarily expressed in philosophic and aesthetic discourses. In other words, while works of art differ in styles incorporating in the course of artistic development technical and nontechnical dictates, the works may, nevertheless, reveal similar *attitudes* on the part of their artists and audiences.[71] Similar attitudes, however, have different antecedents. An understanding of the atti-

[71]"A style is not so much a 'way of seeing the world' as it is a technique for representing what is already seen . . . Technique influences form, and form, by a kind of reflexive activity, influences the techniques of representation . . . whenever the representation is conventionalized into formal patterns by craft and medium, these patterns themselves acquire symbolic meanings and emotional values." See Wylie Sypher, *Four Stages of Renaissance Style*, New York: Doubleday and Company, 1955, p. 8.

tudes requires the incorporation of their antecedents. If points of concurrence are preceded by seeming similar factors that bring about the change (and the resultant similarities), it would be appropriate to speak of operatic history in terms of cycles. It can be shown, in fact, that such cycles do occur and, indeed, that the unfolding of operatic history may be analyzed in these terms. The aesthetic history of Italian opera from its inception to the middle of the Eighteenth century represents a major cycle of operatic development in which the predominating emphasis moves gradually from drama to music and then to drama once more. In these hundred and fifty years, roughly speaking, Italian opera underwent great changes. It gave rise to theories concerning the medium itself and led to criticism of particular works and specific operatic trends. The preceding pages, by way of introduction, attempted an examination of opera as a medium without regard to its historical unfolding in order to facilitate the analysis of its moment of birth.

Whatever the substance of change, and regardless of approach, the *problem* remains unchanged: opera is a melodrama, *sui generis*, in which people tell each other how they feel in song. No matter how one slices it, action is necessary to the drama in which feelings seek expression. And if drama is dependent on well-chosen words, music-drama is dependent on the few chosen words dictated by the music. The recognition that the simultaneity of action and emotion in the musical drama comes "naturally" and that verbosity is alien to opera did not have to wait for the insight of a Stendahl. In fact the recognition is there from the start that the "powers" of music make music into the mood-building art *par excellence*. The question remains: how to unleash it with best results. This is what preoccupies all those who have tried to refine and define, experiment and theorize, about the conditions under which the powers of music are most effectively made manifest.

Chapter Three

The Camerata as Invisible College

Writings which attempt to downgrade the role of the Florentine Camerata as the cradle of early Italian opera seem as far from the mark as those which insist on the exclusivity of its birthright. It is likely that members of the so-called Camerata—that Renaissance salon or "academy" of amateurs, musicians, artists, astrologers, philosophers and scientists who met informally under the aegis of Bardi and Corsi—were largely unaware of the role that history would accord to them.[1] The goal they set for themselves was certainly not to create what the next four centuries would know as opera. Their aim was to reform the polyphonic music of the day and they believed that the best way to do so was to renovate the ancient Greek practice of setting words to music with "power to move the passion of the mind."[2] They did not think of themselves primarily as innovators; they thought they were returning to an earlier and better way.

Recent research, particularly the work of Pirrotta and Palisca, has added much to the refinement of our knowledge of the Camerata, and its proper place in musical history. As we shall see, "the group" was split by rivalry between its two "conveners," one of whom inclined more to talk and amateur music-making and the other to experimentation in dramatic productions with music.[3]

There was also a stylistic difference between its two musical stars. Moreover, this informal academy was only one of five or more Florentine academies which dabbled in drama and aesthet-

[1]See Nino Pirrotta, "Temperaments and Tendencies in the Florentine Camerata," *Musical Quarterly*, 1954, vol. XL, pp. 169-189.
[2]Giulio Caccini, Foreword to *Le nuove musiche* (1602) in Strunk, *op. cit.*, p. 379.
[3]Bardi's group, the Camerata, and Corsi's group, which was something of a workshop, were somewhat overlapping, but distinct. Strictly speaking, therefore, there is not a single group with two conveners, but an "invisible college." The latter will become increasingly clear in the following pages.

ics. One of these, the Alterati, apparently deserves major attention, because it contained the greatest numbers of musical amateurs.[4] Nevertheless, one immediately discovers that the overlap
in membership between the Alterati and Camerata was very
high. For that matter, the overlapping of memberships among
all these groups "makes it hard to keep their contribution distinct," says Palisca.[5] Nor were the Camerata so naive as to think
that they were reviving ancient Greek tragedy; their aim, rather,
was to revive a certain style of singing which they associated
with classic drama. They were primarily interested in communicating more "effectively."[6] Certain of the members may have
been aware that they were developing a new style (or genre),
and salient or not, the infighting over who-did-what-first suggests that a subconscious realization of their innovative role was
alive in the others.[7]

Additions and subtractions make the story more interesting, but the fact remains that the experiments of the Florentine
group did make history. Ironically, their case is even *stronger* in
that they did not explicitly pronounce their paternity of the opera; in that they differed in the conception of how to reach their
goal; in that they were part of a larger network consisting of
other groups similarly occupied. The Camerata, and possibly
their allies, acted as midwives to the sixteenth century, which
was pregnant with the peculiar conjunction of social, ideological
and cultural ideas and practices from which the opera emerged.
Not only were the musico-aesthetic theories of the Camerata influenced by the social, ideological and cultural context of the
century, but its very existence as a social institution, was a product of the time. Analysis of the structure and composition of the
group has direct bearing on its thought, just as its thought has
direct bearing on the birth of opera. And as may already be apparent, the kind of artistic creativity that arose from the salon of
the Camerata has a number of parallels in the dynamics of creativity in science. This should not be confused with the long-

[4]Claude V. Palisca, "The Alterati of Florence, Pioneers in the Theory of Dramatic Music," in *New Looks at Italian Opera, op. cit*, pp. 10-11.
[5]*Ibid.*, p. 10.
[6]*Ibid.*, pp. 35-37; 53.
[7]See Claude V. Palisca, "Musical Asides in the Diplomatic Correspondence of
Emilio de'Cavalieri," *The Musical Quarterly*, vol. XLIX, no. 3, 1963. Also see
Nino Pirrotta, "Early Opera and Aria," *op. cit*, pp. 40-53.

standing alliance of theoretical music with science as part of the quadrivium. Practical musicianship was not a part of it, much less a recognition of commonality as far as the dynamics of creativity are concerned. In fact, the Camerata contributed to further the gap between "musical science" and practice, between objective truth and subjective determination, between acoustics and aesthetics.

The Camerata—Custodian of a Paradigm

The geography of the Renaissance is dotted with groups of learned men—laymen and professionals—who came together for serious talk. In his much-quoted letter to G.B. Doni (1594-1647), Bardi's son, Pietro, tells how his father "who took great delight in music and was in his day a composer of some reputation always had about him the most celebrated men of the city, learned in this profession, and inviting them to his house, he formed a sort of delightful and continual academy from which vice and in particular every kind of gaming were absent. To this the noble youth of Florence were attracted with great profit to themselves, passing their time not only in pursuit of music, but also in discussing and receiving instruction in poetry, astrology, and other sciences . . . "[8] Pietro De'Bardi goes on to mention Galilei, the theorist and composer (and father of the astronomer); Caccini, the renowned singer; Peri, singer-organist and composer; Rinuccini, the famous poet and librettist; and Jacopo Corsi, who succeeded his father as patron of the group and its creative activity. Extending the net, one can trace the links between Bardi and Galilei and the classicists Francesco Patrici and Girolamo Mei to the humanist Piero Vettori, and to an allied, but rival, group in Rome, centering on de'Cavalieri, leading indirectly to Monteverdi.[9] Seated in the parlor as full participants in

[8]Pietro de'Bardi, Letter fo G.B. Doni (1634) in Strunk, *op. cit.*, p. 363.

[9]"Nor was there," writes Pietro, "any want of men to imitate them, and in Florence, the first home of this sort of music, and in other cities of Italy, especially in Rome, these gave and are still giving a marvelous account of themselves on the dramatic stage. Among the foremost of these it seems fitting to place Monteverdi." In Strunk, *Ibid.*, p. 365. On membership of musicians other than those mentioned above see Claude V. Palisca, "The 'Camerata Fiorentina': A Reappraisal," *Studi musicali*, 1972, pp. 208-12. Also see Palisca, "Girolamo Mei, Mentor to the Florentine Camerata," *Musical Quarterly*, 1954, vol. XL, and Mei's *Letters on Ancient and Modern Music to Vincenzo and Giovanni Bardi*,

the conversation and as members of the audience were the nobles and clergymen of the Medici court, their officials and the
rising middle class of the city.

"Indeed," writes Caccini, "in the times when the most vir-
tuous Camerata of the most illustrious Signor Giovanni Bardi,
Count of Vernio, flourished in Florence, and in it were assembled not only a part of the nobility but also the first musicians
and men of talent and poets and philosophers of the city, and I
too frequently attended it, I can say that I learned more from
their learned discussions than I learned from descant in over
thirty years; for these most understanding gentlemen always encouraged me and convinced me with the clearest reasons not to
follow that old way of composition whose music, not suffering
the words to be understood by the hearers, ruins the conceit and
the verse . . . [causing] a laceration of the poetry . . . but to hold
fast to the manner so much praised by Plato and other philosophers, who declare that music is nothing other than the fable,
and last and not the contrary, the rhythm and the sound, in
order to penetrate the perception of others and to produce those
marvelous effects, admired by the writers . . ."[10]

In his foreword to his *Le nuove musiche*, Caccini established,
among other things, his own affiliation with the Camerata. His
flowery praise, however, accompanied by the dedication of his
version of *Euridice* to Bardi were part of a concerted campaign by
Caccini to prove that he had been writing in *stile rappresentativo*
since the days of the Camerata. Hence his *Euridice*, though it
followed Peri's, was in a style for which he could claim first
rights.[11] Yet, Peri's *Euridice* had preceded his; it was performed

---

Palisca, ed., Rome: American Institute of Musicology, 1960. Also see Pirrotta,
op. cit. Francesco Patrici expressed the view that Greek tragedies were sung in
their entirety in his treatise *Della Poetica* of 1586. With the aid of the tables of
Alypius, Patrici analyzed a fragment of Galilei's document on Greek music.
Though not a member of the Camerata, he discussed the matter with Bardi.
Patrici, Bardi and Mei were acquainted with the work of Piero Vettori, the com-
mentator on Aristotle's *Poetics* and editor of Greek tragedies. See Leo Schrade,
Tragedy in the Art of Music, Cambridge: Harvard University Press, 1964, pp. 53-
54. Most poetic theorists, however, relying on Aristotle's *Poetics*, considered the
chorus to have been the only musical part of ancient tragedy. See Barbara Hanning, *Of Poetry and Music's Power: Humanism and the Creation of Opera*, Ann
Arbor, Michigan: UMI Research Press, Microfilms International, 1980, pp. 15-
19.
[10]Strunk, *op. cit.*, p. 378.
[11]Giulio Caccini, Dedication to *Euridice*, in Strunk, *op. cit.*, p. 370.

in 1600, also to Rinuccini's libretto, on the occasion of the wedding of Maria di Medici to Henry IV. While Peri did not protest against Caccini, Cavalieri did. Among Cavalieri's reports to the Tuscan court about the social, political and artistic affairs in Rome during his mission in Rome, there are some "musical asides" which are indeed most revealing. After having been discharged from the job of coordinator of music at the Florentine court and replaced by Caccini, Cavalieri writes with indignation: "That I [Cavalieri] should have been set aside by Giuilio Romano, who if he lived a hundred years could learn from me!"[12] And after having seen the printed score of Caccini's *Euridice* he writes: "I find nothing in it that annoys me. For my *rappresentatione*, which is printed, having been printed three and a half months earlier, settles all the contentions. And it will be recognized what is science and what is the difference between starlings and partridges."[13] Cavalieri also challenges Rinuccini who acted "as if he had been the inventor of this way of representing in music, never before found or invented by anyone," and relates: "I spoke to him about all this, for it seemed to me that he had done me wrong. Because this [style] was invented by me . . ."[14]

Rinuccini is willing to give Peri credit for having surmounted the "difficulties this style presented."[15] Peri, however, aware of Cavalieri's annoyance at Rinuccini, writes in his preface to his score of *Euridice*: "Although Signor Emilio del Cavalieri, before any other of whom I know enabled us with marvelous invention to hear our kind of music upon the stage, nonetheless as early as 1594, it pleased the Signors Jacopo Corsi and Ottavio Rinuccini that I should employ it in another guise . . ."[16]

---

[12]Quoted in Palisca, "Musical Asides," *op. cit.*, p. 353.
[13]*Ibid.* p. 354.
[14]*Ibid.*, pp. 343-54. La Tragedia as prologue, according to Hanning, is supposed to have conveyed the transformation of tragedy from the "spectre of pity and terror" to "the sweet songstress of melancholy," capable of moving the hearts of audiences by singing. Prologues in this period, Hanning has shown, functioned to establish the mood of that which followed and were often used as "defensive expressions" of authors who were "conscious of innovating." For Rinuccini, moreover, as well as for Peri, the "novelty" of "testing" the power of music goes back to their first opera, *Dafne*. See Hanning, *op. cit.*, pp. 3-8.
[15]Ottavio Rinuccini, Dedication to *Euridice*, in Strunk, *op. cit.*, p. 367.
[16]Jacopo Peri, Preface to *Euridice*, in Strunk, *op.cit.*, p. 373. Rinuccini's interest in the "power of music" was undoubtedly affected by his association with Bardi in the 1589 *intermedi*. Hanning suggests that in addition to his own humanistic

While the claims of priority help to make the chronology of the first monodic musical dramas more accurate and provide insight into the personalities involved, their significance from a phenomenological point of view should not be lost on us, for it contributes a major point to the characterization of the group as a whole.[17] Peri and Caccini were highly accomplished singers, and Caccini was also a theorist of sorts and a most demanding and disciplined teacher of singers. While Cavalieri was only indirectly in touch with the Camerata, Caccini and Rinuccini were full-fledged members. Caccini also appeared at the meetings of the Alterati, although he was not formally a member.

Whether Pietro Bardi and Caccini overstate the case, whether the other groups such as the Alterati were of equal or greater merit, whether music was or was not the group's predominant concern are interesting questions, but probably not critical ones.[18] The fact is that we have something to go on, with respect to the Camerata. Some of their theoretical writings and statements have been preserved, as well as some of their music. Records of the proceedings of the Alterati are even more complete, because the Alterati—unlike the Camerata—was an official literary academy rather than an informal group. Even if the Camerata was merely an example of other such groups, it would be worth dwelling on it; but clearly it was more than that, for *Dafne*, the two *Euridices* and other works in similar manner are its products.

The Camerata, then, was not just another salon of the type with which later literary history is replete. Like the Alterati, whose theoretical discussions reached a very high level, the Camerata constituted a forum for theoretical discussions, but it was also a workshop, a "laboratory" for the creation and perfor-

---

training and participation in the academies he must have learned of Mei's and Galilei's theories from Bardi so that by the time he frequented the home of Corsi his interests were already well formed. See Hanning *op. cit.*, p. 12.

[17]For clarifications on chronology see Palisca, " . . . A Reappraisal," *op. cit.*, pp. 203-208.

[18]"When we remember that the same intellectual climate produced a true literary academy, the Crusca (in which Bardi was l'Incruscato), we have reason to doubt whether musical discussions loomed as large in the activities of the Camerata as we think they did." Pirrotta, "Temperaments . . . ," *op. cit.*, p. 171. The above notwithstanding, one can argue that theorizing about music within a larger frame of reference contributed to the crystallization of the new musical aesthetics.

mance of music. Above all, it was marked by a determination to find a new way as far as the composition and performance of music was concerned, despite differences over how to get there.

In the parlance of the sociology of science, the Camerata fits rather closely the model of "invisible college."[19] This concept refers to a group of scientists who share a focal problem or "paradigm" and by addressing themselves to the problem and to each other create the kind of "continual academy" which the younger Bardi invoked as a description of the Camerata.[20] In modern science, this means shared laboratories, a system of mutual criticism, a specialty journal, a water cooler, a faculty club, periodic conclaves and the like, together with tacit agreements concerning the appropriate methods of research, priority problems, and shorthand communication such shared work implies. Science is a "community based activity" and a paradigm governs not only a subject matter but a group of practitioners.[21] Thinking of the Camerata as a kind of "invisible college" may be helpful.

The applicability of the idea of "paradigm" and "invisible college" in art has been noted by others as well. The sociology of art "requires analysis of the developments of belief systems of such groups as well as sociometric analysis of the relations between their members, of the relations between such groups, and of the relationships of such groups to the larger social structure."[22] Of course, the idea of the salon, the coffeehouse or the cafe as a breeding place of artistic creativity is nothing new in the history of art or intellectual history generally. Indeed, the centrality of such meeting places for the exchange of views has often been noted.[23] More, the weaving of bonds of mutual support among artists, of liaisons between artists and dealers, and the forging of common understandings between artists and critics

[19]See Crane, *op. cit.* Also see D.J. de S. Price and D. Beaver, "Collaboration in an Invisible College," *American Psychologist*, 1966, vol. XXI, pp. 1011-18.
[20]Pietro de'Bardi, *op. cit.*
[21]The above postulate is the basis for the sociology of science as well as for Kuhn's theory of paradigms.
[22]Crane, *op. cit.*, p. 131.
[23]To mention but a few, see L. Coser, *Men of Ideas*, New York: Free Press, 1965; Arnold Hauser, *The Social History of Art*, London: Routledge & Kegan Paul, 1951; B. Rosenberg and N.E. Fliegel, *The Vanguard Artist*, Chicago: Quadrangle Books, 1965; White & White, *op. cit.*, Arthur Loesser, *Men, Women and Pianos*, New York: Simon & Schuster, 1954.

has often been both the cause and consequence of sitting to-gether.[24] The idea that social circles of this kind—brought to-gether through mutual interest—should share a common puzzle, which all are trying to solve, has recently come to the fore in the sociology of science, and as a result, in the sociology of art. Here, one has only to think of a group such as the Impressionists to realize that they were coping—as an "invisible college"—with a puzzle which each, separately and together, was trying to solve.

Gombrich notes how, in the Renaissance, new pieces of art came to be viewed as "contributions" and as "solutions" to problems, and thus another analogy between work in the arts and the new arena of experimental science should not be over-looked. [25] Indeed, as Crane notes in this connection, "the simi-larity between this [Gombrich's]concept and Kuhn's idea of par-adigm is startling."[26]

For the Camerata, the puzzle was to discover the ideal com-bination of words and music such that text and music, each in its own way and in juxtaposition to the other, could be maximally effective in communicating not just sensory pleasure but the specific meaning and emotions appropriate to the text. Reading the theoretical writings of members of the Camerata, their letters and the introductions to their compositions, one cannot but be struck over and over again by the attempt to solve this problem. No matter that they did not know exactly how the Greeks had done it (if they had); that was all the more reason to return again and again to the inadequacy of contemporary music, and to try yet another time to achieve the formula that would "move the understanding."

The paradigm that guided the Camerata was also "revolutionary"—even though it was not new. It was an at-tempt, as already noted, to overthrow the predominance of an earlier paradigm related to polyphony.[27] Experiments within the new paradigm consisted of marrying words to music in such a way that the text would be clearly understood and its underlying meaning communicated, through music, to the listener. Guiding

---

[24]See White & White, *op. cit.*
[25]Gombrich, *op. cit.*, pp. 8-9.
[26]Crane, *op. cit.*, p. 134.
[27]For a discussion of the dynamics of the "overthrow" of paradigms see Kuhn, *op. cit.*

the experimentation were ideas about Greek monody and the likelihood that Greek drama was declaimed in a song-like manner. Reviewing the work and the writings of the Camerata, Grout derives three basic concerns: the solo singer; the search for forms of "natural" declamation; and the effort to use melody to interpret the feeling of the text rather than to depict graphic detail.[28]

Far from concentrating exclusively on music-drama, the solo aria and madrigal won the greater part of the Camerata's attention, as is well known. But the selfsame process of continual experimentation within the monodic paradigm also led to a variety of attempts to set dramatic texts to music, in the presumed manner of the ancient Greeks. Thus, the solo aria and the madrigal, no less than the music and text in the *stile rappresentativo*, are "contributions" to the origin of opera. However self-serving, Caccini makes this clear in his dedication to Giovanni Bardi. "His Lordship," he writes, "will recognize that style which, as your Lordship knows, I used on other occasions, many years ago, in the eclogue of Sannazaro . . . and in other madrigals of mine at that time . . . This is likewise the manner which Your Lordship, in the years when Your Lordship's 'Camerata' was flourishing in Florence, discussing it in company with many other noble virtuosi, declared to be that used by the ancient Greeks when introducing song into the representations of their tragedies and fables . . . This manner appears throughout my other compositions, composed at various times going back more than fifteen years, as I have never used in them any art other than the imitation of the conceit of the words, touching those chords more or less passionate which I judged most suitable for the grace which is required for good singing, which grace and which manner of singing Your Most Illustrious Lordship has many times reported to me to be universally accepted in Rome as good."[29]

It by no means detracts to repeat that the group was split in several ways. Corsi and Bardi had their differences over the kudos of sponsorship and the character of group activities, with Corsi tending to be more interested in actual experiments with the role of music in drama and Bardi, perhaps, more interested

[28]Donald Jay Grout, *A Short History of Opera*, New York: Columbia University Press, 1947, p. 44.
[29]Guilio Caccini, Dedication to *Euridice* (1600) in Strunk, *op. cit.*, pp. 370-71.

in theorizing. But Bardi's theorizing probably stimulated Corsi's experiments.[30] Peri and Caccini had their differences, too, and their differences provide a nice illustration of the "working out" of a paradigm. Both accepted that their main goal was to enhance communication through singing, and that modern tragedy might be effectively presented by adaptation of the manner of ancient tragedy. Peri sought to bring singing nearer to speech, allowing the text and the action to dictate to the music; Pirrotta calls this *recitar cantando*. Caccini, more concerned with the perfection of singers and the art of singing, was committed to "affective reactions to dramatic situations,"[31] to words finding expression in the music; Pirrotta calls this *cantar recitando*.[32] Galilei, influenced by Mei, tried his hand at applying the theory of the predominance of words; the results, says Palisca, were more lyrical than dramatic. Outsiders, says Pirrotta, would be impressed by the similarities rather than the differences.[33]

Indeed, the vocabulary and techniques used by the two men were the same, and Pirrotta remarks that this could only have been the product of their joint membership in the salon, where shared concepts arose from theorizing and socializing. The effortless and graceful singing style known as *sprezzatura*, and the continuo accompaniment (preferably self-accompaniment) mark the compositions of both Peri and Caccini.[34]Palisca also remarks on the criticism of colleagues from which members of the salon could profit. Much like the "refereeing" or "discussant" functions in scientific institutions, presentations made by members of the Alterati were commented upon formally by "defenders" and "censors" who were nominated for the occasion.[35] All this is duly recorded in the minutes of the Alterati sessions.

Even the competition over "priorities" is reminiscent of the behavior of scientists. The race to be first has to be reconciled in science with the need and the norm of sharing. The scientists' role is above all to advance knowledge, and knowledge advances through originality. "Recognition and esteem," explains Merton, "accrue to those who have best fulfilled their roles, to

[30]See Palisca, "The Alterati . . . ," *op. cit.*, p. 10.
[31]See Pirrotta, "Early Opera . . . ," *op. cit.*, p. 52.
[32]*Ibid.*
[33]*Ibid.*, p. 45.
[34]*Ibid.*, pp. 53-55.
[35]For an example, see Palisca "The Alterati . . . ," *op. cit.*, p. 22.

those who have made genuinely original contributions to the common stock of knowledge. Then are found those happy circumstances in which self-interest and moral obligation coincide and fuse."[36] Merton goes on to explain that the frequency of struggles over priority does not result merely from the traits of the individuals involved but rather from the institution of science "which defines originality as a supreme value and there by makes recognition of one's originality a major concern. When this recognition of priority is either not granted or fades from view, the scientist loses his scientific property. Although this kind of property shares with other types general recognition of the 'owner's' rights, it contrasts sharply in all other respects. Once he has made his contribution, the scientist no longer has exclusive rights of access to it. It becomes part of the public domain of science . . . In short, property rights in science become whittled down to just this one: the recognition by others of the scientist's distinctive part in having brought the result into being."[37]

The behavior and rhetoric of Caccini, Peri and Cavalieri, as already noted, is relevant in this respect. Interestingly, Pirrotta proposes three reasons why these men fought over "priorities," though the reasons are not mutually exclusive. One possibility is that they really believed they were in a race; a second possibility, which does not contradict the first, is that they failed to appreciate the differences in the kinds of experiments they were conducting; and, finally, they may each have experienced the fear of being overshadowed![38]

Attention should be drawn to the fact that the conflict centers over priority rights with regard to a new style. Unlike individual compositions, style is a contribution to which the composer may cease to have "recognition of the 'owner's' rights." As in science, property rights with regard to style are limited to the mere recognition by others of the composer's "distinctive part in having brought the result into being." The increased awareness with regard to musical styles in the early baroque may be explained in part, by the tangible spirit of the scientific revolution.

[36]Robert K. Merton, *The Sociology of Science*, Chicago: The University of Chicago Press, 1973, p. 293.
[37]*Ibid.*, p. 294.
[38]Pirrotta, "Early Opera . . . ," *op. cit.*, p. 45.

The above analysis suggests that there was a sense of innovation in the air, a sense that the experimentation was leading somewhere. Pirrotta feels that Cavalieri was most aware of this, and indeed, that Cavalieri actually deserves credit for the invention of a new form of theatre, all in music, an invention that expanded the already strong musical component of the literary pastoral, while simplifying the pastoral form to adjust it to the particular exigencies and slower pace of a musical performance. The *recitar cantando* style was employed by Cavalieri, as it was by Peri, but it was Cavalieri's contribution —according to Pirrotta—to bring to the stage "such dramatic actions as could be developed completely in songs and music" as opposed to use of music incidentally.[39] Pirrotta does not credit Cavalieri's claim that his concern was with moving the passions; nor does he think his contribution to sung speech or spoken song matches those of Caccini and Peri.

The fact that Cavalieri was not a member of the Camerata suggests why "invisible college" may be a more accurate term than academy or salon or social circle. The flow of influence was not limited to those who attended the meetings, or to formal membership as in the Alterati, but extended to those who were part of the informal network of social and professional connections. Nor was the network limited to residents of Florence, since Cavalieri lived in Rome and much of the early operatic activity centered there; indeed, Bardi himself ultimately moved to Rome. The same thing holds for Girolamo Mei. Not a musician but a serious scholar of Greek music, Mei is thought to have influenced Galilei in his treatises and compositions, though he did not attend Camerata meetings. He argued strongly against polyphony, insisting that the Greeks did not sing in "harmony." He pressed for monody, arguing that only a single melody could arouse the "affections," and emphasized the necessity for distinguishing between scientific and artistic facts so that art may "exploit as it sees fit without any limitation those tones about which science has learned the truths."[40] Mei's influence on members of the Alterati, also through his letters (he was honored with nonresident membership), was similarly great and he

[39]*Ibid.*, p. 46; pp. 49-50.
[40]Quoted in Palisca, "Scientific Empiricism in Musical Thought," in *Seventeenth Century Science and the Arts*, Hedley Howell Rhys, ed., Princeton, N.J.: Princeton University Press, 1961, p. 125.

is credited by Doni (a later member of the Alterati) with having guided his own research into ancient Greek music.[41]

Thus did an "invisible college" of Florence and Rome at the end of the sixteenth century usher in the new medium of opera as an unintended consequence of its single minded preoccupation with something else. It was determined to overthrow the polyphonic paradigm and to replace it with expressive music of a kind that would both carry the words of a text to the listener and express the feelings implicit in the words. Words assumed a new importance as a result, and the search for the proper juxtaposition of the words and music ensued. Although the text was accorded a predominant role, the question of exactly how music should be grafted to the text led to a renewed interest in the "powers of music." This concern of the ancient Greeks was shrouded in mystery; Palisca feels that the members of the Camerata were too educated to hold any naive belief in those powers, but rather were seeking legitimation for the new paradigm. A good recipe for public success, says Palisca, was a "head full of classical poetics, but an ear to the ground."[42] They were classicists in aesthetics, adds Pirrotta, not classicists in the sense of imitating the ancients.[43]

The emphasis on expression and communicability was joined, in the monodic paradigm, with the commitment to beautiful singing. The term "aria" was much used in the sixteenth and seventeenth centuries and the notion of aria underlies the attack on the inability of polyphony to move its audience. However pleasing, polyphony was thought to be unable to communicate the emotional message of a text. Galilei's interest in vocal monody, in fact, predates his *Dialogo* and goes back to his arrangements of madrigals and other part-song compositions for solo voice and lute.[44] He is supposed to have entertained the Camerata by singing the bass part of part songs while accompanying himself with a lute reduction of the original composition, thus enhancing the music with the text and the "expressive accents of the voice."[45] The individual line gradually gained

[41]See Palisca, "The Alterati . . . ," *op. cit.*, p. 17.
[42]*Ibid.*, p. 37.
[43]See Pirrotta, "Early Opera . . . ," *op. cit.*, pp. 86-9.
[44]See Alfred Einstein, "Galilei and the Instructive Duo," *Music and Letters*, 1937, vol. XVIII, pp. 360-68.
[45]See Claude V. Palisca, "Vincenzo Galilei and Some Links between 'Pseudo-Monody' and monody," *The Musical Quarterly*, 1960, vol. XLVI, p. 345.

prominence in the experiments with aria-like singing. The idea of *sprezzatura*, those "intangible elements of rhythmic buoyancy and dynamic flexibility of the performance" together with continuo accompaniment were technical features related to the aim of communication.[46] Caccini's set pieces are more lyrical, as might be expected from his adherence to *cantar recitando*; while Peri is more dramatic. Nevertheless Pirrotta thinks that Peri's music is the richer in melody.[47]

Although he rarely uses repetitions, as befits *recitar cantando*, he focuses on a passion and "follows it through" seeking to express its meaning and dialectics, and "not just counting on the text." In view of all this, it is curious, Palisca notes, that so little explicit attention was devoted either in the Camerata or the more literary and systematic Alterati to the question: What kinds of texts are best suited to the new paradigm?[48]

While questions remain unanswered, it is evident that much is known about the invisible college from which the earliest operas derived. It is now time to ask where these ideas came from. How did it happen that creativity in music became a focus of attention in salons like that of Bardi and Corsi and in groups like the Alterati? Why were they concerned about reforming music? These questions—in the spirit of what was declared in Chapter One—require explanations from the domain of intellectual and social history. And for all its seeming simplicity, so does the question of how the Bardi-Corsi group, with its mélange of amateurs and professionals, artists and scientists, poets and philosophers, noblemen and successful bankers, happened to come together at all. The following pages will show that the nature of the group and the subject of its conversation are by no means unrelated.

Individualism: Ideological Infrastructure of the Camerata

Neither the Camerata nor its theoretical preoccupation comes as a surprise from the point of view of intellectual history. The Bardi-Corsi coterie represents a point of crystallization of certain

[46]See Pirrotta, *op. cit.*, p. 53.
[47]*Ibid.*, pp. 66-68.
[48]See Palisca, "The Alterati . . . ," *op. cit.*, pp. 34-35.

musico-aesthetic theories that had been in the making during the sixteenth century and were fully and consciously adopted only toward the turn of the century. Moreover, the group itself as a social institution was made possible only as a result of the political and socioeconomic changes in the organization and cultural outlook of the larger society.

Most historians see the beginning of opera as part of the early baroque. To be sure, their decision is not based merely on dates; it incorporates a consideration of stylistic features as well. However, when these historians treat the theoretical and cultural background of experiments by such groups as the Camerata, they avail themselves extensively of Renaissance and late Renaissance ideas. Some solve the problem by choosing to talk in terms of "anachronism," while others simply ignore the incongruity, arbitrarily using the customary labels "Renaissance" or "baroque" depending on the aspect to which they refer.

Indeed, it is difficult to speak of the style of a time as uniform, or to see in a given style all the characteristics of a period. For example, in describing the transition from the Renaissance to the baroque, Hauser points out that Wölfflin overestimated the importance of subjectivism in the baroque while overlooking its manifestation in the Renaissance, presumably because it is in the nature of cyclical theories to emphasize contrast rather then continuity;[49] hence, for example, Sach's reliance on Wölfflin.[50] Hauser asserts that Wincklemann, Lessing, Goethe and Burckhardt rejected the baroque on account of its "irregularity" and "capriciousness," neglecting to consider some classicist elements in the seventeenth century. Sypher claims, on the other hand, that the baroque is a direct continuation of the "grand style" of the High Renaissance.[51] Mueller goes so far as to dismiss the integrity of a baroque "culture epoch" altogether, arguing that too many of its traits are applicable to other periods. He demonstrates how the concept "baroque" has been transformed from a simple adjective to a comprehensive philosophy of history. He endeavors to show that in musicology, as elsewhere, the term is employed alternately as description, evaluation and

[49]Hauser, op. cit., p. 424.
[50]See Sachs, op. cit., p. 260, also his "Barockmusik," *Jahrbuch die Musikbibliotek Peters*, vol. XXVI, pp. 6-15.
[51]Wylie Sypher, *Four Stages of Renaissance Style, op. cit.*, p. 183.

explanation.[52]Whatever theory one is inclined to endorse, two points should be borne in mind. The first is that much of Renaissance thought and feeling found expression in the baroque, and vice versa; the continuity of thought over different periods is often ignored in the attempt to stress the distinctiveness of each. The second point is that there is a "strain toward consistency" among the arts, the leading ideas and the dominant social patterns of a given period—even Mueller admits this[53] —and that these clusters of ideas, integrated or not, often justify a collective label. The customary "Renaissance--baroque" classification still serves well.

The thoughts and activities of the Florentine group must be seen in this light, and it is useful to think of the Camerata as bridging the two periods. While largely reflecting Renaissance thought, their theoretical utterances were enlisted in the support of expressionism and subjectivism, a movement away from pleasure derived from either elegant design or sensuous extravagance in favor of affect and emotional involvement. This particular combination of "old" and "new" reflects the social changes that took place during the course of the sixteenth century.

The affirmation of individualism in the early Renaissance and the later attempt to implement it as a conscious program in daily living led to a broadening of the concept itself. Indeed, if there is a concept that underlies both the existence of the Camerata as a social institution and the character of its ideas, it is the concept of individualism. The deposing of polyphony by the individual line of monody may be seen as its symbol. That is far too simple a statement, of course, as will become clear immediately, nor is it the only explanatory concept of which we have need, but it is a good place to begin.

Individualism as attitude and doctrine is associated with the emergence of a powerful middle class. The urban commercial economy began to take shape in the late Middle Ages and led first to the political and cultural independence of the middle class, and ultimately to its intellectual predominance. The allegiance to region and locality that accompanied this process clashed with the universalist striving of the Church and its attempt to maintain a uniformity of culture. It was the insistence

[52]John H. Mueller, "Baroque—Is it Datum, Hypothesis, or Tautology?" *The Journal of Aesthetics and Art Criticism*, vol. XII, pp. 421-37.
[53]*Ibid.*, p. 437.

on differentiation—of collectivity from collectivity, of individual from collectivity and individual from individual—that spans the period from the late Middle Ages to the baroque.The ethic of "free competition" that accompanied the rise of the urban middle class in Italy inevitably led to the granting of recognition to those who "made it." The rural aristocracy adapted itself very early to the new urban financiers. Trying to enlist the support of the public for the ruling houses, the courts were bound to take notice of this new power and to use it to their own advantage. As a result, the traditional aristocracy, even in its social relationships, accepted the principle of "individual achievement" on a par with the "ascriptive" basis of its own status. Thus, bankers and merchants, artists and plebeian intellectuals were fitting company, and were even sought after by the princes and noblemen of the courts. "In contrast to the exclusive moral community of court chivalry," says Hauser, "a comparatively free, fundamentally intellectual type of salon life develops at these courts which is, on the one hand, the continuation of the aesthetic social culture of middle-class circles . . . and represents on the other, the preparatory stage in the development of those literary salons which play such an important part in the intellectual life of Europe in the seventeenth and eighteenth centuries."[54] Society was becoming pluralistic and heterogeneous. The courts admitted a variety of people with and without the traditional social credentials. Salons and social circles, equally diverse in composition, were made up of people who voluntarily sought each other out on the basis of shared ideas and interests. This freedom of association—bridging the barriers of class and propinquity—brought shared interest to the fore as a basis of social life.

Individualism—or individual "achievement"—was thus the basis of the kind of salon over which Bardi and Corsi presided. The Camerata was representative of the cultured strata of Florentine society. Bardi's home was open to all those interested in the discussion of matters of culture: scientists, poets, intellectuals and musicians, as well as bankers and merchants. It is essential to an understanding of salons of this kind to emphasize the mingling on equal terms of amateurs of various degree and professional artists and scientists.

The route to the salon traversed by the merchant or banker

[54]See Hauser, *op. cit.*, pp. 269-71.

is implicit in the rise of the middle class to social status and to cultural pretension, simulated or real.[55] The laymen had an important voice in the salon and their presence, obviously, had direct influence on the quality and content of the discussion. The issue of whether laymen had the right to discuss art was even publicly aired. Lodovico Dolce in his *L'Aretino* (1557) raised the question and reached the conclusion that it was perfectly all right for the layman to discuss art as long as he did not propose to discuss it from a technical point of view[56]

No less than the layman, however, the artists' presence needs explaining. The artist, too, had a long socioeconomic route to traverse on his way to the salon. Again, it is the individualism implicit in the breakdown of the guilds and the emergence of the stature of artist as distinct from craftsman, with all of the individuality that the new term implies, that is the key to the story.

In the thirteenth and fourteenth centuries, as is well known, artists were typically organized together with craftsmen in guilds of glaziers, saddlers, goldsmiths and the like.[57] Art and artists neither commanded special recognition nor were they treated with awe. Compared with the merchant guilds, they exerted little influence on the economic and social life of the society. [58] Although there were isolated cases in which artists were treated as members of a free profession, these cases did not represent societal recognition of the special kind of work artists engage in, nor do they result from a desire to contribute to the unhampered development of art; rather they result simply from a lack of recognition that artists need protection. Musicians, for example, had little recourse to courts of law as late as the fourteenth century. Along with prostitutes, jesters and criminals,

[55]Bardi himself came from an old established family of bankers. See Pirrotta, "Temperaments and Tendencies . . . ," *op. cit.*, p. 171. For the historical importance of the Bardi family in the economic and financial life of Florence see Armando Sapori, *La crisi delle compagnie mercantili dei Bardi e dei Peruzzi*, Florence: S. Olsheki, 1926.

[56]See Hauser, *op. cit.*, p. 386. Also Lodovico Dolce, *L'Aretino ovvero Dialogo Della Pittura*, Milan: Daelli e comp., 1863, pp. 13-14.

[57]See Hans Huth, *Künstler und Werkstatt Der Spätgotik*, Augsburg: Filser verlag, 1923, p. 7.

[58]For a comprehensive picture of the Florentine guild organization, the relative importance of the various guilds, the differences among them, their constitutions, financial positions, etc., see Alfred Doren, *Entwicklung und Organisation der Florentiner Zünfte in 13 und 14 Jahrhundert*, Leipzig: Duncker E. Humblot, 1897.

they had no legal rights and could act neither as plaintiff nor as witness.[59]

Even where greater homogeneity of craft prevailed, the nature of guild organization suggests that the artist shared his society's view of himself as nothing more than a trained craftsman. In line with this, the acceptance of new members into the guild was highly regulated and depended less on quality or work than on years of experience. Children of members stood a better chance than did 'ordinary outsiders.'[60] The guilds maintained their hold on the artist as long as he was viewed primarily as a craftsman. The guilds, for example, were able to control the number of artists and keep artists out of the market simply by increasing the required years of apprenticeship. This took place in fact as a protective measure, in the fifteenth century when the movement from country to town intensified perceptibly, constituting an economic threat.[61] Musicians first organized when they turned to the towns for work, as the available opportunities in courts became more limited. Since the towns, too, offered fewer jobs than there were musicians in need of employment, musicians felt the need to organize in order to regulate the competition.[62] However, given the scarcity of available jobs, the new arrivals began to compete with guild members by offering to work as unorganized labor at reduced prices. And as time went on, complaints were voiced about the lowered quality of work, which in most cases was attributable directly to the forces of economic competition. The distinction between individual artists was inevitable in such a situation.

With the strongly shaken position of the guilds, technical proficiency, which was never doubted in the thirteenth and fourteenth centuries, was no longer taken for granted in the fifteenth and sixteenth. Proof attesting to his proficiency was often required of the artist applying for a job, since many were those who tried to execute works of art without any formal training whatsoever.[63] At the same time, the individuality of artists was no longer ignored and artists now began to "specialize" and to

[59]See Abram Loft, *Musician's Guild and Union: A Consideration of the Evolution of Protective Organization Among Musicians*, unpublished Ph.D. dissertation, Department of Music, Columbia University, 1950, p. 38.
[60]Huth, *op. cit.*, p. 11.
[61]*Ibid.*, pp. 13, 17.
[62]See Loft, *op. cit.*, pp. 38-39.
[63]Huth, *op. cit.*, p. 14.

do what was most expressive of their personalities and technical abilities. The work of art was now treated as a unique work, and artists who still engaged others to help in the execution of their designs made sure to erase all signs that might make the work seem not to have been produced by a single master. The fact that painters no longer made their own frames emphasized the separation between artist and craftsman.

It can readily be seen how the doctrine of individualism applied to the world of art shifted the emphasis from technical proficiency to artistic creativity, focusing more on the artist than on his art, more on the man than on his product. This shift eventually led to the thesis that art, save for some techniques, was basically unteachable. Admitting that "il comporre in Musica non sia altro che una practica," Pietro Aron Adds: " . . . i buoni compositori nascono, et non si fanno per studio, ne per molto practicare, ma si bene per celeste influsso, et inclinatione, Gratie veramente, che a pochi il ciel largo destina."[64] Such a thesis was bound to break the craft tradition even further. Moreover, emphasizing the power of the artist's personality rather than his "know-how" changed the conception of art itself. The role of true art was no longer to imitate nature as it is, but as it appears to be, i.e., to express it. The main contribution of the artist was now seen to be the depiction of life in its inner reality. Indeed, the individual artists now endeavors to "contribute" to the realization of this goal. Thus did the artist find his way into the salon, alongside the scientist, each "contributing" in his own way.

If the presence of the layman and the artist in the nobleman's salon needs explaining, the nobleman's presence seems self-explanatory. Yet it is worth recalling that period when the nobility itself underwent a transformation of its "class consciousness"—albeit centuries earlier—when hereditary nobility opened its ranks to new recruits and the fact of "noble origin" made way for the idea of "noble character." This transformation was accompanied by the rise in the status of the court poets, whose origins in the lower strata were also submerged. "Now that the words 'gentle' and 'simple' had come to signify not merely differences of birth but of education, so that a man

---

[64]See Pietro Aron, *Lucidario in musica* (1545), Oppinione XV, 2nd Book. By 1545, such a statement no longer came as a surprise.

was not necessarily gentle by mere birth and rank but must become so by training . . . They [the salaried court poets] are no longer content to enjoy the favor and generosity of a great lord; they now aspire to be teachers of their patrons." Hauser credits them with being "the true forerunners of the Renaissance poets and humanists."[65] The very presence of laymen and artists— given the recent blossoming of their status—constrained the conversation in this direction. And as we shall try to show, their thoughts and feelings, and their activities, were reinforced not only by the social and economic changes which their very presence represented but by religious and political doctrines as well.

Since non-artists were engaged in the discussion of art, the technical aspects of art were relegated to a lesser place. Aesthetic and philosophic problems came to the fore instead, and became common ground. "Theorizing" of this kind increasingly gained in importance. It led, ultimately, to the discovery of the affinity among the arts, that is, to Art as a concept that cuts across the several branches of art and their technical peculiarities.

The recognition of the affinity among the arts and the importance of "theories" of art was responsible for the transfer of training from the workshop to the academy and contributed in turn to the transformation of homogeneous artistic circles into "cultured" circles, which, like the intellectual court circles, admitted poets, artists, amateurs and laymen alike.[66]

The cathedrals and the courts were the workshops for musical teaching in the early Renaissance. In addition to employing organists and choirs for their services, the cathedrals and other important churches employed choirmasters whose task was not only to compose music for various occasions, but more importantly, to train and teach the singers of the choir. Many Renaissance theorists were choirmasters. Their treatises and compositions were largely connected with their position and activities, and the technical emphasis in their work may attest to the technical proficiency of their students.

While the importance of the Renaissance courts as centers of musical life is well known, the fact that they also served as important centers of musical instruction has been less emphasized. Musical instruction played an important part in the educa-

[65]Hauser, *op. cit.*, pp. 211-229.
[66]See Huth, *op. cit.*, p. 150.

tion of princes and courtiers. The courts, however, were not the only ones to employ musicians and train privileged sons and daughters in the musical art; cardinals and private nobles also kept musicians as players and teachers in their retinue.

In the later Renaissance, the musical activities and instruction of the Church and the court were likewise replaced by the academy. Musical education in the academy was more theoretical and less closely connected with actual music making. If an earlier period distinguished among the arts on the basis of technique, and even classified arts and crafts together when they shared techniques, this later period sought out the commonalities among the arts based on the shared ideas about creativity, function and effect. The social composition of the salon was responsible, in no small part, for the changed agenda.

The discussions about music, judging from the writings of certain members of the Camerata, were of this very theoretical nature. Regardless of the actual qualifications of the discussants, the primary concern was with musico-aesthetic questions, and the issues discussed apparently required little or no musical training. They required a theoretical grasp of art in general and of the role of music in particular. Composer, poet and layman felt equally competent to participate. If Mei and Galilei also engaged in traditional theoretical polemics, it was nonetheless in the service of the musico-aesthetic ideas to which the group was strongly committed. Indeed, it is a curious characteristic of music reformers, the Florentine reformers included, to *state* their music theories in prefaces, letters or even complete books discussing music primarily from an aesthetic-philosophical point of view.

The depictions of the Camerata portray very clearly their allegiance to the new conception of art: no longer a tool for the imitation of nature, but an expressive vehicle for the feelings and

[67]Gombrich, *op. cit.*, p. 8.

[68]Goodman, *Languages of Art, op. cit.*, p. 248.

[69]Caccini did not write much music until the age of forty when he first attempted to write in the "new style," which emphasized expressive qualities over beauty of design and craftsmanship. See Alfred Ehricks, *Guilio Caccini*, Leipzig: Hesse & Becker, 1908, p. 11.

[70]Galilei dedicated his famous *Dialogo*, to Giovanni Bardi. He used Bardi's name for one of the discussants through whom he expresses his own opinions. Bardi also commanded Mei's respect as is evident from Mei's letters addressed to Bardi.

perceptions of individual artists. The role of music was not to "delight the ear" but to "move the passion of the mind."

The phrase "delight the ear" recalls a passage in Gombrich on the growing gulf between the "intellectual pursuit of art" and the craft from which it arose. "A new hierarchy is created," says Gombrich, "by which true nobility in art has no need to 'flatter the eye' or to rely on surface attractions. On the contrary—such attention to a polished surface is in itself the symptom of a less aspiring mind"[67] Similarly, "move the passion of the mind" recalls a passage from Goodman who says that "in aesthetic experience emotions function cognitively."[68]

Thus, in a group like the Camerata, Caccini could be held in great esteem not only as a singer but also as a composer, although he considered some of his musical training to have been a waste of time.[69] And Galilei, himself respected for his theoretical and technical proficiency, venerated and respected the theories and observations of his host who was but an amateur—even if the flattery was partly self-serving, as we have seen.[70]

Indeed, a social institution on the order of the Bardi "salon" is inconceivable without the redefinition of the layman's relationship towards art and the discovery of the affinity among the arts. The latter is directly related to the importance attached to the aesthetic-philosophical discussions of art, and the former to the changed status of art and the artist.[71] Jumping back several generations once again, consider the analogy of the plebeian minstrel who enjoyed, in spite of his lower rank, enormous advantage through his professional association with the knightly poet. He would otherwise never have been allowed to give public expression to his own individuality, his private subjective feelings, or, (putting it another way), to turn from epic to lyric poetry. Only the new social position of the poet and the shared social prestige of the knight made possible this poetical subjectivism.

[71]The implementation of individualism as a conscious program in daily living reached its utmost limits toward the end of the sixteenth century. The seventeenth century again praised birth more than ability, but it could no longer retrieve the basic recognition that was accorded to man. Man from now on could only be mistreated, usurped of rights, but rights which he was believed to possess. For a comparison between life in the sixteenth and seventeenth centuries, see Cecily Booth, *Cosimo I, Duke of Florence*, London: Cambridge University Press, 1921, Chaps. I, II, IV, X, XI, and Lucy Collison-Morley, *Italy After the Renaissance*, London: George Routledge & Sons, 1930, Introductory Chapter and Chaps. VI, VIII, X.

The new noblemen of Florence found themselves in a very similar situation. Sixteenth-century Italy was prospering, despite political unrest. "Ask your merchants," writes Bendetto Dei, boasting about the economic prosperity of Florence at the beginning of the century, "ask those who should know as they visit the fairs every year, whether they have seen the banks of the Medici, the Pazzi, the Cappinu, the Buondelmonti, the Corsini, the Falconierei, the Portinari and the Ghissi, and a hundred of others which I will not name . . . We have round about us thirty thousand estates, owned by noblemen and merchants, citizens and craftsmen, yielding us yearly bread and meat, wine, and oil, vegetables and cheese, hay and wood, to the value of nine hundred thousand ducats in cash."[72] Florence was one of the most important centers of trade in the Italian Renaissance,[73] frequented by merchants from all over Europe. Its industry was developed and fostered by all its citizens, and its rulers were in a position to confer high social status on the arts.[74] In a community where rank and title were absent, wealth conferred distinction not only on itself but on those who could adorn it. "Florence in those times," says Biagi, talking about changes that came over the city during the Renaissance, "beheld new customs come to life, and listened to many kinds of poetry, from the triumphs and masquerades in the streets to the Platonic banquets at Careggi, from Carnival songs and street ballads to country-dances and sacred representations. The thoughtless gaiety, and the ease with which both spiritual and material desires were gratified, seemed to compensate the people for their diminished liberty."[75]

While it is true that the Medici were continuously trying to

---

[72]From *Florentine Merchants in the Age of the Medici, Letters and Documents from the Selfridge Collection of Medici Manuscripts*, Gertrude Richards, ed., Cambridge: Harvard University Press, 1932, pp. 45-46.

[73]"Die kapitalistische Wirtschaftsform," says Davisohn, "hat sich in Florenz nict früher als in andern Städten Italiens entwickelt, aber ihre Erscheinungsformen treten plastischer hervor als anderwärts, und die politischen Wirkungen veränderter ökonomischer Verhältnisse lassen sich auf dem Boden der Arnostadt besonders deutlich erkennen." See "Über die Enstehung des Kapitalismus," p. 268, in Robert Davidsohn, *Forschungen zur Geschichte von Florenz*, Berlin: Siegfried Mittler, 1908, vol. IV.

[74] See Bella Duffy, *The Tuscan Republics*, London: Fisher Unwin, 1903, pp. 236-252.

[75] Guido Biagi, *Men and Manners of Old Florence*, London: Fisher Unwin, 1909, p. 137.

consolidate their power by all possible means, their patronage of culture was genuine. The culture which they fostered represented a mixture of middle-class taste touched and refined by the more cultivated taste of a complacent financial aristocracy which by then had already acquired a tradition of its own. Thus Giovanni Bardi came from an old established family of bankers who exerted a considerable influence on the economic and financial life of Florence. In his mode of life and intellectual interest, Bardi represents a conservative financial aristocracy whose influence reached beyond matters of finance to the intellectual and cultural life of the Florentine court. But whereas Bardi was fashioned after the old type of nobility, Emilio de Cavalieri, his rival at court, was a typical representative of the cultivated urban middle class, which left its marks in all areas of culture in the Italian Renaissance. As superintendent of all the artists at court, including musicians, Cavalieri exerted even greater influence at court than did Bardi and eventually replaced him altogether.[76] Thus, Cavalieri more than Bardi symbolizes the gifted, though untitled, member of the urban middle class to whom Cardinal Ferdinand de'Medici, the Grand Duke of Florence, could look.

The cultural aspirations of the new ruling class, supported by wealth and fanned by competition with the older nobility and by rivalry with other cities added its impetus to the trend toward expressivity in the arts. After all, the *intermedi* and the early operas were closely connected with court festivities. But if the stability of the economic situation contributed in this way, the contribution to expressivity from the religious realm was more likely the product of instability.

Though profoundly affected by the Counter-Reformation, Italy was shocked by and unreceptive to the Reformation itself. She was already beyond the age of theology and was "accustomed by long habit to making fun of the very corruption that aroused indignation in Germany . . . "[77] The new theology, founded on reintegration of the spirit and an indifference to

[76]Pirrotta, "Temperaments and Tendencies . . . ," *op. cit.*, p. 176. The main object of the appointments, however, says Pirrotta, was to limit Bardi's influence at court since the latter had supported the marriage of Grand Duke Francis I with Bianca Cappello. Cardinal Ferdinand de'Medici, the new Duke who disapproved of the marriage, replaced Bardi with Cavalieri whom he knew from his self-imposed exile in Rome.
[77]Francesco de Sanctis, *History of Italian Literature*, Jean Reford, trans., New York, 1931, vol. I., p. 463.

form, could hardly appeal to a people among whom art reigned supreme. Luther, who condemned the Catholic Church for idolatry and artistic externalization of all sorts, was a heretic in the eyes of the papacy; however "in the eyes of the Italian bourgeoisie, he seemed merely a barbarian like Savanorola," says de Sanctis.[78]

The Church at first attempted to halt the change, but after long, futile religious wars it abandoned the fight against historical reality and adapted itself to its new position. Though the Church continued to fight the heretics, it became more tolerant toward the "faithful." It granted its members greater freedom to enjoy the delights of secular life. In contrast to the Reformation's hostile attitude towards art, the Counter-Reformation, primarily engaged in the fight against free intellectual inquiry and threatened by the Giordano Brunos who fought the battle from within, promoted the arts and made use of their emotional appeal for the deepening of religious experience. The Church, too, was now concerned with art that reached its audience on a personal level, the main purpose of which was to intensify religious experience rather than to elucidate theological convictions.[79] The Church was now consciously engaged in replacing the symbolic, superpersonal, spiritual approach with subjectivism. It became aware of the expressive void which science could not fill. Indeed, though the Counter-Reformation was on the whole not hostile to the arts, it was above all interested in their utilitarian aspects.[80] If the extremists among the members of the Council of Trent were ready to sacrifice polyphony to the single line of the Gregorian chant, it does not result primarily from an interest in the new aesthetic trend in music, but was rather for the purpose of propagating and enhancing the liturgy. The fact is that church reformists joined hands, willy-nilly, with the revivers of classic forms to encourage experimentation on ways of moving audiences by means of the expressive message of the single musical line.

The realism exhibited in the actions of the Church is expressed everywhere, but it is most clearly articulated in the political theory of the age. In contrast to the return to pure spirit

[78]*Ibid.*, p. 462.
[79] See E.H. Gombrich, *The Story of Art*, London: Phaidon Press, 1950, pp. 344-45.
[80]The art, churches and theatre of the Jesuits—the order expected to combat the Reformation all over Europe—attests to that.

advocated by the Reformation, Italy produced the revolutionary concept of Machiavellism, emphasizing man not as he ought to be, but man as he is. While liberating man from external authority, the new concept placed greater responsibilities upon him by declaring that the forces and laws of society, and man's social and historical problems, are a product of the desires and reflections of human will and thought. Man, therefore, should not only be free from external dictates to express himself; the world which surrounds him *is* his expression. Thus, while primarily identified as a theory justifying political realism, Machiavellism, like the changed attitude of the Church, reinforced cultural changes outside the political sphere as well. Its conception of man was well suited to a period in which man was no longer cognizant only of his rights, but was prepared to experiment and assert himself, a man ready to express his will.

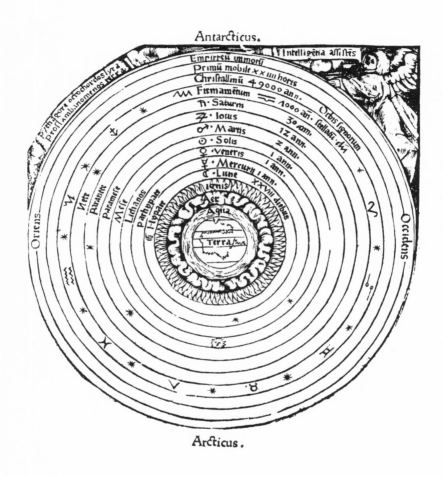

Plate 3. The Universe as a Composite Image. Aristotle, *Libri de caelo* IV, Johann Eck ed., (Augsburg, 1519). The central rings represent the four elements. The rings that follow represent the spheres of the planets accompanied by the musical notes they play (on the left).

Chapter Four

Divining the Powers of Music

The absence of the Humanists and the Platonists will have been noted in what was said so far, especially by those who know that Galilei and Mei and their friends have come to be called, by some, Musical Humanists.[1] There is no doubt, of course, about the influence of the Humanists on the theorists of the Camerata. Yet the relationship is not a simple one, even if it is often presented simply as antecedent and consequent. The society which embraced the Camerata was evolving in the time of the Humanists and helps to explain Humanists and Humanism, too. Ironically, this point can be more clearly made by starting afresh in a new chapter than by dealing with both developments simultaneously. A photographic montage or even a composition in counterpoint might be a more faithful representation of events, but historical writing is better served by sequence and monody, even if these require the reader to bear in mind what came before.

After all, this book is an attempt to impose an organization on historical records and on the historians and philosophers who have interpreted them, in order to synthesize a major theme or themes that illuminate a critical moment in music history. Having admitted this unabashedly, we shall pursue the argument by asserting that the academies and social circles with which we are dealing, and the historians and philosophers who deal with them, do the same thing. Synthesis is a creative act, and however much one criticizes the methodology of Geist theorists, more disciplined scholarship also must rise above the facts and figures to assign a name or a label to what it has found. Likewise, the student of ideas, no less than the proponents of those ideas, looks selectively to his predecessors for support.

Thus, every account of the Humanists reveals not only the influence that the ancient world exerted on them but also the

[1]See D.P. Walker, *Spiritual and Demonic Magic from Ficino to Campanella*, London: The Warburg Institute, University of London, 1958, p. 20.

way in which they enlisted that world for reinforcement of their ideas, and in the process were influenced by what they found. Similarly with the Camerata. Indeed, the complexity of the historical account is made salient thereby because the Humanists were influential for the Camerata in somewhat the same way that the ancient world was influential for the Humanists. The Humanists were linked to the Camerata, then, both by sharing some of the same sources of cultural and social influence, and by constituting a kind of continuum or bridge with its origins in antiquity, or more accurately, antiquity as they perceived it.

The historians, too, in analyzing the ways in which the Humanists occupied themselves with accommodating paganism and Christianity to each other, put their own stamp on the process. Trinkaus sees unity in plurality.[2] Spitzer sees it as part of a larger span, as part of the growth of European cultural solidarity reaching into the eighteenth century and governed by the theme of "musicalization," reflecting the spirit and influence of Classical and Christian ideas of world harmony.[3] In the opinion of most scholars however, some of this unity began to come apart toward the end of the sixteenth century. Differentiation was setting in. There was a pulling apart of different social and cultural institutions so that each was governed by somewhat different rules.[4] Secular areas were identifiably distinct from non-secular ones: indeed the very process of differentiation is a secularizing one, even if Martin disagrees.[5]

The baroque fits this period of differentiation. There was no longer a single common musical style in the baroque, but a choice of styles as well as a diversity of idioms.[6] And the Camerata stood at the point of transition from the unity of the Renaissance to the pluralism of the baroque. Both within the group itself, and between the group and others, there were clearly discernible differences.

[2]See Charles Trinkaus, *In Our Image and Likeness*, Chicago: The University of Chicago Press, 1970, pp. 761-75.
[3]Leo Spitzer, *Classical and Christian Ideas of World Harmony*, Baltimore: The Johns Hopkins Press, 1963.
[4]On this subject see the introduction to Chapter V.
[5]The concept secularization, argues Martin, attempts to simplify historical complexity "in the interest of ideology or of an over-neat intellectual economy." David Martin, *The Religious and the Secular: Studies in Secularization*, London: Routledge & Kegan Paul, 1969, p. 6.
[6]See Manfred J. Bukofzer, *Music in the Baroque Era*, New York: Norton, 1947, pp. 1-19.

The most important center of Platonic influence in the Renaissance was the Platonic Academy of Florence headed by distinguished leaders such as Nicholas of Cusa, Marsilio Ficino and Giovanni Pico. The Bardi-Corsi gatherings took place decades after the Platonic Academy was established. By that time, Platonic teaching was well entrenched in the intellectual life of Florence and affected the thinking of all who were interested in matters of culture, not excepting the Camerata.[7] The influence of Platonism on the thought of the later Renaissance was even deeper than was the influence of the Humanistic movement at an earlier stage. Nonetheless, the contributions of both Humanists and Platonists to the shaping of the intellectual elite as well as the cultural circles in which they participated can hardly be overestimated.

The classicism brought about by the Humanist movement, along with its cultural and educational ideals, survived long after the Renaissance. Indeed, the real contribution of the Humanists was not in the development of a new philosophy—except perhaps in the field of ethics—but in the rediscovery and translation of a considerable number of ancient philosophical texts, which were unknown to the Middle Ages or had receded to the background, and the concomitant revival of several ancient philosophies besides that of Aristotle.[8] Rejecting Aristotle and his fundamentally scientific interest for other concerns, artistic and moral, they chose Plato, the "natural refuge for those fleeing Aristotle."[9] The Renaissance, after all, did not forsake religion; it only modified its attitude towards the authority of the Church and the place of the individual vis-a-vis the collective. And although the Renaissance is renowned for its confidence in Nature, it could forsake Aristotle for a while in favor of a conception of *human* nature that wrested man free and gave him dignity and worth as an individual. The stance of the Humanists was in the name of a more personal interpretation of the world.

Not that Aristotle was neglected.[10] As Palisca has shown, the theory of imitation and emotional purgation expressed by

---

[7]See Nesca A. Robb, *Neoplatonism of the Italian Renaissance*, London: George Allen & Unwin, 1935, chapt. VII.
[8]See Paul Oskar Kristeller, *Renaissance Thought: The Classic, Scholastic, and Humanist Strains*, New York: Harper & Brothers, 1961, chapt. V.
[9]*Ibid.*, chapt. III.
[10]*Ibid.*, chapt. II.

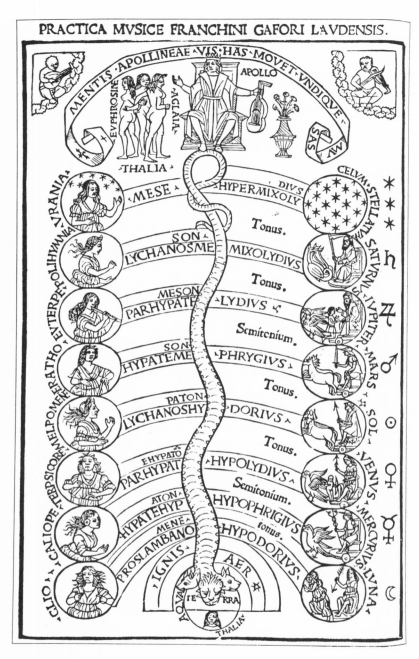

Plate 4. The Music of the Spheres. Franchino Gafori, *Practica Musicae* (Milan, 1496), frontispiece. The spheres are accompanied by: musical notes (left of center), musical modes (right of center), Gods (circular vignettes on the right), and muses (circular vignettes on the left). They all contribute to a larger whole represented by the figure of Apollo (on top).

80

Aristotle in his *Poetics* furnished Mei and Galilei, the leading theorists of the Camerata, with several of the main concepts out of which they evolved their musical aesthetics. Also, they rejected the neo-Platonist commitment to Pythagorean "numerology" in favor of unmathematical equal-tempered tuning in their effort to free practical music from speculative science.[11]

While this position was based on the *Harmonics* of Aristoxenus and minor writings of Aristotle, members of the Camerata repeatedly quote Plato as their authority. In light of the writings of Kristeller and others, there is no reason to doubt that both scholasticism and Humanism lived side by side throughout the Renaissance, and Plato and Aristotle were enlisted where appropriate. As it turned out, as far as the sixteenth century was concerned the controversy over whether "reason" or the "senses" should judge matters concerning music eventually dictated that empiricism should be the approach in musical theory, and, despite reservations about certain aspects of Platonic doctrine, expressionism in musical aesthetics.[12]

The desire to actively affect the world, to exercise will, and to give expression to the passions of the mind: these were the contributions of the Humanists, drawing as they do on their blend of classic, Christian and "humanistic" doctrines. The Humanists, says Trinkaus, "offered through their writings a new affirmation of the possibility and value of human action. They presented a vision of man controlling and shaping his own life . . . and they stressed a new conception of human nature modelled on their own image of the Deity."[13] Whereas the Greeks were satisfied with speculation, and medieval Christians humbled themselves under the strict surveillance of God, the Humanists began to think of themselves as masters of the world, as men who should act in the image of the God after whom they were fashioned. The determination "to operate" was their innovation, says Yates.[14] It was "man making trial of his own power," says Trinkaus.[15]

[11]See Claude Victor Palisca, *The Beginnings of Baroque Music: Its Roots in Sixteenth Century Theory and Polemics*, unpublished Ph.D. dissertation, Department of Music, Harvard University, 1953, chapt. IV.
[12]See *ibid.*; also see Palisca, "Scientific Empiricism in Musical Thought," *op. cit.*
[13]Trinkaus, *op. cit.*, p. 767.
[14]Frances A. Yates, *Giordano Bruno and the Hermetic Tradition*, New York: Vantage Books, 1969, p. 155.
[15]Trinkaus, *op. cit.*, foreword, p. xiii.

These doctrines pervaded the arts. Petrarch, an early Humanist, treated will on a par with intellect. His lyricistic view of the world drew on poetry, literature and history more than on dialectic and natural philosophy because the former reveal the actualities of human life and feeling. Man's action is his focus, and action—notes Trinkaus—is related to persuasion: "the consequence of the human word used in discourse to direct and influence the feelings of others."[16]

Lorenso Valla went beyond Petrarch in all these ways. Trinkaus calls Valla's view of human nature "passional." "Man," for Valla, "became an emotional force, imbued with love and hate . . . careless of the voice of the intellect when his passions were sufficiently powerful to sweep him beyond it." Again, it is the meanings perceived through language that mediated his passions and channeled them into action. "Words to Valla were quite literally actions since they pronounced a view of reality which helped to shape the direction of the passions."[17] Or, as Kristeller would have it, "It was the novel contribution of the Humanists to add the firm belief that in order to write and to speak well it was necessary to study and to imitate the ancients."[18] Plato's idea of the creative process, whereby the poet is seized by a *furore*—an inspiration, we would call it—was widely accepted and later discussed seriously by the Alterati.[19]

Altogether, the central importance of words and their persuasive powers, the concern with rhetoric and expressiveness, the weaving together of intellect and passions—all these continued high on the agenda of the Florentine Camerata and of the invisible college of which they were a part. Of course, the commitment to will—to the idea of "acting" on the world—underlay the drive to experiment.

"Musical humanism" also concerned itself with moving the passions. It was during the late Humanistic period that music began to weaken its connection with arithmetic, geometry and astronomy and to assume its place among the humanities, first as a separate branch of literature and then as sister to dialectics, rhetoric and poetics.[20] Music was aimed at the affections,

---

[16]*Ibid.*, p. 769.
[17]*Ibid.*, pp. 771-72.
[18]Kristeller, *Renaissance Thought, op. cit.*, p. 13.
[19]See Palisca, "The Alterati . . . ," *op. cit.*, p. 22.
[20]See Kristeller, *op. cit.*, p. 65.

and was also seen—in Aristotelian terms—as an agent of respite and relief. The new aim of the composer, says Giacomini to the Alterati, is not just ethical in the Platonic sense, but to move the passions, perhaps to purge them.[21] But Palisca warns against jumping too quickly to the Aristotelian analogy, though Aristotle's aesthetic theories were no less important than Plato's. The taste of the time favored a mixture of genres, he writes, and the arts were expected not only to purge the senses but to feast them as well.[22] The pluralism that characterized the late Renaissance and early baroque is reflected here. The functions of music are, variously, to instruct, entertain, persuade, purge, and impassion.

It remained for the Camerata and their like to attempt to define a systematic approach to the aesthetic problems of linking words and music within the terms of reference of the humanistic commitment to passion and persuasion. Their predecessors had not altogether ignored these relationships, as we have already seen. Further, as will immediately become clear, early experiments with words and music occupy an important place in Humanist theories of magic. What became increasingly important, at any rate, was the desire to communicate through music, and not simply to titillate, soothe, or portray words literally. Galilei's tirade against the contrapuntal composers of his day explicitly decries the absurd attempts to portray words literally, as if the idea of "dark" could be communicated by a black note or the idea of "descending" by having "one part of the composition descend in such a way that the singer has sounded more like someone groaning to frighten children and terrify them than like anyone singing sense." Singing sense is what matters to Galilei. For him, "the most important and principal part of music [is] the imitation of the conceptions that are derived from the words." "Unhappy men," says Galilei of his contemporaries,

> they do not perceive that if Isocrates or Corax or any of the other famous orators had ever, in an oration, uttered two of these words in such a fashion, they would have moved all their hearers to laughter and contempt and would besides this have been derided and despised by them as men foolish, abject and worthless. And yet they wonder that the music of their times produces none

[21]See Palisca, "The Alterati . . . ," *op. cit.*, pp. 26-7.
[22]*Ibid.*, p. 29.

Plate 5. The Conquest of Jericho (Joshua V, 1-21). An engraving by Franscias Chauveau (1613-1670) depicts the fall of Jericho with the "power" of sounding trumpets.

of the notable effects that ancient music produced, when, quite
the other way, they would have more cause for amazement if it
were to produce any of them, seeing that their music is so remote
from the ancient music and so unlike it as actually to be contrary
and its mortal enemy . . . and seeing that it has no means en-
abling it even to think of producing such effects . . . For its sole
aim is to delight the ear, while that of ancient music is to induce in
another the same passion that one feels oneself.[23]

Music as the communication of passions, that is, music to
underline meaning rather than to please; this is what occupied
the theorists of the Camerata. Words as the key to the concepts
and passions are what occupied the Humanists, however
"empty" their rhetoric sometimes sounds.[24] Divining the formulae for moving men's minds and hearts in poetry, prose and
music was the problem that they shared. They drew on the
wealth of new aesthetic possibilities arising from the emergent
unity of the arts, where music had become the partner of poetics
and rhetoric. They looked to the classics for the key, but also for
legitimation of their efforts.

More immediately, however, the significance of the fact
that Ficino, the foremost fifteenth-century interpreter of Plato,
thought of sound and sight as the media of meaning may not be
overlooked. According to Ficino, sound and sight are superior to
the lower senses because they are able to convey intellectual
content. But sound—words and music—is the more effective of
the two. And musical sound, "more than anything else perceived by the senses," transmits the thoughts and feelings of
"the singer's or player's soul to the listeners' souls."[25] Music, in
other words, has communicative powers: it facilitates contact, a
kind of "meeting of minds," and "hearts."

Words are a sign of man's divinity, according to Ficino.
"Speech," he says, "is granted to us for a certain more excellent
task, namely as the interpreter of the mind." The human mind,

---

[23]Strunk, *op. cit.*, p. 317.

[24]Kristeller, *op. cit.*, p. 101.

[25] Walker, *op. cit.*, p. 9. Ficino expressed his ideas about music in his three
books, *De Triplici Vita*, which deal with the health of scholars, the prolongation
of their lives and the astral influences on them. We rely heavily on Walker's
study and will not specify the particular book in which Ficino states a particular
opinion. The aim here is to present a synthesis of relevant passages, and references to Walker will clarify details.

in Ficino's view, is capable of conceiving "as many things in itself as God in knowing makes in the world. By speaking it expresses as many into the air." Indeed, "the use of innumerable words" is one of four great gifts that make possible man's achievements in the arts and thus his ability to restructure physical reality.[26]

The concepts of air and spirit are central to Ficino's theory and to his conception of the influence of music. Music is more influential than visual art, according to Ficino, because sound, which is moving air, makes direct contact with the air residing in the ear, which *is* the human "spirit." Thus, without the music having to be transmitted by a sense organ of another nature—as does even visual art—body and soul are affected.[27] More than this, says Walker, Ficino argues the superior influence of music because it moves and transmits movement:

> Although visual impressions are in a way pure, yet they lack effectiveness of motion, and are usually perceived only as an image, without reality; normally, therefore, they move the soul only slightly . . . Smell, taste and touch are entirely material, and rather titillate the sense-organs than penetrate the depths of the soul. But musical sound by the movement of the air moves the body: by purified air it excites the aerial spirit which is the bond of body and soul: by emotion it affects the senses and at the same time the soul: by meaning it works on the mind: finally, by the very movement of the subtle air it penetrates strongly: by its contemperation it flows smoothly: by the conformity of it's quality it floods us with a wonderful pleasure: by its nature, both spiritual and material, it at once seizes, and claims as its own, man in his entirety.[28]

In thus attempting to explain why Plato said the soul was more similar to musical consonance than to the harmonious objects perceived by other senses, Walker adds that Ficino is also probably answering two of Ps. Aristotle's problems on music, which discuss the questions: "Why is hearing the only perception that affects the moral character?" and "Why are rhythms

---

[26]See Ficino, passages in Trinkaus, *op. cit.*, pp. 485-6. "Conceiving" and "expressing," together with constructing things in the material world and miracle-making, constitute the four signs of man's divinity and immortality.
[27]See Walker, *op. cit.*, p. 8.
[28]*Ibid.*, p. 9.

and melodies, which are sounds, similar to moral characters?"[29] Whether he is answering one or both propositions, Ficino here invokes his music-spirit theory, which rests largely on the contention that sound alone, of things sensed, has movement. The aerial spirit that resides in the body unites body and soul. The spirit needs to be nourished and purified, and this is especially so for the studious because the spirit is consumed in the course of exercising it. Wine and aromatic foods, odors and sunny air, and —most important of all—music is the diet prescribed by Ficino: " . . . if the vapours exhaled by merely vegetable life are greatly beneficial to your life, how beneficial do you think will be aerial sounds to the spirit which is indeed entirely aerial, harmonic songs to the harmonic spirit, warm and thus living, endowed with sense to the sensitive, conceived by reason to the rational?"[30]

Musical Magic

The magical and hermetic elements in the writings and accounts of the Humanists reveal their profound preoccupation with the powers inherent not just in nature but in the arts. The magic of the Humanists is also oriented to action on the world, of course, and the media of words and music have a share in shaping its manipulative—or should we say persuasive?— powers. Thus, beyond the spirit which flows in man there is an all-embracing *spiritus mundi*. It serves to bind the "soul" and "body" of the cosmos and transmits the particular influences of each of the several planets, just as the astrologers believed. The human spirit is capable of connecting with, and being enriched by, this cosmic spirit. In the same way, the cosmic spirit can transfer to the human spirit the desired characteristics of the planets. Here again, Ficino provides the recipes and regimens for doing so and, once more, music is especially recommended. First of all, music, having movement, can be made to correspond to the movements of the celestial bodies, and thus the human spirit—through music—can refresh itself through contact with the cosmic spirit. Secondly, because of the ability of music to arouse singer and listener to particular emotions and moral atti-

[29] *Ibid.*, p. 11.
[30] *Ibid.*, p. 5.

tudes, it is also capable of arousing those emotions and attitudes that correspond to the moral character of the gods whose names the planets bear. A singer of music that is "grave, earnest, sweet and joyful with stability" can hope to attract the spirit of Jupiter, while "music which is voluptuous with wantonness and soft-ness" will, by natural sympathy, attract the spirit of Venus.[31] Or compare Laura's voice, in Petrarch's sonnet 134, which is "chiara, soave, angelica, divina,"[32] to the vibrations of Apollo, attuned to music that is "venerable, simple and earnest, united with grace and smoothness."[33]

"In his aesthetic contemplation of the act of weeping," says Spitzer, "Petrarch has given equal weight to the seen and the heard; in both, Laura shows supernatural powers over nature (the eyes are a subject of envy to the sun, the music of her speech has the power of Orpheus) . . . The Pythagorean music of the spheres has been made accessible to the poet on this earth . . ." "Petrarch," continues Spitzer, "is the first Western poet to frame a person in 'air', an atmosphere, a kind of secular halo." It is a Christian achievement, insists Spitzer, flavored perhaps "with a touch of revised pantheism, which tends to deify the individual being . . ."[34]

Ficino, however, cautions that his formula for reaching the stars is not the equivalent of worshipping them. Rather, it is imi-tating them in such a way as to benefit from their spirit. And once again he gives rules for stargazing and for attuning words and music to particular stars: include the powers of the star in the text of the song; discover the people and places under the influence of a star and include their modes and meanings in your songs; imitate the variations in speech, songs and actions that are induced under various aspects of the star, and include these in your song.[35]

Notice the operations: Ficino calls for systematic observa-tions of movement of the stars in the heavens. He calls for infer-ential analysis of the influence of different stars from the changes in human behavior that accompany the changes in stellar behav-

[31]*Ibid.*, pp. 16-18.

[32]See Spitzer, *op. cit.*, p. 63.

[33]See Walker, *op. cit.*, p. 18.

[34]Spitzer, *op. cit.*, p. 62. Giacomini's explanation of spirits, tears and quality of voice (in his exposition on the nature of purgation in tragedy) both echoes Ficino and lends support to Spitzer's analysis. See Palisca, "Alterati . . . ," *op. cit.*, p. 25.

[35]See Walker, *op. cit.*, p. 17.

ior. He prescribes imitative behavior. He calls, in short, for a kind of applied science, as Galilei called for systematic and empirical analysis of the various situations, the better to match them to appropriate music.

Magic is a form of doing, not just of contemplating and calculating; hence its kinship to science. It is a form of manipulating a supernatural world; hence its proximity to religion.[36] It gives the power to influence; hence its proximity to the spirit of individualism. It gives the individual access to the harmonies in the world; hence its proximity to the spirit of the Renaissance. As Spitzer says, the "musicalization" of the soul enables "the individual human soul, though a minimal thing in this infinite space, [to]attune itself to the whole world."[37]

There is good reason to believe that Ficino actually practiced his astrological music. His texts were Orphic hymns sung to the accompaniment of some sort of lyre. The Orphic hymns are suitable because Orpheus among the ancient theologians is the most ancient of the Greeks, the master of Pythagoras and through him of Plato. As Pico says, "In natural magic nothing is more efficacious than the Hymns of Orpheus, if there be applied to them the suitable music, and disposition of soul and other circumstances known to the wise."[38] They call upon the gods and invoke their powers.

Ficino's song was probably some form of heightened speech, "neither like someone reading nor like someone singing." Or perhaps, suggests Walker, it was like plain-song since the singing was so near to being a religious rite. Walker feels certain in asserting that it was surely monodic, and that Ficino was aiming "at the same ideal or expressive, effect-producing music as the later musical humanists."[39] Indeed, Peri's foreword to his Euridice makes this point.[40] And Pirrotta, discussing the prayer of Act III of Monteverdi's Orfeo, has the following to say: "the double version in the score provides us the privilege of catching some glimpse of the growth of a poetic conception. There is no doubt in my mind that the unornamental version of

[36]In his classic essay, "Magic, Science and Religion," Malinowski says it all and better. See reprint of essay in Anchor Books, 1948.
[37]Spitzer, op. cit., p. 128.
[38]Walker, op. cit., pp. 22-3. Also see Yates, op. cit., p. 177. More will be said about Orpheus in Chapter V.
[39]Walker, ibid., p. 20.
[40]See Strunk, op. cit., pp. 374-5.

Plate 6.   Crucifixion and World Harmony. From an evangel from Regensburg (c. 1020). The small letters on the sides of the cross in the upper oval read:

M			M		I NE		P L I N	
O S	(mors);		D U U S	(mundus);	N F	(infernus);	T E S	(?).
R			N		U S R		P I L O N	

The number of letters, starting with the first word, are: 4, 6, 8 and 12. These create the relationships: 2:3 (the fifth), 3:4 (the fourth), and 1:2 (the octave), i.e. perfect consonances. Christ, his death, and hell are all part of world harmony.

this piece is not a schematic one, to be embellished at will by the performer, but a full realization of the prayer following the oratorical principles of the early 'stile rappresentativo.' It is also a prayer in the familiar terms of human misery and of confident hope in a superhuman power. It took a stroke of genius, after having quite effectively conceived the whole series of strophic recitative variations on a repeated bass line, to give the same basic material—the same aria I would call it, and not in a merely formal sense—a completely new and more sophisticated twist reworking it into an 'orphic' rite, a highly stylized and hieratically formalized incantation, through which a superhuman singer soothes and subdues the forces of darkness crossing his path. Both as a prayer and as an incantation Orpheus' song left its mark on history."[41]

It is altogether clear that Ficino's music-spirit theory involves both music and words. If anything, the latter is more important than the former. In his hierarchical scale of what media influence which stars, it is evident that music alone can reach, through the spirit, to sense and feeling, fantasy and imagination. But only the text carries the kind of explicit intellectual content that reaches the mind.[42] Thus, it is the combination of words and music that can affect the whole man, just as the theorists and practitioners of the Camerata were trying to say.

Walker finds two different kinds of magic in Ficino and his followers. One kind he calls "natural"; the other "demonic." The demonic magic draws its strength from various types of sympathetic tuning to the movement of the planets and their character. Demonic magic tends to be more transitive than natural magic, i.e., one gains power over natural or heavenly forces and these can be employed to act on other people.

Natural magic, on the other hand, devolves primarily on the operator himself. Its influence stems not from the unveiling of occult astrological forces but rather from the intrinsic beauty of the magical formula itself. It feeds back on its creator. Natural magic did not exclude sympathetic tuning to astrological vibrations, but it did not involve summoning up demons or otherworldly creatures.

Each of the arts divides in this way, according to Walker. Thus, the visual arts have a demonic dimension when figures

[41]Pirrotta, "Early Opera . . . ," op. cit., pp. 101-2.
[42]See Walker, op. cit., pp. 21, 26.

and characters are emphasized in talismans, for example; words used as essences of things as in incantation, for example, are demonic; and demonic music emphasizes proportion and number. It implies a tuning into the stars. By contrast, the modes of natural or "spiritual" magic, as it is called alternately, are identifiable in their striving for meaning and beauty rather than crude manipulation. This striving, of course, is precisely what leads natural magic onto the path of art, science, psychology and religion. Ultimately, this transformational process undermines the very belief in magic and other rules—those of art, science and religion—displace them. The musician and the listener remain to enjoy the effects on themselves.

Humanists who followed Ficino accepted one or the other—sometimes both—aspects of Ficino's magic, and consequently differed over its effects. Pletho and Tyard believed that rites of musical magic were effective, but only subjectively, because they transform the singer, particularly his imagination, or prepare the worshipper for religious contemplation.[43] Taking an extreme demonist stand, Agrippa, however, believed that incantations could be used in order to project the operator's spirit into "the enchanted thing in order to constrain or direct it."[44] Lazarelli believed that music does not only invoke extra-worldly creatures; it calls them into being.[45] Others, however—even those who did not dissent from the possibility of supernatural forces—emphasized that the power of music is intrinsic. "The sweetness itself of the concert," writes Del Rio, "and the harmonious modulation, distract the soul from thought of pain, and by inciting to joy, sooth and temper the humours . . ."[46]

The processes through which magical influence operates were similarly varied. One dominant theory—derived from Ficino—emphasizes, the sympathetic vibrations that result "when a tonal relationship corresponds to a solar relationship," as Giorgi maintained. Another is Pomponazzi's idea of compatibility achieved between operator and patient through musical incantation. Campanella, on the other hand, argued that certain sounds are compatible with certain emotions. And La Boderie ex-

[43]Tyard's two dialogues on poetry and music (1552; 1555) present the fullest account of the aims of the early Pleiade and foreshadowed the aims of the Baif Academy. See *ibid.*, pp. 61; 121.
[44]See *ibid.*, p. 92.
[45]See *ibid.*, p. 70.
[46]*Ibid.*, p. 179.

tended these theories—à la Spitzer—arguing that the underlying principles of harmony and proportion are "the causes both of the order of the heavens and of musical consonance."[47] It is most interesting that even Kepler, whose major contribution to re-vamping astronomy was his attempt to replace the metaphysical accounts by physicalistic explanations still linked astronomy with music—following the quadrivium tradition—in order to discover the "harmony of the universe." One should not forget, of course, that the link between music and astronomy was also "natural" since both could be expressed mathematically. Bacon, however, became interested in the moving and dynamic nature of sound, thus echoing one of Ficino's more natural explanations. "From Ficino through the Renaissance," says Abrams, "Hermetism . . . had been a reputable, indeed an almost universally accepted part of the intellectual universe. During the course of the seventeenth century this mode of thought had been displaced by philosophies based on the new science, whose immensely effective working hypothesis were forthwith translated."[48]

Not all of these theorists advocated, or experimented with, the practical implications of their ideas. Some did, of course, par-ticularly those who sought to reconcile magic and religion, or to preserve religion from magic. Thus, La Boderie urged the use of Orphic Hymns, which, together with Catholic liturgical hymns, would have a salutary effect and repair the impious and heretical psalms which threatened to divide France.[49] Long before the mid-dle of the fifteenth century, Pletho had combined his knowledge of ancient Greek music with Byzantine music for his polytheistic pantheon.[50] One hundred and fifty years later, Jean Bodin con-demned all planetary magic as idolatrous and inveighed against the Orphic Hymns.[51]

Walker's discussion of Bodin emphasizes that Bodin's fear of Orpheus is the result of his belief in the magic of words—and particularly names—and thus the un-Christian combination of words and music in the Orphic Hymns seemed to him particu-larly dangerous. The original Hebrew in the hymnal settings of the Psalms of David—written for the worship of the One God—

[47]See Ibid., pp. 116, 109, 231, 124 respectively.
[48]M. H. Abrams, Natural Supernaturalism, New York: Norton, 1971, p. 170.
[49]La Boderie was afraid of both the "paganism" of Ronsard-like poetry and of the Protestant Psalms. See Walker, op. cit., p. 125.
[50]See ibid., p. 60.
[51]See ibid., pp. 174-5.

represented a proper use of words and music. This concern for "authentic" combinations has both kabbalistic and hermetic overtones.[52] Discarding the magical and celestial aspects of music altogether, Tyard argued for a combination of religious and philosophical poetry with powerfully effect-producing music. His aim, like La Boderie's, was to enlist music in the service of religious contemplation. He insisted that monody was the desired form and held up the poet-musician as his ideal, much as Caccini and Peri did later.[53]

Paolini, contemporary and compatriot of the Gabrielis and a friend of Zarlino, also proposed the reform of the "softening, decadent modes and the multiplicity of instruments" in modern music in order to make the effects of music more powerful. He regrets that the metric of poetry is lost in modern music. Paolini claims to see divine inspiration in Ficino's matching of planets and musical modes, and although rejecting the magical aspects of the theory, enlists a planetary scheme as a mnemonic device for orators to call up listeners' associations with the planets. Of course, explains Walker, these are shared symbols and obviously learned behavior.[54]

Baif's academy in the mid-sixteenth century experimented with *musique mesurée* and with monody, much as Paolini would have liked. While the academy was devoted to "measuring" together music and poetry in order to produce the "effects" on the hearers attributed to ancient music, the question, however, "whether such products are 'incantations' in the magical sense or incantatory for their artistic quality alone," says Yates, "is a very difficult one, for the border line between magic and art is as hard to trace in this period as the borderline between magic and religion."[55] Compared with *musique mesurée*, the Italian experiments were more decisive, as has already been shown.[56] Peri may be

---

[52]On the interchange between Kabbalism and European Hermeticism, Abrams explains that though Kabbalism undertook to "explicate the secret meaning of Scriptures" and Hermeticism to "expound a secret practice," they share certain principles. These principles, according to Abrams, deal with the mutual alienation of elements that were originally one within nature, within man, or between man and God--and the subsequent quest for re-union. See Abrams, *op.cit.*, pp. 155-158.

[53]See fn. 43.

[54]See Walker, *ibid.*, pp. 133-44.

[55]Yates, *Giordano Bruno . . . , op. cit.*, p. 175. Also see Yates, *The French Academies . . .* , *op. cit.*, pp. 85-90.

said to have continued in the Orphic tradition; his interest in the primacy of words led to the special kind of monodic speech Pirrotta calls *recitar cantando*. Caccini's *cantar recitando* is more in the tradition of accompanied monody, perhaps. And altogether, the notion of compatibility between certain modes of music and certain affections—as an agreed-on set of associations—found its way into both composing and listening in the two centuries of music that followed.

The Heritage of Musical Humanism

The tendency throughout the sixteenth century to set music more closely to its text, has been attributed by many historians to the influence of Humanism. But it was a Humanism transformed and elaborated: it was a Humanism on the road to secularization. From the Humanists came the basic commitment to "bonae litterae," together with their particular reverence for ancient texts. Via the Humanists came the belief in the divinity of the Word and the power of music to attune man to the cosmic spirit. These were "religious" conceptions, but they were a step on the road to more secular theories of the powers of music— and its combination with words—that sought to make contact not only with the stars and their gods, or even with the Christian God, but to make contact with other men, without having to resort to intermediaries.

With all their belief in ancient music, however, neither the Platonic Academy nor its successors had any real idea of what Greek music sounded like, let alone the secrets that would unleash its powers. Neither do we. Nor did the professional musicians delude themselves into thinking—as Ficino and even more

---

[56]Although the Italian experiments were more decisive, Hanning calls attention to the influence of Gabriello Chiabrera, a recognized classicist poet, on Rinuccini's poetic meters and verse form. Chiabrera, in turn, is supposed to have imitated the French poets, especially Ronsard. "The influences of French sources," says Hanning, "first on Chiabrera and through him on Rinuccini, is also evident in the external forms of their poetry . . . " Moreover, claims Hanning, Chiabrera may have imparted to Rinuccini the "Ronsardian ideal with regard to the union of poetry and music, thereby transmitting not merely new rhythmic patterns, but an entire concept of *poesia musicale*." See Hanning, *op. cit.*, pp. 13-15.

Plate 7A. The Reception of the Just. There is music both in heaven and in hell. Each of the places is associated with different musical instruments.

Plate 7B.   The Reception of the Doomed.

knowledgeable theorists may have—that their practical composi-tions had any real basis in ancient music. Yet being aware of the inability of their contemporaries to reproduce such effects, they seized on the one element that could most easily be emulated, namely the closer alliance between music and text. In doing so they may be said to fit well the widespread theme of unification (coniunctio) that Abrams identifies in Hermetic philosophy, Christianized versions of kabbalistic doctrines and, of course, Neoplatonism.[57]

An additional type of alliance between music and text was brought about by the many efforts to understand Aristotle's the-ory of *Katharsis*, for the function of purgation was extended to include not only different kinds of poetry but music as well. This, in turn, contributed to the formulation of theories concern-ing the affections.[58] Giacomini, for example, a committed Aristo-telian whom we have already mentioned in connection with the Alterati, believed that the effect achieved in tragedy is due to the ability of people to empathize.[59] The road from here to the in-ducement of desired passions is not long. The power to move the affections finds anchorage in "harmony" and "rhythm," which are elements common to both music and poetry and, for that matter, to the art of oratory as well. As we have seen, Mei, who like Giacomini was of Aristotelian persuasion, believed that music could use the above elements to imitate the "con-ceits" of the soul by employing the texts in "such a way" as to stimulate the same emotions in the listener. These ideas, which

[57] Abrams' discussion of the interchangeability of the languages of spiritual and physical alchemy in joining male and female, sulphur and mercury, Sol and Luna, king and queen seems applicable also to the union of words and music. In his discussion of Kabbalistic and Hermetic influences on radical Christian theology of the 17th Century, Abrams cites a "first principle" left to philosophy by Boehme, which is most interesting for it "becomes creative by generating its own contrary, which it then proceeds to reconcile to itself." According to Abrams, Boehme also left "the compelling vision of a fallen universe which is constituted throughout by an opposition of quasi-sexual contraries, at once mu-tually attractive and repulsive, whose momentary conciliations give way to re-newed attempts at mastery by the opponent powers, in a tragic conflict which is at the same time the very essence of life and creativity as well as the neces-sary condition for sustaining the possibility of progression back to the strenu-ous peace of the primeval equilibrium." See Abrams, *op.cit.*, p. 162.

[58] See Baxter Hathaway, *The Age of Criticism: The Late Renaissance in Italy*, Ithaca, Cornell University Press, 1962, pp. 205-300.

[59] *Ibid.*, pp. 251-55. Also see Bernard Weinberg, *A History of Literary Criticism in the Italian Renaissance*, Chicago: University of Chicago Press, 1961, vol. I, pp. 322-24.

were explicit in Giacomini and Mei, are implicit in Peri and Caccini; they are, in a sense, already taken for granted.[60] A musical aesthetics centered on the "power" of music was on its way to acquiring permanence.

For all that, the call for a closer alliance between music and text did not give rise to the new aesthetic ideals as much as it was enlisted in their support; for Humanism itself was a product of the Renaissance. This is not to say that the ancient world exerted no influence whatsoever on Renaissance music, as is believed by some, but rather that the conception of ancient music derived from Greek literature (in the absence of musical examples) did not serve as a guide for the Renaissance composer.[61]

Almost all sixteenth-century scholars exploited the original sources of classical Greek musical theory. Yet, although they arrived at very much the same general conception of ancient music, they varied considerably as to the degree to which they wished to reform their own music using ancient music as a model. Gaffurio, Artusi, Salinas and Cerone had a purely scholarly interest in ancient music because by and large they were satisfied with the music of their time. Galilei and Mei, on the other hand, who were dissatisfied with the music of their time, wished to revive ancient music as much as possible. Vicentino and Zarlino, though interested in some reform, believed that modern music had advanced beyond ancient music in many ways.[62] "These differences in outlook," says Walker, "are important since they explain why two Humanists, such as Galilei and Zarlino, advocated very different styles although both had arrived at much the same conception of ancient music. Whereas Galilei seems to be ready to sweep aside all polyphony in order to revive his version of Greek music, Zarlino would, at most, only have wished his disciples to learn from the ancients how to correct some of the abuses of contrapuntal style."[63]

[60]See Hanning, op. cit., chapt. II.
[61]"'Renaissancemusik' im buchstäblichen Sinne [kann] nur ein relativer Begriff sein, da die Musik damals [nich wie die bildende Kunst] greifbare Vorbilder der Antike, höchstens die Metrik und Rhythmik der antiken Poesie, zur Verfügung hat. Was damals 'antike Musik' heisst, ist belanglos." Theodor Kroyer, "Zwischen Renaissance und Barok," *Jahrbuch der Musikbibliotek Peters* 1927, Vol. XXIV, p. 49.
[62]See Walker, "Musical Humanism," *The Music Review*, vol. II (1941), p. 5; Ambros, *Geschichte der Musik*, Reprografischer Nachdruck, Leipzig, 1891, vol. III, p. 162; Palisca, *The Beginnings of Baroque Music*, op. cit., chapts. I, II.
[63]Walker, ibid., pp. 5-6.

Indeed, the degree to which one adhered to the model of ancient music reflected one's prior commitments. Even those who adopted it most thoroughly were not converted by it, but rather found it most congenial. Yet even when an idea is selected as a reinforcement for a prior position, it may have unanticipated effects.

The affinity between the writers on ancient music and those who now wished to follow their model was expressed in their conception of music. Both expected music to possess expressive powers, directly and clearly communicable to the listener. But whereas the ancients believed their music to have effective powers, the moderns tried to recapture these powers, which they claimed were lost as a result of emphasizing the wrong aspects of the musical art. If the music of the ancients could be used as a model, it was because the ancients had the "right" conception of music. The influence of Humanism is not to be found, therefore, in the attempt itself to revive the effective powers of music, but rather in the ways that were chosen for this purpose.

Some of the musical Humanists, in their attempt to recapture the effective powers of music, advocated not only a closer relationship between the music and the text, but also the revival of the chromatic and enharmonic genera as well as the revival of the Greek systems of intonation. The questions of the genera and intonation, though they produced an enormous theoretical literature, had no practical results;[64] neither did the consideration of the Greek modes.

The modes were another factor seen by both classical authorities and Humanists as a means of producing effects. All agreed on the characteristics of each mode and that the choice of mode affected the ethical quality of the music, but the Humanists could not agree on one system of modes. Before choosing his mode, therefore, the composer had to choose between different systems.[65] The conclusiveness of the characteristics of the individual modes was thus challenged. When the question of the modes, like that of the genera and intonation, also turned out to

[64]Chromaticism and the popularity of chromatic works in the late sixteenth century have at times been attributed to the influence of Humanism. Vicentino, for example, who was a great champion of chromaticism and its use in the Italian madrigal, tried to apply the Greek genera as he understood them in the famous book *L'antica musica ridotta alla moderna prattica*. The experiments in chromatic and enharmonic music also inspired organ builders, but it had no lasting effect.
[65] The following systems are quoted by Walker, *ibid.*, pp. 221-22.

be largely of theoretical interest, the close relationship between music and text remained the most important means of reproducing the effects. Through the vivid expression of the text, music could once again become what it "ought" to be —expressive and effective.

Here too, however, differences of opinion were unavoidable, since in the practical application the setting of music closer to its text raised a number of questions. Was the sense of the text to be portrayed literally, or translated into musical terms? Should the rhythm of the text be preserved through writing music that was as near as possible to emotional speech, or by preserving the meter of a poem in its original setting? How was one to assure the audibility of the text, through homophony, or by further reduction to monody? (Nearly all agreed that counterpoint obscured the words.)

The position taken by the different theorists on these questions, and the degree to which they wished to implement them, reveal their own predilections, regardless of their overall consensus about ancient music. Most theorists, for example, with but a few exceptions, believed ancient music to have been monodic. Nor were they original in thinking this: the idea that the expressive power of Greek music could be attributed to its monody can be traced as far back as Glareanus.[66] But not all were in favor of reintroducing a monodic style; in fact, with the excep-

---

	Glareanus, Tyard, Vicentino:	
Dorian	A.	D - a - D
Hypodorian	P.	a - D - a
Phrygian	A.	E - b - E
Hypophrygian	P.	b - E - b
Lydian	A.	F - c - F
Hypolydian	P.	c - F - c etc.
	Zarlino, Mersenne:	
Dorian		C - g - c
Hypodorian		g - C - g
Phrygian		D - a - D
Hypophrygian		a - D - a etc.
	Galilei, Mei, Doni:	
Dorian		E - E
Phrygian		D - D
Lydian		C - C etc.

[66]See Fano's discussion of the Dodekachordon in the introduction of *La Camerata Fiorentina: Vicenzo Galilei*, Fabio Fano, ed., vol. IV, *Instituzioni e monumenti dell'arte musicale italiana*, Milan, 1934, pp. xvii-xviii.

tion of the Florentines, they were prepared to accept any modification of the polyphonic style, provided it conformed in other ways to their new conception of music. The homophonic style seemed equally suited to their purposes because it was capable of both adhering to the rhythm of the text and of expressing its content musically. In fact, most of the sixteenth-century music that was strongly influenced by Humanism such as *musique mesurée* in France and its counterparts in other countries was not monodic but polyphonic.[67]

Was the pro-monodic aesthetic then "only an extension and exaggeration of the belief in the ethical power of music"?[68] Mei concluded on the basis of his studies of the Greek musical system that the music of his time was incapable of producing the effects that Greek music did because "it [modern music] conveyed to the soul of the listener at one time diverse and contrary affections", thus echoing what Abrams calls the "traditional wisdom" according to which perfection is identical with simple unity.[69] Modern counterpoint, according to Mei, was the best demonstration of the fact that Greek music could not have been anything but monodic. Yet it is difficult to prove that the monodic style really had intrinsic advantages over the homophonic style as far as the ethical power of music was concerned. Indeed, if the pro-monodic aesthetic was an "extension" at all, it was an extension of the emancipation of the individual in addition to the belief in the ethical power of music. The emancipation of the individual, which had already found expression in other areas of life, was now finding expression in music.

Monody and the Art of Singing

If the commitment to monody is the major outcome of theorizing about the ancient powers of music, the art of beautiful singing is a major outcome of monody, and thus, indirectly, part of

[67]See Walker, *op. cit.*, vol. IV, pp. 69-70. Also see Gustave Reese, *Music in the Renaissance*, New York: Norton, 1954, pp. 383; 839.
[68]*Ibid.*, p. 70.
[69]Mei is quoted by Palisca, *The Beginnings of Baroque Music*, p. 178. As sources for his generalization, Abrams cites the convergence of Biblical, Neoplatonic, Gnostic and pagan sources in the Hebrew tradition of Kabbala and in the Christian version of Hermetic lore. See Abrams, *op. cit.*, p. 155.

the heritage of Musical Humanism. While homophony made it possible for the composer to assert his individuality, it left little room for the performer to assert his. The monodic style, on the other hand, enabled the singer to project his own emotions onto those of his song. The listener, too, could more readily identify with a solo singer conveying the emotions of an individual than with a group of singers trying to do the same.

With the development of the monodic style, the singer appeared for the first time as a true soloist. His singing was no longer a part of a whole, but was a whole "belebt von Ausdruck, von Empfindung er wird individuelle Gefühlssprache."[70]

The expression of the music no longer solely depended on the music itself but on the interpretation of the performer. "Es is bekannt," says Ehrichs, "Dass in den damaligan Zeit eine Komposition von dem ausübenden Musiker durchaus nicht bis in alle Einzelheiten ebenso ausgeführt wurde wie der Komponist sie niedergeschrieben hatte. Vielmehr war es bei den Virtuosen allgemeiner Brauch die Tonstücke, welche sie vortrugen, beliebig zu verändern. Die Komponisten billigten dieses Verfahren nicht nur, sondern erwarteten es geradezu, dass ihre Werke von den ausübenden Künsten in der verschiedenartigsten Weise verziert wurden. Die schrieben daher auch nur wenige Vortragsbezeichnungen hin und überlissen es dem Geschmack des Vortragenden, die Kompositionen mit allen möglichen Zierrat auszuschmücken. Der Brauch des Verzierens war allmählich zu einer regelrechten Kunst geworden, und in den Traktaten der Schriftsteller des sechzehnten Jahrhunderts finden sich oft lange Kapitel, die sich eingehend mit den verschiedenen Regeln über die Verzierungskunst beschäftigen."[71]

Though the freedom of the performer was limited by the "rules" that governed the ornamentations ostensibly left to his discretion, his role as interpreter could no longer be overlooked.[72] Music, which only comes to life through performance, always depended on the interpretation of the performer, but now the listener was conscious for the first time of the performer's double role: he judged him not only for his technical

---

[70]See Ambros, *Geschichte der Musik*, op. cit., vol. IV, p. 320.
[71]Ehrichs, *op. cit.*, p. 66. See also Caccini's foreward to his *Le Nuove Musiche*.
[72]See Pirrotta's discussion of the subordination of vocal virtuosity and embellishments to the expressive requirements of music. Pirrotta, "Early Opera . . . " *op. cit.*, pp. 63-65.

Plate 8A.   The Last Judgement. Depicting blowing angels awakening
the dead (A), and "heavenly" music making (B). From Hieronymus
Bosch's (1450-1516) 'The Seven Deadly Sins'.

Plate 8B.   Paradise.

skill but also for his creative abilities. Consequently, like the artist before him, the performer gained in stature as he gradually became the composer's equal.

The rise of the virtuoso singer was a direct outcome of this development. The singer, in contrast to earlier periods, now appeared as an individual conscious of his individuality. He no longer aimed only at the attainment of the skills expected of all singers, but cultivated additional skills that would set him apart from other singers. The skills he developed first were those that would enable him more faithfully to convey the music as he experienced it. In time, however, the skills themselves became worth displaying, and a singer's technical ability became as much a part of his personal mark as his musical understanding.

The equality between composer and performer, between musical understanding and technical ability, which grew out of a desire to serve music diverted in time the attention from the music itself to its performance. The entrenchment of monody, deriving from an aesthetic theory that rejected mere sensuous beauty, made it possible, paradoxically, for beautiful singing to develop a system of its own, and thus was born a separate art of singing.[73]

It is no coincidence that this development took place first in Italy, where such high value was placed on gratification of the senses. During this period, singers were admired and appreciated everywhere in Italy, even in the private homes of the clergy. And when the Church itself came to tolerate the new trend in non-liturgical sacred music, it was not only instrumental in furthering its dissemination, it also contributed to the cult of singers.[74] "Sogar die Nonnen in Rom," says Ambros, "fingen an mit Pri-

---

[73]"Der Sänger erlernte im Rahmen des allgemeinen Musikunterrichts wohl das Treffen der Noten, ihren Wert usw., kurz und gut, alles was nötig war, um korrekt zu singen; die Schönheit des Tones, die Eleganz und Fertigkeit der Verzierungen, insbesondere das Verständnis, wo sie anzubringen seien, kommen bis dahin nur nebenher in Betracht." Hugo Goldschmidt, *Die italienische Gesangsmethode des XVII, Jahrhunderts und ihre Bedeutung für die Gegenwart*, Breslau, S. Schottlaender, 1982, p. 27.

[74]See Ambros, *op. cit.*, pp. 424-425. The text of the rituals as well as freely composed religious texts were now set in the new style. An example of the latter is Ottavio Durante's "Arie divote." The following inscription is of interest: "Arie divote, le quali contengano in se la maniera di Cantar con gratia, l'imitation della parole, et il modo di seriver passaggi et altri affetti Nuovamente composti da Ottavio Durante, Romano, appresso Simmoni Verovio 1608, con Licenza de Superiori.

madonnen gelegentlich eine sehr Bedenkliche Aehnlichkeit an-
zunehmen."[75] But nowhere was the performer as welcome as in
the private salons.

It is significant, indeed, that beautiful singing was not only
appreciated by the Camerata, but that its members also contributed to the development of its method. Pietro della Valle, who
pays tribute to the Florentine group on many accounts, does not
fail to mention their contribution to the art of beautiful singing.[76]
And Doni mentions Caccini as the one to whom he attributes "la
nuova e graziosa maniera di cantare."[77]

Caccini was identified with a method of singing that was
the most esteemed in all of Italy. His students, and especially his
daughters, were invited to take part in all important musical
events that called for the participation of singers. From a few
extant letters it is known that Caccini himself, together with his
daughters, spent some time in Paris and performed at the court
of Henry IV.[78] These letters not only testify to the singing ability
of the Caccini family, but are important documents for tracing
the dissemination of the Italian method of singing exemplified
by Caccini.[79] Moreover, Caccini is also explicitly mentioned by Michael Praetorius in his discussion of the Italian method of singing
and the recognition it had been gaining in Germany.[80]

The Secularization of Musical Powers: Conclusions

Reviewing the attempts to revive ancient music, from the
Platonic Academy to the academy of the Camerata and after, it is
evident that the effort failed. In the most elementary sense, it
failed because no one could truly say that he had a record of how
ancient music sounded. Nevertheless, the preoccupation with
the music —and the words—of the ancients had important consequences. First of all, it led to a doctrine that insisted on the
primacy of the communication of affects, that is, of meaning,

[75]Ambros, *ibid.*, p. 423.
[76]See Pietro della Valle, *Della musica dell'eta nostra che non e' punto inferiore, anzi e migliore di quella dell'eta passata* (1640) in Solerti, *Le Origini, op. cit.*, p. 162.
[77]See Giovanni Battista Doni, *Trattato della musica scenica*, in Solerti, *ibid.*, p. 211.
[78]See Ehrichs, *op. cit.*, p. 58. Also see Angelo Solerti, "Un viaggio in Francia di Giulio Caccini," *Rivista musicale italiana*, 1903.
[79]See Henry Prunieres, *L'Opera italien en France avant Lulli*, Paris: Champion, 1913. pp. xxvi-xxxiii.
[80]See Ambros, *op. cit.*, pp. 316-18.

over the entertainment implicit in delighting the ear (or flattering the eye). Secondly, it led to the primacy of the word, and the role of music in heightening and clarifying its persuasive message. Thirdly, it led to practical experimentation with the art of musical persuasion as the ancients "might have" practiced it, and thus to a wedding of theory and practice.

Although he was not a serious musician, theory and practice guided Ficino in his musical astrology, just as theory and practice met again in the Bardi salon. The members of the Camerata, as much as their illustrious predecessor theorized about the powers of music, believed that the ancients had answers, and however inadaquate the answers at hand, experimented with practical music.

Ficino, of course, believed in musical magic. He believed that the ancients could attune themselves to the cosmic spirit through music, and tried to do so himself. In his theorizing he provided an explanation of the process by which the spirits inherent in man and in the universe could be contacted by musical rituals. The method for doing so he defined by observation and experimentation.

The members of the Camerata were no less practical than Ficino, and no less theoretical. While they still believed that the ancients held the secrets to the powers of music, they left off trying to understand them exactly, convinced only that a major clue to the nature of that music resided in some form of monody, that is, some way in which music could enhance the spoken word. Their theorizing insisted that music must cease to distort the words or merely to embroider them, but must cope with the problem of conveying their latent meaning. This meaning, they believed, could be transmitted from composer to listener.

From the Camerata through the doctrine of affections, the powers of music were not simply described in empty words, but became part of the technical aspect of the theory of composition. Thus, the campaign against music that "delights the ear" argued, in part, that the use of many notes was "artificial" and that the limitation of means held the secret for success. Galilei, who was chiefly responsible for this claim,[81] also tried to sup-

[81]Galilei based his claim on simple songs of the populace, which he thought were more "natural," and on the odes and hymns of the ancient poets, which he thought were limited to four notes since they were sung to four-string citharas. See Palisca, "Galilei and Links . . . ," *op. cit.*, p. 347.

plant Zarlino's contrapuntal theory with a theoretical formulation of the harmonic practice of his contemporaries, thereby satisfying the need for a theory of chromatic and enharmonic
music.[82] The latter, as is well known, loomed large in the attempt
to endow music with greater expressive powers.[83] In addition,
musical elements such as range, tempo and meter were employed to qualify emotions. Such experimentation centered
around the effort to match affects to musical procedures, since it
follows logically, of course, that if the foremost goal of music is
"to move the affect of the soul," there must exist more, and less,
affective "manners" of doing so. With his *esclamazione, trillo,* and
ribattuta di gola, etc., Caccini pointed the way.[84] Indeed, like
Ficino, the Camerata tried to show how latent meanings could
be transmitted from composer to listener—through observation,
experimentation, composition and performance. While Ficino
aimed primarily at healing the body and refreshing the spirit of
man by connecting him to the cosmos, the primary aim of the
Camerata was to connect men with men. Ethical persuasion pre-
occupied them all, but the Camerata took a further step toward
the humanizing, and secularizing, of music.

It is fashionable nowadays to speak of the origins of modern science in the hermetic tradition of magic, operating on the
will and the world. Magic itself—for all its mysterious ways—is a
more secularized form of religion, giving man something "to
do." Joined with a theory based upon empirical observation,
magical operations become increasingly scientific. And so it is
with music: Aesthetic theory addressed to the nature of music
found itself in the corridors of the same laboratory from which
empirical science was emerging. Theorizing about the powers of
music, divining them, then joining composition and performance with theory and empirical observation, the theorists and
musicians of the late Renaissance and early baroque connected
music with both magic and science.

Indeed, Galilei almost sounds like an applied social scien-

---

[82]See *ibid.,* p. 346.
[83]In an illuminating article concerning Galilei's counterpoint treatise, Palisca
shows how Galilei, with "prophetic vision," set out already in 1588 to defend
the principles of the *seconda prattica.* See Claude V. Palisca, "Vincenso Galilei's
Counterpoint Treatise: A Code for the *Seconda Prattica,*" *Journal of the American
Musicological Society,* 1956, vol. IX, pp. 81-96.
[84]See preface to *Le Nuove Musiche, op. cit.*

tist. If you wish to be a (serious) composer, he says, study natural conversations:

> When the ancient musician sang any poem whatever, he first considered very diligently the character of the person speaking; his age, his sex, with whom he was speaking, and the effect he sought to produce by these means; and these conceptions, previously clothed by the poet in chosen words suited to such a need, the musician then expressed in the tone and with the accents and gestures, the quantity and quality of sound, and the rhythms appropriate to that action and to such a person.[85]

[85]See Strunk, *op. cit.*, p. 319.

Chapter Five

Orfeo: Unleashing the Powers of Music

In his report on the proceedings of the Academia degli Uranici in Venice during the last few years of the sixteenth century, Walker allows himself to wonder how "a group of highly educated adults should spend hours seriously discussing, as if it were a historical fact, a story which they knew and admitted to be legendary," namely that Orpheus' music influenced not only men and animals but also produced effects in rocks and stones and trees.[1] The explanation, Walker suggests, lies in the symbolic function of Orpheus for Renaissance Neoplatonism, specifically,

> he was a theologian who linked the ancient gods to Christianity, a magician, astrologer, poet, orator, musician, lover both plebian and heavenly, and child of the sun. By discussing the effects of Orpheus' music one could range, with easy suppleness, over every possible practical application of Neoplatonism, from the whitest to the blackest magic, from the most intellectual religious to the most crude superstition, from the beauty of music to the power of a whispered incantation.[2]

Orpheus sums up the culture of the Renaissance as well as the gaining impetus of expressionism and operationism that led to the baroque. The centrality of the image of Orpheus and his lyre, and the preoccupation with this theologian-magician-musician, is basic to the early history of opera and, more generally, to the history of music. Orpheus personifies the concept of man's ability to divine the powers of music, discussed in the previous chapter. And above all, he is the symbol of "unleashing" the powers of music, which will be discussed in this one.

[1]Walker, *Spiritual and Demonic Magic*, pp. 128-31. Also see Abrams, *op. cit.*, pp. 146-155.
[2]*Ibid.*, p. 101.

Musicians, both practical and theoretical, see in Orpheus' artistry and dignity the humanism of man become God. The mastery of music is one of the achievements that elevate the human being to the spirituality of the gods. Moreover, to this day the aesthetics of music is still fascinated by the idea of the practical use of music to move the animate and inanimate, the human and the supernatural, and thus to affect change in the individual, his society and his cosmos. Most important of all, perhaps, to use Spitzer's phrase once more, Orpheus stands for the "musicalization" of the world. Music stands for harmony and "stimmung," and of all the sentiments, love is paramount. Love is the epitome of music, and it is no coincidence that throughout centuries of operatic history music has dealt primarily with love and has spoken resolutely of the inner experience of "being."

As has been pointed out already, the Orphic Hymns play a central part in the rituals of magic practiced by Ficino and his followers. This is not the place to reenter the debate over whether or not Ficino actually meant what he said when he insisted that his musical magic was not demonic, and was intended rather more as a benevolent influence on the practitioner himself than a communion with the established gods. It is important, however, to recall that these incantations are artistic. Talismanic or natural, Ficino's magic is elegant and refined, and "the question whether such products are incantations in the magical sense or incantatory for their artistic quality alone" has to do, as Yates has said, "with the difficult borderlines between magic and art and magic and religion."[3] Pico's *Conclusiones Orphicae* is apt once more: "In natural magic nothing is more efficacious than the hymns of Orpheus, if there be applied to them the suitable music, and disposition of soul, and the other circumstances known to the wise."[4] The Orpheus theme was adopted by the lyric stage as its motto. In other words, it became both a motive force for the musical expression of the individual, and the subject to which this creativity could be devoted. From musical inspiration, Orpheus became musical material to work upon. It will be recalled that the Orpheus theme occupied the members of the Camerata as well. Two of its members wrote

[3]See Ch. IV, fn. 56.
[4]See. ch. IV, fn. 38.

music for Rinuccini's *Euridice*. And Monteverdi, who explicitly acknowledged that he was adopting the *stile rappresentativo* to tell his version of Orpheus eventually designated any composition set for stage as belonging to the "representative species."[5] From Orpheus' lyre to the Magic Flute, musical instruments likewise have been favorite subjects of opera. Pirrotta might say that they give legitimacy to the convention of the music drama, but magic-making instruments clearly have a special fascination. As Spitzer says, "The Greek musician-god was brought back to life to prove in person on the stage the magic power of music, which, when put to the service of love, can master nature and conquer hell."[6] In other words, opera is the self-glorification of music on the stage of the theater.[7]

Poliziano's *Orfeo*

A contemporary and compatriot of Ficino and Pico, and a classical scholar and poet in the court of the Medicis, Angelo Poliziano early (1480) chose "La Favola di Orfeo" as a theme for a dramatic poem.[8] In his monumental work on the history of the

[5]See Leo Schrade, *Monteverdi*, New York: Norton, 1950, p. 209. For a comparison between the treatments of the Orpheus legend by Poliziano, Rinuccini and Monteverdi, and the musical implications of the different poetic structures, see Hanning, *op. cit.*, ch. III. Altogether,the chapter deals with the formulation of the new recitative style.

[6]Spitzer, *op. cit.*, p. 121.

[7]In the Prologue of Striggio's libretto to Monteverdi's *Orfeo*, La Musica—the personification of music on the stage—states this clearly and distinctly:

I rule the realms of Music sweet,
And with my skill soothe troubled minds
Or stir with passion and inflame
The coldest hearts with furious love.

On golden strings I play and sing
To calm the ears of mortal men,
And so exalt their souls to heaven,
And to the music of the spheres.

My theme is Orpheus, loved on Pindus,
Glorious child of Helicon,
Who melted hearts of savage beasts
And made Hell bow before his pleading.

[8]For the establishment of the exact dates of Poliziano's *Orfeo*, see Nino Pirrotta, *Li Due Orfei: da Poliziano a Monteverdi*, Einaudi, Torino, 1975, pp. 8-9.

Plate 9.   Orfeo. A Seventeenth century engraving by Daret, depicting
Orpheus taming animals with the "powers of music".

theater in Italy, D'Ancona relegated the *Orfeo* to a transitional species that arose between the *sacra rappresentazione* and the revival and imitation of the classical theatre of Greece and Rome. Drawing its argument from mythology, the *Orfeo* was an early attempt to break away from the *sacra rappresentazione* towards the classics. Nonetheless, though it detached itself in subject from the religious tradition, it was not yet enmeshed in classic imitation and therefore could not be called an example of ancient dramatic art restored.[9] According to D'Ancona, it was but "a theatrical ornament to a festival of a prince."[10]

In discussing this point, Pirotta relegates the *Orfeo* to the kind of representations that provided entertainment at banquets in between courses. Such entertainments lasted long especially at carnival times. The imperfections of the *Orfeo*, which Poliziano himself considered imperfect, Pirotta attributes to the speed in which it was prepared and to the function it served. He does not believe, as does D'Ancona, that the theatrical techniques of the *Orfeo* followed those of the contemporary sacred theater, but rather that they developed and amplified the characteristics of "fabule" that were inserted at intervals during banquets or official receptions. Unlike sacred representations, which dealt with a level of existence remote from the viewer, the mythological world of the *Orfeo*, stresses Pirrotta, did not obstruct reality; the characteristic traits of the *Orfeo* remained graspable and immediate. Nothing about the *Orfeo* pointed to a didactic or symbolic function; everything was staged in a manner that would provide Orfeo with a natural and persuasive setting for his kind of expression. While the play is admittedly replete with classic allusions and citations, according to Pirrotta the classic tale of the *Orfeo* myth was not the only source of literary inspiration for Poliziano's play; the eclogue was an additional important source. The latter had nothing in common with sacred representations, either in poetic structure or in its scenic elements. Moreover, the *Orfeo* originally consisted of three episodes— "bucolic," "heroic" and "bacchic"—with similar dynamic developments that start calmly and increase in pace towards the end. The five-act tragedy with additional parts and characters is

[9] D'Ancona, *Origini del teatro italiano*, Turin, 1891, vol. II, pp. 140-143. Also see Vittorio Rossi, *Il Quatrocento*, Milan, 1938, pp. 375-376, and the chapter following for a discussion of Italian dramatic genres and their musical implications.
[10] D'Ancona, *ibid.*, p. 144.

a later transformation of the play that formed the original structure. Not only were many of the meters used in the *Orfeo* unknown to the sacred representations, but the overall rhythm of the presentation was fast, whereas that of the sacred theater was slow. According to Pirrotta, there was a difference in the use of music as well. "Too much or too little" music characterized the sacred theater, whereas the *Orfeo* followed the tradition of bucolic court representations where verbal recitations alternated with songs.[11]

Whatever the differences among scholars, they all seem to agree that Poliziano brought to the *Orfeo* the poetic qualities in which he excelled. Since a mastery of the complexity of human nature is totally absent from the play, *Orfeo* has been praised more for its poetic quality than for its dramatic merit. The play is most convincing where the situation is less dramatic than lyrical. Orfeo's devotion to Euridice, his complete subjugation to love, present him as a lyrical personage whose character as a whole remains unknown. Indeed, Orfeo's part rises to its height in the passages where he sings of his love, lamenting his separation from his beloved. This outpouring of the heart is likewise the finest scene of the play because in it the dramatic motive could be lyrically expressed. Despite its intensity, Orfeo's love does not seem eccentric, since it exists in a world powerfully perfumed with love. Nor do the acts it inspires seem dramatic. Invading Hell and risking life for love are but logical acts for one whose life is not worth living without it. The decision to try to bring Euridice back does not create emotional conflict, since love is not merely a part of Orfeo's existence, but permeates his entire being.

Even Pluto takes Orfeo's great love for granted. After all, didn't he himself experience the powers of love? But just in case he has forgotten, Orfeo makes a point of reminding him of his "ancient famed love." So there is understanding in Hell for the invader who comes in the name of love.[12]

---

[11]Pirrotta, *op. cit.*, pp. 10-20.

[12]Orfeo takes this for granted or else he would not have addressed the infernal spirits in the following way: "Pity, pity a poor lover, Pity ye infernal Spirits. Love alone hath brought me here below. Thither have I flown on his wings. O Gerberus, lay aside thine anger, for when thou shalt hear all these my woes, not thou alone but all the others here in this blind world shall weep with me. "Ye Furies, ye need not shriek at me nor curl your serpent locks, for if he knew my bitter woes ye would join me in my lamentations. Let pass this woeful man,

Indeed, in the world in which Orfeo lives, there is no pity anywhere for one who scorns love and resolves to live without it. He who loves should not desire to heal "a pain so sweet," but rather should praise it the more because he suffers from it.[13] For him that scorns love, no punishment is too severe; he is torn "limb from limb in many pieces with cruel torture."

Pluto is moved to grant Orfeo's request by his "sweet note" and "glorious lyre," for his love alone would not have sufficed. Strong love, it appears, constitutes a legitimate reason for the invasion of Hades, but it is neither new nor unusual to Pluto. It is Orfeo's "sweet" expression, rather than the fact that he truly loves, which stirs Pluto to pity. Indeed, so powerful is Orfeo's expression that all the infernal spirits are affected by it.

Orfeo's complaints are expressed in song. In the lyrical world in which Orfeo breathes, emotions find vent in song. However, his song is not only the "sweet" expression of his feelings, capable of arousing sympathy. It is more. It is the expression the *effective* powers of which are capable of making "Ixion's wheel stand still" and the water no longer "shrink from Tantalus."[14] The shepherds, too, reach for their pipes in order to express their love, but even more in order to *move* the hearts of their beloveds.

Poliziano's *Favola di Orfeo* is one of the most representative expressions of the period. The ideas, style and general atmosphere of the play embody the spirit of the High Renaissance in Italy. It expressed the sentiments of its audience not only by satisfying their aesthetic expectations, but by capturing their longings and fulfilling their dreams at one and the same time.

---

hated of heaven and all the elements, who comes to win a boon from Death. Therefore open for him the iron gates." From Louis E. Lord's translation, London:Oxford University Press, 1931, p. 92.

[13]*Aristaeus*: "Mopsus, 'tis to the dead thou speakest. Spend not thy words—words that the wind may idly bear away. Aristaeus loves, nor would not give his passion o'er, nor heal his pain so sweet. He praises Love who suffers most from Love. But if thou carest aught for wish of mine, come, take thy shepherd's pipe from out thy pocket and we will sing beneath this leafy shade. For well I know that song to my Nymph is dear." *Ibid.*, pp. 77-78.

[14]"Who is he that with so sweet a note and with his glorious lyre moves the abyss? I see Ixion's wheel stand still, Sisyphus sitting on his stone, and the Danaids standing with empty urn. Nor does the water longer shrink from Tantalus, and I behold Gerberus of the triple mouth listening and the furies grow calm at his command." *Ibid.*, p. 92.

The scholarly enthusiasm of the age also finds expression in the play, though therein does not lie its importance. A certain degree of enthusiasm for classical ideas and literature is to be expected of a man who, in addition to being one of the greatest poets, was also one of the foremost classical scholars of his time.[15] To D'Ancona, looking at the *Orfeo* as a transitional work, a work on the road to classical imitations, it seemed the *Orfeo* had not yet achieved the stature of ancient art restored. However, examined on its own merits, it is clear that Poliziano, aware of the psychology of the age and himself no less affected by it, was able to fuse in his *Orfeo* the scholarly, philosophical and aesthetic outlook of the period.

Poliziano's poetry, the sweetness of his style, and the smoothness of his expression were capable above all of quenching the thirst for artistic beauty so characteristic of the age. Moreover, the world of shepherds, nymphs and woods found an echo in his soul, and like the idyllic dreamers of the nation, he too escaped into nature, hoping to internalize its tranquility. Though it cannot be considered a pure example of the genre, in spirit and mood the *Orfeo* anticipated the style of the best pastorals. Yet the *Orfeo* created a unique synthesis of its own, combining pastoral and tragic elements with artistic beauty and classical literature.

Arcadia was a wonderland for a society seeking to escape the new complexities of city life. Indeed, as the following chapter will maintain, the pastoral drama may also have served as a substitute for the heavenly city, which for the men of the Renaissance was no longer the only source of solace. Orfeo was the hero of the Arcadian world, the hero of a world that fulfilled all dreams and aspirations. In this world of fulfillment, gods no longer manipulate the fate of man; on the contrary, man possesses the power to manipulate the gods. Mirroring Renaissance thought, the love for beauty, art, and poetry constitute Orfeo's power, the power of man. His is the power of civilization, capable of "humanizing" the barbarous world of the gods.[16]

---

[15]By the time the *Orfeo* was written, Poliziano was already famous for his translation of the *Iliad* and had gained the title of "Homericus Juvenis" first given to him by Ficino. He attended lectures in philosophy given by Ficino. Although influenced by the latter's Neoplatonic ideas, he remained more attracted by poetry and philology.

[16]"Unerring instinct guided Poliziano in the choice of his subject. Orpheus was

The *Orfeo*, however, was more than a Renaissance representation of the Orpheus myth incorporating elements of the pastoral kingdom of Theocritus. It was a mixed work of melodramatic art in which music had a significant part. "To do the *Orfeo* justice," says Symonds, "we ought to have heard it with its accompaniment of music." He further remarks that "we find in *Orfeo* a charm of musical language, a subtlety of musical movement, which are irresistibly fascinating. Thought and feeling seem alike refined to a limpidity that suits the flow of melody in song. The very words evaporate and lose themselves in floods of sound."[17]

In itself, the insertion of music into the *Orfeo* play was not significant. It was simply a continuation of a long-established tradition. However, in the *Orfeo* music was not merely employed to enhance the performance; it was an intrinsic part of the play. While the simplicity of the shepherds and the overall pastoral charm bespoke internal and external tranquility, music became the expressive vehicle for the passions of the soul.

The role of music, as all but explicitly defined in the play, represents the musico-aesthetic theories of the ancients. The Orpheus myth was a dramatic embodiment of the theory that professed the expressive and effective powers of music.

The play as a whole contained the full apparatus for the enchantment of the senses, the chief attraction of the lyric stage of the following century. Moreover, it professed the aesthetic theories that were later so firmly stated by the members of the Florentine coterie, though the actual music employed in the *Orfeo* was not yet especially fashioned for the unique role to which it was assigned.[18]

---

the proper hero of Renaissance Italy—the civiliser of a barbarous world by art and poetry, the lover of beauty, who dared to invade Hell and moved the iron heart of Pluto with a song. . . . This was the ideal of the Renaissance: and, what is more, it accurately symbolised the part played by Italy after the dissolution of the Middle Ages. In the myth of Orpheus the humanism of the Revival became conscious of itself. This fable was the Mystery of the new age, the allegory of the work appointed for the nation." Symonds, J.A., *Renaissance in Italy* (New York: Modern Library, 1925), p. 105.

[17]*Ibid.*, p. 106.

[18]"Ci fu chi volle riguardare cotesto Orfeo del Poliziano come il primo saggio del dramma musicale, togliendone la gloria dell'invenzione al Caccini ed al Peri. Certo v'ha parte la musica: la canzone d'Aristeo, il coro della Driadi, la preghiera d'Orfeo agli spiriti infernali e il coro delle Baccanti dovettero essere e in parte vi si dicono cantati. Ma cio' non basta: il canto soleva spesso introdursi

Frottola and Madrigal: The Problem of Alliance Between Words and Music

All records of the music of the *Orfeo* are lost, yet conjectures have been made as io its style. These conjectures all point to the musical language and practice believed to prevail at the time the play was first produced at the Mantuan court. It has long been contended that the choral parts of the *Orfeo* were written in the form of the Italian *frottola*, since the *frottola* was the reigning form of part song at that time. It has likewise been suggested that the solo parts also followed the customary practice of singing *frottole* as solos by giving the polyphony to the lute or other accompanying instruments.[19]

After all, the insertion of music into dramatic representations was not limited to the *Orfeo*. Music was regularly introduced into the plays in vogue at that time.[20] According to Rubsamen, it has been impossible to identify the music sung during such performances because more often than not the inserted *canzonette* were improvised by those who sang them.[21] Yet several *frottole* have been identified: those written by dramatic poets closely associated with Isabella d'Este, who requested the aid of her singers, Marchetto Cara and Bartolomeo Tromboncino, in the composition of musical *intermezzi*.[22] Some dramatic poets were especially prone to use both solo and choral pieces in their

---

anche nelle rappresentazioni sacre delle eta piu grosse. 'In ogni tempo,' dice bene G.B. Doni (*Opere*, I. II, Della mus. scen., c. IX), 'si e costumato di frammettere alle azioni drammatiche qualche sorte di cantilena o in forma d'intermedii tra un atto e l'altro, o pure dentro l'istesso atto per qualche accorrenza del soggetto rappresentato . . . .conviene pero sapere che quelle melodie sono molto differenti dalle odierne che si fanno in istile communemente detto recitativo . . . .en non hanno che fare niente con la buona e vera musica teatrale.'" See Pietro Canal, "Della musica in Mantua. Notizie tratte principalmente dall'Archivio Gonzaga" in *Memorie del R. Instituto Veneto di Scienze, Lettere et Arti*, 1879, vol. XXI, p. 658.

[19]See Alfred Einstein, *The Italian Madrigal* (Princeton: 1949), vol. I, pp. 35-43, and Walter Rubsamen, *Literary Sources of Secular Music in Italy (ca. 1500)*, (Berkeley, 1943), p. 32. Two choral pieces and two soli are the musical pieces referred to in the discussion of the music of Poliziano's *Orfeo*. (Rubsamen, *op. cit.*, p. 32; Einstein, *op. cit.*, vol. I p. 35; Canal, *ibid.*, p. 658; Angelo Solerti, "Precedenti del Melodramma", *Rivista musicale italiana, vol. X (1903), p. 208).*

[20]See Rubsamen, *op. cit.*, chapter VI.

[21]*Ibid.*, p. 33.

[22]See Rubsamen, *op. cit.*, chapter II.

dramatic works.[23] Though the identified examples are few in numbers they leave little doubt about the style of the music inserted into dramatic representations during the reign of the *frottola*.

The many secular dramas, comedies and tragedies in which music played a sufficiently important role to warrant their mention in a discussion of the precursors of opera[24] all availed themselves of the musical language of the day. Doni's oft-cited remark about the place music held in theatrical performances prior to the invention of the recitative style explicitly states that there was no special type of music particularly suited and adapted for the theater.[25] Even the immediate precursors of opera had not yet developed a musical language of their own, but made use of the music practiced at the time. The pastorals, the many celebrations of marriages, the receptions of distinguished guests, the grand tournée and the like all benefited from the services of the famous madrigal composers of the day.[26] Malvezzi's *Intermedi et Concerti* (1591), which preserves the music of the *intermedi* written for the famous festivities on the occasion of the marriage of the Grand Duke Ferdinand with Christine of Lorraine, also contains valuable notes about the performance. It is evident from Malvezzi's publication that all the pieces were written in madrigal style.[27]

It has been argued that the *frottola*, which was used in con-

---

[23]*Ibid.*, p. 33.

[24]See Solerti, "Precedenti . . . ", *op. cit.*, pp. 208-213.

[25]See fn. 18.

[26]Francesco Corteccia wrote the music for the *intermedi* of Antonio Landi's *Il Commodo* performed at the wedding festivities of Cosimo de' Medici and Eleonora of Toledo in 1539. Alfonso della Viola composed the music for Beccari's *Il Sacrefizio* (1554), for Lolio's *Aretusa*(1563), Giraldi's *Orbecche* (1541), and Agostino Argenti's *Lo Sfortunato*. Alessandro Striggio together with Corteccia provided the music for Giovanni Battista Cini's *intermedi* based on the tale of Cupid and Psyche, given between the acts of d'Ambra's *La Cofanaria*, which was performed at the wedding of Francesco de Medici and Johanna of Austria (1565). Pietro Strozzi together with Striggio and Merulo composed the music for the wedding festivities of Francesco de' Medici and Bianca Gapello in 1579, in which Caccini took part as singer. All of the above musicians were famous madrigal composers of the day. For a full account of these *intermedi* and other dramatic presentations, see Solerti, *Gli Albori del Melodramma, op. cit.*, Oscar George Sonneck, "A Description of Alessandro Striggio and Francesco Corteccia's Intermedi Psyche and Amor, 1565," *Miscellaneous Studies in the History of Music*, New York, 1921; and Einstein, *op. cit.*, vol. I, pp. 300-306.

[27]Several different composers contributed to the *intermedi* of 1589, including

nection with dramatic representations around the turn of the fifteenth century, came closer than the madrigal (which was used in the course of the sixteenth century) to solving one of the major problems inherent in the alliance of words and music, namely, ensuring the audibility of words.[28] This the *frottola* was able to achieve primarily because contrapuntal techniques played an insignificant part in its overall structure. The *frottole* were essentially chordal in style. For the most part, they were constructed of four voices with the soprano part standing out as a melody. The bass had many leaps of fourths and fifths and acted as a harmonic foundation.[29] It is believed that in the process of composition these outer voices were written out first and the inner voices were added as harmonic fillers.[30] Fugato passages or imitation, though not characteristic of the *frottola*, did take place; but where they occurred, they did not interfere with the main flow of the melody. Paraphrasing a passage from Cerone's *El Melopeo v Maestro*, Ambros says, "Wer eine Frottola mit fugen, Machahmungen u.s.w. ausstatte, gleiche einem, der einen werthlosen Stein in Gold fasst. Eine so veredelte Frottola werde sum Madrigal, wahrend ein allzuarmlich behandeltes Madrigal zur Frottola herabsinke."[31]

Though Cerone's description is over-simplified and is more applicable to the later *villote* and *villanella* than to the collection of

---

Luca Marenzio, Emilio de' Cavalieri, Cristofano Malvezzi, Peri and Bardi. From Malvessi's account we also learn that some of the choral pieces were sung as solos and accompanied by instruments. See Solerti, Albori, *op. cit.*, vol. II, p. 19; also Solerti, *Precedenti, op. cit.*, p. 226; also Ambros, *op. cit.*, vol. IV, pp. 254-58.

[28] Obviously, the polyphonic madrigal is intended. The solo madrigal is a development of the late sixteenth century, and itself represents a chapter in the history of monody. For the latter, see Einstein, *op. cit.*, vol. II, pp. 850-58.

[29] For a summary of the stylistic features of the *frottola*, see Reese, *op. cit.*, pp. 156-65. For a thorough musical discussion of the *frottola* proper and the other poetic-musical types that are included within the generic term *frottola*, see Einstein, *op. cit.*, vol. I, pp. 75-107.

[30] It is difficult to establish the performance practice of the *frottola* because of its stylistic features. "Das Problem [in answer to the question 'vocal or instrumental'?], says Schwartz, "ist auch heute noch nicht restlos gelöst. Soveit aber wird man sagen können, dass bei den Frottole der Canto durchaus vokalen charakter hat . . . .Dagegen lässt sich die Frage nach der Vokalität der übrigen Stimmen nicht generall beantworten. Man wird hier von Fall zu entscheiden haben." Rudolf Schwartz, "Nochmals 'Die Frottole in 15. Jahrhundert'," in *Jahrbuch der Musikbibliotek Peters*, vol. XXXI (1924), p. 56.

[31] August Wilhelm Ambros, *Geschichte der Musik, op. cit.*, vol. IV, p. 490.

frottole published by Petrucci,[32] the fact remains that the *frottole* did not much employ the elaborate polyphonic techniques characteristic of the Franco-Netherlandish style, indicating a consideration for clear-cut phrases in which all voices began and ended together. The syllabic treatment of the text plus the simultaneity, to a greater or lesser extent, with which the voices moved, made possible the clear enunciation and audibility of the text.

The importance attributed by historians to the audibility of the text with respect to the *frottola* has largely been dictated by the theoretical concerns of the Renaissance with the powers of music. Indeed, once language was identified as one of the keys to the powers of music, the audibility of the text was logically conceived not just as a starting point, but as a *sine qua non*. In the attempt to unleash the powers of music, however, experimentation concerning the alliance between music and words had to and did traverse a long road in adding to the clarification of such an alliance. If Poliziano's *Orfeo* is supposed to have come closer to the birth of opera than subsequent developments did, it must contain more than an apparatus to start the ball rolling or, as it seems in retrospect, to create a proper setting for it. It is for this reason that Pirrotta's unique approach to the subject is all the more welcome, because it fills a lacuna that was overlooked.

Pirrotta, unlike many other scholars, suggests that artistic polyphony was altogether limited at the time of the *Orfeo*, so that even the chorus of the bacchantes, was not performed polyphonically but in the manner of the contemporary carnival songs. These consisted of a single singing line with the accompaniment of one or two musical instruments, in contrast to the later type, which was cast in three or four voices. The bacchantes, accordingly, sang the refrain together, though not polyphonically, and took turns singing the stanzas. Performances of this type and others have created interest for their intrinsic value because of later developments, claims Pirrotta. At the time, he suggests, they represented a concept of music characterized by spontaneity and improvization, reflecting humanistic mistrust of the written "scholastic" tradition. For Poliziano and his contemporaries music was first and foremost poetry, or (alternatively) poetic words were already considered music. "Contrary to our habit of thinking about text and music as two heterogeneous

[32]See *ibid.*, p. 491.

Plate 10. A Pig Playing A Rebec. From a fragment of a capital from Cluny (twelfth century). Attributing to swine a familiarity with the world of music is both funny and interesting, even if we doubt their ability to play.

things arbitrarily associated," says Pirrotta, "the humanist poets adhered to the classic tradition where music is conceived as an extension of the poetic form."[33] They were not insensitive to polyphonic music, he adds, but they preferred to sing their poems by themselves. The most common way of making music was singing to the accompaniment of an instrument. Singers improvised verses and poets invented melodies. To sum up, Pirrotta sees the *Orfeo* as a symbol of this broader conception of poetry as singing, and the choice of a singer—Baccio Ugolini for the role of Orfeo—as a clear indication that Orfeo had to sing.[34]

For the Italian literates in the fifteenth century the *stramboto* was the most cultivated form of poetry for music expressing lyric feelings. Many of their texts became part of the contemporary poetic collections. They were not written, however, in the musical codices until the end of the century. Having identified the written tradition with polyphony does not mean that the non-written tradition was only monophonic.[35] In the rising period of the *stramboto*, singing with an instrument may also have been accompanied by a tenor. Pirrotta suggests that the tenor melody relationship remained a fundamental element of all the music that directly or indirectly reflected the non-written practice, namely the *frottola* approach. The four-voiced compositions resulted from the addition of a contratenore and altus. The latter, however, were less essential and were omitted in the execution of the non-written tradition or else rendered by an instrument.[36]

Conceptualizing this kind of music-making, Pirrotta emphasizes the love for harmonization. Thus the accompanied line is not conceived of as a reduction of polyphony, a kind of "pseudo monody," but rather as an amplification of a single line. The distinction made is not between monophony and polyphony, but rather between oneness and the multiplicity of contrapuntal lines. In the former, polyphony is the end result, whereas in the latter it is a starting point. Inequality of voices (the supremacy of one line, for example) should no more surprise in the former than equality of voices would in the latter.

Pirrotta's insightful and novel approach to the issue at hand should not be lost on us, for viewing music and poetry as

[33]Pirrotta, *op. cit.*, pp. 21-22.
[34]*Ibid.*, p. 23.
[35]*Ibid.*, p. 25.
[36]*Ibid.*, p. 26.

Plate 11.   A Cat Playing a Fiddle. From a choir seat from the cathedral of Wells (c. 1300).

organically combined rather than successfully wed introduces the main road to articulation in song.

Poliziano's *Orfeo*, it is agreed, occupies not only an important position in the development of literature, but also in the history of opera. As such, the points usually stressed were not simply the use of music, but the particular way in which it was used and most of all the compatibility between the play (genre and content) and music (nature and practice). The organic connection between poetry and music, (the revitalized classic tradition on which Pirrotta insists) admits, in fact, a kind of interdependence, which assumes incompleteness on the part of the participating components as they stand unto themselves. Indeed, if it is the powers of music that are at stake, here is a way to unleash them. Moreover, the powers unleashed (or evoked) are, in turn, the very powers that are observed. Observation and interpretation are inseparable, united as they are in the "operation" itself. To make the argument more lucidly, one could state squarely that doing means arriving at an interpretation of the done, for evoking powers means labeling them. Doing and naming are two sides of the same coin.

Poliziano was well aware of Ficino's type of "singing." His description of it in a letter to Pico della Mirandola is of heuristic interest without implying some kind of impact as far as musical practice is concerned. "His voice," writes Poliziano in describing a young boy chanting half-way between song and speech, "was neither like someone reading, nor like someone singing, but such that you heard both, yet neither separately; it was varied, however, as the words demanded, either even or modulated, now punctuated, now flowing, now exalted, now subdued, now relaxed, now tense, now slow, now hastening, always pure, always clear, always sweet . . . "[37]

The history of opera is largely the story of musical powers evoked and labeled. It is paralleled by the *Affektenlehre* which also sought the proof of the pudding in the eating. The realization that music may be metaphorically possessed, rather than possessing powers, is not easily arrived at, for metaphors strike us as literal truths with repeated applications, yet repeated applications are necessary so as to communicate that which music is possessed by.

[37]Walker, *op. cit.*, p. 20.

"Das tragende Gefühlsmoment," says Schwartz, discussing the *frottola*, "bestimt die Haltung der Musik. Und wie heir erscheint bei den besseren Frottolisten die Musik nicht blos den Worten hinzugefügt, sondern aus den Worten erzeugt—sie ist Ausdruckskunst."[38] As "Ausdruckskunst," however, the *frottola* was but a transition to the sixteenth-century madrigal, in which music was intended to express the content of texts of literary quality. And whereas in the *frottola* the structure of the poem often affected the structure of the music, bringing about musical repetitions, the madrigal, based on the principle that the same music could not express the varying content of successive stanzas, was through-composed. In general, the music of the madrigal was more affected by the content of the poem than its structure. Moreover, in the madrigal all the voices were engaged equally in the beautiful and precise declamation of the text, in contrast to the *frottola*, in which attention was primarily focused on the upper voice.

The combination of voices of equal importance, each voice asserting a certain independence of the others, was bound to lead to an emphasis on musical structure. Music, however, could still aim primarily at conveying the content. Experimenting with music in this way contributed its share to the clarification of the "powers" of music, though the audibility of the text was sacrificed. The growing realization that music is a synthetic art, capable of conveying "emotions generalized," constituted an important step in the conceptualization of the aesthetics of music.

The increased emphasis on contrapuntal techniques, and on form dictated by musical principles was primarily fostered by Netherlanders who resided in Italy and contributed to the splendor of the Italian courts. The growing complexity of the madrigal, made less apparent by stylistic refinement, seems to have satisfied the taste of the splendor-loving nobles whose craving for extravagance manifested itself in all the artistic productions to which they lent their support.[39]

---

[38]Schwartz, *op. cit.*, p. 52. See p. 55 for examples. "Die Frottole, der sich übringens bei Petrucci auch Ode, Sonetti, Versi Latinie, Strambotti und Capitoli anschliessen, erscheint vielmehr als Bundesgenossin, in gewissen Sinne sogar als Dienerin der Kunstpoesie." Ambros, *op. cit.*, vol. IV, p. 492.
[39]See Alfred Einstein, "Die mehrstimmige weltliche Musik von 1450-1600" in Guido Adler, ed., *Handbuch der Musikgeschichte* (Berlin, 1930). Also Rubsamen,

The widespread taste for part singing and the constantly growing skill of composers at adapting the polyphony of the church to secular ideas overshadowed for a while the need for some method in which the individual, strengthened by the "power of music," could express himself. Yet with the growing interest in subjectivism, the need for a musical style suited to individual expression had to be met. Although they came a century earlier, the ends realized as well as the means employed in Poliziano's *Orfeo* seem closer to the spirit of the Florentine reformers than the music and performances with which they were familiar and to which they contributed. The carefully cultivated secular music, incorporating the improvements in artistic skill and devices, led through a natural process of growth to the secularization of the impersonal style of the Church before it could once again stand on the threshold of monody and give fit expression to the individual. In retrospect, it is evident that the *frottola* was closer than the madrigal, its offspring, to the idea of monody, the final goal of music in the Italian Renaissance and the beginning of the baroque.[40]

---

op. cit., chapters I, VII. The whole book is devoted to the study of the changing quality of texts, and consequently to that of music.

[40]As was stated earlier, however, there is reason to believe that intricate polyphonic music never became rooted enough to be considered "Italian." Taking note (prior to the full blooming of the *frottola*) of the predominance of Franco-Flemish composers in Italian courts and not altogether pleased about it, the Duke of Milan writes to the Mantuan Marquis in January 1473 about his project, which is nothing less than the "revival of music in Italy." See Antonino Bertalotti, *Musici alla corte dei Gonzaga in Mantova del secolo XV al XVIII* (Milan, 1890), p. 9. Einstein makes the following remark: "The *frottola* and the old *frottola*-like canzone had been forms of monody. Thus the trend towards the *a cappella* ideal seems like a deviation and the trend away from it like a return." Einstein, *The Italian Madrigal, op. cit.*, vol. II, p. 836.

Summarizing the characteristics of the *frottola*, Ambros says:

Das Madrigal näherte sich, schon weil es wieder von der höheren Contrapuntik Gebrauch macht, wiederum mehr der durchcomponirten Motette. In der Villote kommt dagegen das Liedmassige, der Strophengessang sehr entschieden zur Geltung. Die Frottole steht gewissermassen in der Mitte. Sie ist strophenweisse zu singen (oft mit einer ganz betrachtlichen Strophenzahl), aber ihr musikalisches Schema ist meist viel breiter gefasst als jenes der Villote und gibt ihr fast das Ansehen eines durchcomponirten Stückes. Aber gewisse gleichreimende Verspaare, gewisse wiederkehrende Refrainverse werden Anlass zur Wiederholung und Wiederkehr ganzer musikalischer Perioden. Dadurch erhält, von der Poesie her und durch sie, die Frottole jene regelmässige, gleichsam architektonische Anlage, jenen Bau, der sie eigenthümlich gegen die contrapunktisch hinströmende Chanson der Niederländer contrastiren lässt . . . .Und ebenso und eben deswegen werden die Rhythmen und Accente

Although their music was simple in technique and predominantly chordal in texture, the madrigal dramas of the late sixteenth century contributed little to the attempt to suit the music to the purposes of dramatic dialogue and to the utterance of individual characters. In fact, they confounded the situation by trying to meet the solistic demands of the theatrical performance with music sung by an ensemble. And although there may be germs of opera buffa in these works,[41] the choral mass does not allow for an individual character to advance to the center of the stage and thus engender for singers and audience alike, a process of identification with the protagonists.[42]

Monody: A Musical Means for Individual Expression

Choral settings of dialogues and soliloquies were further from being a means for individual expression than were the solo adaptations of polyphonic compositions. Curiously, the solo madrigal was not used in the madrigal comedy. Indeed, the complete disregard for the tentative method of solo song is interesting. It seems that nothing is experienced as new in history,

---

nicht durch das Bedürfniss contrapunktischer Führung, sondern durch das Versmass und den natürlichen Accent der italienischen Sprache und es tritt solches am entschiedensten in der Oberstimme hervor, wo auch die herrschende Melodie und zwar oft schon in liedmassiger Form durchbrechen möchte, aber meistens es nur zur Halbbildung bringt—etwa wie ein aus dem Rohesten Bildwerk die künftige Gestalt schon deutlich aber einstwailen noch unformlich erkenen lässt. In der Textur der Stimmen treten allerdings wohl Nachahmungen u. dergl. auf, aber in sehr beschiedener Fassung und nur untergeordnet. Alles dieses drängte nach der Monodie, dem letzten Ende und Ziel italienischer Tonkunst, wo sich, recht im vollsten Gegensatze gegen die niederländische "Verbrüderung" (Confrèrie), jenes Geltendmachen der eigenen Persönlichkeit jener Subjectivismus bethätigte der schon anderweitig (Z.B.von Burkhardt in seiner "Cultur der Renaissance in Italien") als das eigentliche Kennzeichen der italienischen Renaissancezeit hervorgehoben worden ist," Ambros, *op. cit.*, vol. III, p. 495-96.

[41]Einstein strongly disagrees. *The Italian Madrigal, op. cit*, vol. II, pp 794-95. Einstein views such works as "musical entertainments" and under no circumstances as anticipations of the music drama. Also see Pirrotta, *op. cit.*, pp. 127-132.

[42]The madrigal drama hardly deserves the place in the genesis of opera assigned to it by Romain Rolland. In his consideration of the madrigal drama he was not concerned with the solutions to the solistic demands of the drama, but rather with the very fact that it was sung. See Romain Rolland, *Les Origines, op. cit.*, chapter II.

save for rediscoveries. In the unfolding of history there seems to be a difference between the dynamic force of new developments and their rediscovery. Paradoxically, those involved in a rediscovery are often more conscious of the element of "novelty" than are the original innovators. This is largely due to the fact that rediscoveries usually consummate a conscious search for a change, whereas original discoveries are often but a stage in a process of natural development the significance of which is perceived mostly in retrospect.

Although they lacked the means to make individual identification with the characters of the drama possible, the madrigal comedies were part of the search for a musical means of individual expression. In abandoning polyphonic techniques in favor of a chordal texture, and thus assuring the intelligibility of the text, they also reflected the growing concern with the listener's immediate enjoyment of secular music, a factor that contributed greatly to the rise of opera.[43]

Monody, the musical means for the expression of the individual, was born from solo performances of polyphonic music. The line of demarcation between accompanied monody and its forerunners is in the final adoption of *basso continuo* notation, emphasizing clearly the distinct individuality of the outer parts and the complementary relationship between them.[44] Of course, the liberation of the melody from a polyphonic web gave rise to new problems. Now that the solo voice served as a vehicle for the expression of the individual, new ways had to be found to meet dramatic demands. For example, composers could no longer rely on the use of inner voices and on contrasting textures to increase or relax dramatic tension, but had to accomplish it within a single line. The bass lines were static at first, due to the unfamiliar emphasis on chordal thinking. However, in the attempt to answer the new needs, the bass began taking a more active part in the musical texture. In addition, the early mono-

---

[43]The concern of church music vis-a-vis the listener has always been less to communicate the music *per se* than to provide religious inspiration. Looked at from this point of view, the listener becomes a full-fledged participant in the "musical activity" of the Church. The opera, however, had no higher objective than itself. In the process of communication in opera, the listener is therefore "addressed" rather than "manipulated." To the extent that he participates, his participation is vicarious.

[44]See Alfred Einstein, "Der 'stile nuovo' auf dem Gebiet der profanen Kammermusik" in Adler-Handbuch, *op. cit.,* pp. 370-73.

dists experimented with the use of harmony for expression. At first, they relied on the dissonance itself rather than on harmonic progressions for expressive effects; yet this practice disappeared, giving way to a new practice based on the principle of related harmonies. The latter, as distinguished from incidental harmonic relationships arising from voice parts that in themselves were melodic, established the basis for modern composition.[45]

The stiff and severe style associated with the recitative of early opera has often been equated with monody as a whole, though it was primarily limited to the early examples of opera and a handful of other songs. While the word "recitativo" was used a great deal, it usually meant no more than "solo song."[46] Indeed, the influence of chamber monodies upon the musical taste of the time was far greater than that of the isolated performances of the earliest operas.

Monody was essentially both a lyric and a dramatic form and was conceived more naturally than the early music dramas, which were hampered by the self-consciousness and contrived intellectual efforts of their creators and, above all, by their attempt to emulate "heightened speech."[47] In fact, it was monody that held the secret of the future of Italian opera, and through the chamber cantatas, of the art of the *bel canto*.

Monodies in the first third of the seventeenth century were written in three main centers: Florence, Rome, and Venice. The Florentines experimented with the use of harmony for expression and dramatic interest. Compared with the essentially bold experiments of the Florentines, Roman monody seems less colorful and simpler, lacking both ornamentation and chromatic interest. The Venetians, in contrast to both Florentines and Ro-

---

[45]In judging the style of any musical period, especially that of the sixteenth century, it is important to take note of the following statement made by Jeppesen: "In any style whatsoever, the presence of tension between the horizontal and vertical musical conceptions may be substantiated: but in the one style the primary interest lies in the line—in the other, it lies in the chord; in the first, one has to do with melodic impulses, which recoil from the impact with the sonorous requirements—in the second, with the sense of sonority which finds an aesthetic corrective in the linear demands." Knud Jeppesen, *The Style of Palestrina and the Dissonance* (Copenhagen: 1943), p. 84.

[46]See Nigel Fortune, "Italian Secular Monody From 1600-1635," in *The Musical Quarterly*, vol. XXXIX, 1953, p. 172.

[47]See Jacopo Peri, "Dedicatoria e prefazione a L'Euridice," in Solerti, *Le origini*, p. 47.

mans, were no longer interested in the "extravagant underlining of passionate texts"; instead they were concerned with problems of design, and with the writing of beautiful melodies. It was the Venetian composers who first seized upon the idea of contrast out of which they developed the idea of recitative and aria. From the strophic variations and from madrigals with smoother melodies and more active basses, they developed the cantata, the laboratory for the grand "experiments" of opera composers.[48]

The desire to give definite musical expression to the words, apparent in both the dramatic madrigals and afterwards in the recitative style, became less and less marked in the cantata. The cantata was increasingly concerned with the general spirit of the text rather than its details, abounding in graceful tunes and vocal ornamentations that were far removed from the ideals of the Camerata.[49]

Once the novelty of the early operas wore off, opera, too, tried to employ the full apparatus of the art of music. While the clarification of the powers of music continued, the emphasis shifted from questions about essence to questions about use. The first made assumptions, which the second sought to realize. The former rested primarily on theorizing, the latter on dictates provided by music *qua* music. That music need not be circumscribed, and that it does not "underlie" texts to which it lends meaning, had to be clarified before it could be realized that the underlying texts need circumscription if they are to label what the music is about.

While the development of monody was taking its own course, the revolt of the Camerata was directed primarily against scenic and musical effects which were essentially for show. Their attempt to reduce purely lyrical forms to a rational musical basis, on which intelligible settings of texts could be built, was short-lived. The return to pictorial and vocal display was swift, and the invention of the Florentines was reduced to a mere thread connecting the episodes of a grand production.

[48]See Henry Prunieres, "The Italian Cantata of the XVII Century," *Music and Letters* (1926) pp. 120-32; also Fortune, *op. cit.*, pp. 181-92.
[49]See Prunieres, *op. cit.*, pp. 38-48. It should be pointed out that what has been said is hardly an adequate summary of the development of monody. But the intent here is less to trace its historical development than to emphasize (1) its essential idea, i.e., the provision of a vehicle for the expression of the individual; and (2) that the recitative style cannot be equated with monody as a whole.

Plate 12.   Initial H in the Shape of a Blowing Centaur. From a Zister-
zien Bible (c. 110). The ''reality'' of music in such that even imaginative
figures, neither man nor animal, take music for granted.

134

Chapter Six

An Invitation to Music

This chapter looks to the literature and drama of the period in an effort to identify the relationship between these and the mixtures of social values, aesthetic theories and musical experiments that have been considered so far. It would be presumptuous, of course, to attempt a systematic review of a hundred years of the literary arts of Italy and of their relationship to music. Great scholars have addressed themselves to both of these questions. Musicologists have written about the many ways in which music was interpolated in the various dramatic genres, and have searched for the seeds of the music-drama in these performances. Literary scholars have provided detailed analyses, as well as sweeping surveys, of the different poetic and dramatic genres; and there is much that still needs further investigation.

While this chapter draws on both musicological and literary scholarship, its search for the link to the prehistory of opera focuses more on the latter than the former. The dramatic arts of Italy—we shall argue—were not precursors of the opera simply because they made room on the stage for music. They did so, of course, and that is a matter of importance; but even more important, in our opinion, is that aspect of the relationship between Italian drama and music that is to be found in the musical "overtones" of the words and action of the theater. The persistent emphasis of the words is on emotions (especially the emotion of love) rather than intellection, and the persistent emphasis of the action is on spectacle and pageantry. It is the tendency to the melodramatic that is the key to the character of both the people and the arts, the seeds from which opera sprouted. The literary and dramatic arts of the Renaissance Italians may be conceived of as an "invitation to music" to join in.

Conjunctions and Disjunctions in Culture

The search for uniformities among cultural institutions or the bearing of one art form apon another is often expressed by invoking the "spirit of the age." The theory of the Zeitgeist, in its extremest manifestation, tends to set aside the social order of economics, politics and society as well as the natural order, which is the realm of physical science, and to concentrate on the humanities as if these were in a "higher realm" governed by intangible spirits. Such spirits are thought to influence each other and to produce a uniformity of style and expression.[1] The possibility that the arts, singly or collectively, may be part of a system of mutual influence, in which social and scientific factors are no less important, is often overlooked.

The Zeitgeist often gains its definition through the description and analysis of the cultural products of its time. Not surprisingly, the offspring are found to have characteristics identical to those of their presumed begettor. The fallaciousness of such tautological argument is brilliantly exposed by Mueller in his discussion of the evolution of the concept "baroque." As noted earlier, Mueller shows that the concept moved from a simple adjective to a label for a comprehensive philosophy of history.[2] While disallowing the baroque as a "culture epoch," Mueller is nevertheless willing to entertain the notion of Zeitgeist, provided that it is not reified. The culture-epoch theory, says Mueller, is not relativistic enough. "Relativism," he argues, "is the only approach which allows for the continuous growth of knowledge" based on persistent study of the interplay of many variables and an openness to reinterpretation based on the emergence of new variables. Spirit-of-the-age theories, on the other hand, are not typically engaged in the "search for correlations subject to revision," nor are they "content with an approximation of 'truth'." Rather, says Mueller, such theories are typically "a non-empirical shortcut to absolute certainty."[3]

The student of the Italian Renaissance is fortunate in this respect. Without having to insist on the necessary interconnect-

[1] See *Meaning in History: W. Dilthey's Thoughts on History and Society*, H.P. Rickman, ed., Allen & Unwin, 1961.
[2] Mueller, *op. cit.*, pp. 431-35.
[3] *Ibid.*, pp. 436-47.

edness of the arts at all times and places, he can persuasively establish their interconnection at this period. And without having to maintain that the arts must always be correlated with science and society, he can claim with considerable certainty that that is the case at least at this time.

In so claiming, he finds strong support in the scholarly community, even from the skeptical. Indeed, Panofsky, who is even willing to entertain the question whether the Renaissance is a discernible period—thus dwarfing Mueller's critique of the integrity of the baroque—argues for the mutual influence during the Renaissance of science and art, theory and practice, liberal arts and mechanical arts. In explanation, Panofsky looks to the social and economic factors reviewed above in Chapter Three: "the concentration of wealth, power and cultural enterprise in the hands of an aristocratic elite as opposed to communal organizations; the growing secularization of education; the formation of private groups and circles of dilettanti interested in all sorts of things; the concomitant disintegration of the Guild System; and, as a result of this, the new prestige of the inventor, the military and civilian engineer and, quite particularly, the artist."[4]

In his quest for etymological symbols of the unity of a period as opposed to "the mystical symbols of . . . geist," Leo Spitzer finds the arts from the Middle Ages to the Enlightenment not only interconnected with each other but unified through expansion of the musical concept of harmony.[5] Spitzer argues that it is musical art that underlies the conception of all art during this period and that artistic music and the music of nature are one and the same. The Christian conception of world harmony is prerequisite to the idea of harmony in music while the latter is responsible for "the musicalization of poetry" and the other arts. The triad, grace, nature, harmony (or if one prefers the number four, harmony and music) ruled the Middle Ages, and, in secularized form, extended into the Renaissance.[6] In other times and places, other affect-complexes predominate, says Spitzer, and the death of the idea of the musical unity of the world can be traced to the growth of "analytical rationalism and the segmentary, fragmentary, materialistic and positivistic view

[4]Panofsky, op. cit., p. 166.
[5]Spitzer, op. cit., p. 50.
[6]Ibid., p. 46.

of the world" ushered in not by Protestantism *per se* but by Calvinists and Cartesians.[7] But during the Renaissance, while proportion and harmony reigned and music was measurable like the other arts and sciences, musical similes were used to describe the working, of nature, man and the other arts.

Not only do different periods vary in the semantic imagery that unifies them, says Spitzer, periods may also vary in the extent of their conjunction or disjunction. Here the way is paved for other theorists about the conjunction and disjunction of culture. Kroeber, for example, agrees that while there is a strain towards consistency in culture, the kind of integration that characterized, say, Spengler's Faustian man—the striving beyond the boundaries of time and space—may be absent during certain periods.[8] Daniel Bell argues that this absence of conjunction among the institutions of society is the hallmark of our own generation. For the first time in history perhaps, thinks Bell, there is not just disjunction but contradiction between artistic values and the predominant values of the economic and civic realms. Adherents of the former disparage and ridicule the latter, and if the strain towards consistency is discernible in modern society at all, it may well be that contemporary culture and its art will destroy what is left of the rationality, frugality and objectivity implicit in capitalism. But until recently, "from the mid-sixteenth to the mid-ninteenth century . . . the aesthetic ideal of congruity operated as regulative principle in which the focus was on a relational whole and a unity of form" incorporating harmony, proportion, rationality and representation. "Contemplation," says Bell, "allowed the spectator to create *theoria* (which meant, originally, looking), and *theoria* meant a distancing of oneself— usually an aesthetic distance—from an object or experience, in order to establish the necessary time and space to absorb it and judge it."[9]

While modernity is well characterized by the "eclipse of distance," Bell overlooks the immediacy of experience that is characteristic also of the expressiveness of the baroque, even if the latter had a much more orderly character. But more of this

---

[7]*Ibid.*, p. 138.
[8]A.L. Kroeber, *Style and Civilizations*, Berkeley: University of California Press, 1963, p. 92.
[9]Daniel Bell, *The Cultural Contradictions of Capitalism*, New York: Basic Books, 1976, p. 110.

below; for the moment, the point being made is that there is virtual agreement—among thinkers of various disciplines and persuasions—that the Renaissance was a time of great coherence in the arts, and that this coherence was a response not only to the proverbial strain towards consistency but also to external forces stemming from social, economic and political change.

This chapter proclaims the coherence of the literary and dramatic arts in Renaissance Italy with the art of music. More, it argues that there was a virtual "invitation" to music to join the other arts, almost as if poets and dramatists were writing "libretti," enacting the "musicalization" that Spitzer so forcefully describes.

In demonstrating the conjunction of these arts, this chapter harks back to the socio-economic and political constraints outlined earlier, but it also goes one step further. It argues that there is something about the Italian "spirit" (in a Hegelian sense), or "national character" that must be added to the list of constraints. The idea that there may be relatively unchanging elements in a culture which "program" certain kinds of response, has lately become fashionable again and is summed up under the rubric "social code."[10] Thus in trying to explain the tendency of Italian arts of the Renaissance toward lyricism, sensory stimulation, patent form and simplicity of structure, the reader will be asked to bear in mind not only society, economy and polity, but two other points as well: the transition from restraint to greater expressiveness that characterizes baroque modifications of Renaissance trends, and the possibility that relatively permanent predilections of the Italian character may play a part in the story. It is the interplay of all these, and the openness to new variables—as Mueller would put it—that informs what follows.

Novelle: Narratives of Action

"In Italy," says Symonds, "the keynote of the Renaissance was struck by the *novelle*, as in England by the Drama."[11] Unlike

[10]See for example Rainer C. Baum, "Authority and Identity: The Case for Evolutionary Invariants," *Sociological Inquiry*, 1975; S. N. Eisenstadt, "Post-Traditional Societies and the Continuity and Reconstruction of Tradition," *Daedalus*, 1973, pp. 1-29.

[11]Symonds, *op. cit.*, vol. II, p. 199.

the novel, which did not flourish in Italy, these narrative tales derive from a tradition of oral storytelling. The drama and the novel typically cope with a longish period of time, and delve deep into the complexity of character and the concatenation of events. The *novella*, on the other hand, is little more than a fable or an anecdote—usually presented in groups of tales illustrating a moral quality or striking situation. *Novelle* were brief and sketchy, and very superficial as to the protrayal of character or emotional conflict. In the *novella*, events lead to immediate actions. Response is either typical or unexpected; but rarely is it the result of reflection or contemplation. Despite its elegant and exquisite form, an overall superficiality pervades the genre. "The narrator went straight to his object, which was to arrest the attention, stimulate the curiosity, gratify the sensual instincts, excite the laughter, or stir the tender emotions of his audience by some fantastic, extraordinary, voluptuous, comic, or pathetic incident."[12] Alternately, the narrator might introduce a carefully detailed descriptive passage, or a digression upon a moral theme, or attempt to arouse sympathy for one of the main characters, all "by elaborate rhetorical development of the main emotions . . . using every artifice for appealing directly to the feelings of his hearers."[13] Unlike the "soap opera" of contemporary radio and television, the *novelle* are not continuing stories and their heroes are less familiar and less "complicated." But the aim, overall, is entertainment through arousal of the emotions of the listener or reader without undue effort.

The *novelle* covered every aspect of Italian society. They appealed particularly to the new upper-middle class, emphasizing reality, tickling the senses and then taking cover behind the thin veneer of a moral or a message. The upper classes, Symonds thinks, were amused, but the tastes were those of the new urban bourgeoisie. So powerful was the attraction of the *novella* that even legends of the saints took this form and, as will be noted below, a goodly portion of the *sacre rappresentazioni* were dramatized *novelle*.[14] Indeed, the preference for the tangible and concrete as opposed to the visionary and abstract, for the sensuous

---

[12]*Ibid.*, p. 202.
[13]*Ibid.*
[14]See Allesandro D'Ancona, *Sacra Rappresentazione dei secoli XIV, XV e XVI*, Florence: 1872, 3 vols. D'Ancona's is the chief work dealing with the *sacra rappresentazione*. It contains forty-three plays on a variety of subjects ranging from bible stories to transformed *novelle*.

rather than the ideal, is not only characteristic of the *novella* and the world of the middle class, but in a larger sense determines the character of the other urban, Italian arts as well.

In the cultural exchange between the upper class and the bourgeoisie, the former typically contribute form and refinement to the content provided by the latter. The stylization of middle-class taste, then, was a product of the union that characterized social life in the Italian cities, as has been emphasized earlier. Preoccupation with elegance of style is one of the marks of Italian creativity—not only in the *novella* but perhaps in all media at all times. Going a step further, it has been argued that not only creativity but conduct is governed, in Italy, by style. Corruption in government, the Church and the economy had long since set in, but manners remained all important in the sixteenth century—even in assassinations.[15] The middle class, lacking in tradition, was acutely attuned to the etiquette of the hereditary nobility. Stylistic conscientiousness is the product of a society which believes more in gaining the status of the privileged classes rather than striving to overthrow them. Avoidance of the abstract, the complex, the heroic and the ascetic: these aspects of Italian middle-class culture give evidence of how different the Italian bourgeoisie were from the capitalists of Weber's Protestant ethic. The culture of these capitalists was aimed at much more "immediate gratification."

If the *novella* is characterized by elegance of form and superficiality of content, the *idyll*, which both antedates and outlives it, goes even further. As we have seen, the turn to the idyllic ideal has been attributed by some to the disenchantment of the Renaissance with the world after death. Indeed, the rediscovery of this—worldliness created a new focus for nostalgia—not in an after-life, but in a different life, pastoral and unpolluted. Recalling the primeval peace of Eden and the frolicking of classic gods and shepherdesses, the idyll and other poetic forms celebrated the withdrawal from urban society, with its intricacies and its corruptions. The pastoral character of Arcadian life in Ancient Greece, together with its isolation, explains why it came to be represented as a paradise not only in Greek and Roman bucolic poetry but also in the literature of the Renaissance. "There rose into existence for the rhymsters to wander in, and for the reader

---

[15]See Symonds, *op. cit.*, vol. II, pp. 665-71.

of romance to dream about, a region called Arcadia, where all that was imagined of the Golden Age was found in combination with refined society and manners proper to the civil state."[16] However, this dream world created by poets had none of the characteristics of a dream. It was made up of tangible and concrete things related to each other in intelligible ways and placed in a setting with direct appeal to sensibility. We are reminded, here, of Schiller's famous characterization of the idyll and the elegie: whereas the latter presents Nature as lost and Ideals as unattainable, the former presents Nature as retrievable and Ideals as attainable.

Cloaked in artistic refinement, Sannazzaro's *Arcadia* expressed the feelings of an urban society. Bearing "a classic stamp," it prescribed the rule for all pastoral romances that followed. More important, it paved the way to pastoral drama, a novel species created by the Italians, which was truly representative of their feelings and spirit.

"Airy Music": Pastoral Drama

The pastoral drama grew out of such romances as the *Arcadia* and court masques, in which the principal parts were played by shepherds and shepherdesses. Castiglione and his cousin Cesare Gonzaga composed a pastoral masque as early as 1506 for the court of Urbino. Urbino was an important cultural center in the Italian Renaissance because of the liberality of its rulers and the concentration of musicians, painters and litterati at its court. Like her sister Isabella d'Este, the Duchess Elizabeth was a patroness of the arts and welcomed artistic experimentation with delight.[17] The "Tirsi," the dramatic eclogue composed by Castiglione in collaboration with Cesare Gonzaga, was presented at court at the carnival of 1506. The Duchess and her intimates took

[16]*Ibid.*, p. 278.
[17]Isabella d'Este was a patroness of literature, the pictorial arts and music at the Mantuan court. She had close relationships with most Italian poets who were productive during the prospering years of the *frottola*. She was in the habit of asking her musicians to write music to the poems she liked. Marchetto Cara and Bartolomeo Tromboncino were in her service;. their works reflect, as a result, the literary tastes of their mistress. They form a primary source for the study of the changing quality of musical texts leading toward the madrigal. See Walter H. Rubsamen, *op. cit.*, ch. II, V.

great pleasure at this performance, in which Castiglione and Gonzaga were dressed as shepherds reciting their verse and displaying their musical abilities.[18] The Duchess was extremely fond of music, and especially of music heard in conjunction with theatrical representations.[19]

The pastoral, stripped of the complexity of urban existence, was a high point in this development. Here, indeed, was the ideal world of sentiment. In this world, feelings attained a purity unattainable in any other, more intricate, world. Love, pain, fear, and hope were not obscured by circumstances, but were affected by simple relationships between men and women. The story of a pastoral, its characters and dialogues were all less important than the emotions engendered by them. The story served only to supply the poet with motives for feelings.

During the great vogue of pastoral poetry, many eclogues, arranged as dialogues and recited in pastoral costumes, were composed as *intermezzi* to vary and enliven court festivals.[20] They were performed at first with few or no stage properties, and served as entertainment for the guests at banquets. The simple pastoral tale was augmented gradually by various theatrical elements, a complexity of scenes, and an increase in the number of personages until it reached the dimensions of an independent play.[21] Poliziano's *Orfeo* and Correggio's *Cefalo* (1487), both based on classical myths, belong in a way to an early series of pastoral plays. It is worth noting, however, that the *Orpheus*, the story itself, bears some marks of tragedy as well. Euridice's final death, after having been rescued from Hades, is caused by a "tragic flaw," and Poliziano, faithful to the myth, included in his *Orfeo* the slaying of Orpheus by the Maenads. The omission of his final scene by later composers from their operas is most interesting, for it is not accidental.

Pirrotta claims that already towards the end of the fifteenth-century court representations were not merely conceived to ornament court ceremonies, but had a function of their own re-

[18]*Ibid.*, p. 34.
[19]References to this art are made in the *Cortegiano*, an analysis of Renaissance courtliness with Urbino as its locale.
[20]At two of the three marriages of Lucrezia Borgia the performance of dramatic eclogues is recorded. See the introductory essay to the translation of the *Orpheus* and the *Aminta* by Louis E. Lord, *op. cit.*, p. 56.
[21]Joseph Spencer Kennard, *The Italian Theatre*, New York: William Edwin Rudge, 1932, vol. I, pp. 161-2.

lated to the idea of the theater as a function of the polis. This public function was generally associated with special buildings. In the initial phase of these court representations the premises of the court itself were modified, creating the illusion that the viewers were actually in a building designed especially for the performance. Here, as elsewhere, Pirrotta's careful scholarship is not only informative but provides new insights affecting our understanding of the historical process itself. While denying classic regularity to the theatrical works of the end of the fifteenth century, he calls attention to their relationship to the idea of theater as a function of the polis. These works were characterized by their attempt to bend the free format of sacred popular theater into some classic regularity. This is not the place to elaborate on the genre that Pirrotta calls "drammi mescidati" except to say that the *Orfeo*, according to Pirrotta was at one and the same time characteristic of the contemporary theatrical mentality and served as its model. The mixed phase of theatrical activity started from plautine and terenzian representations and only gradually, through experience, became aware of problems that called for the study of ancient texts in order to deepen the theatrical representations. Correggio's *Cefalo* which was enclosed by choruses, (a distinctive character of the tragedy), also belongs to this mixed genre, which according to Pirrotta assumed a function between comedy and tragedy characteristic of the pastorals of the sixteenth century.[22]

There are a few works displaying pastoral character in the first half of the sixteenth century, but the first true pastoral drama is thought to be Agostino Beccari's *Sacrifizio d'Abramo*, which was produced in 1554 at the palace of Francesco d'Este at Ferrara. All the demands of pastoral drama were satisfied in this play. It created the gentle atmosphere of the Arcadian world, so conducive to romance. It possessed gracious charm and refined sentiments, which are the core of all true pastorals. Less important than its plot, however, is the fact that it focused on the most profound of all human interests, love.[23] Following the practice of

---

[22]See Pirrotta, *Li Due Orfei, op. cit.*, pp. 45-53. The interval of time that separates the *Orfeo* and the *Cefalo* from their successors is believed by some scholars to indicate that they may have had little influence on sixteenth-century plays. For discussion on this subject see J.H. Whitfield, *A Short History of Italian Literature*, New York: Penguin Books, 1960, p. 157; see also Lord, *op. cit.*, p. 57.

[23]The plot involves the fortunes of three pairs of lovers. The consummation of

the day, Beccari's *Sacrifizio* was enhanced by music. The music was composed by Alfonso della Viola, who also wrote the music for the only pastoral dramas of note between the *Sacrifizio* and Tasso's *Aminta*[24], Alberto Lolio's *Aretusa* (1563) and Agostino Argenti's *Lo Sfortunato* (1567), both produced at Ferrara.[25] It is probable that Tasso witnessed the performance of *Lo Sfortunato*.[26]

Pastoral dramas followed the path set by Beccari. The pace was slow at first, but as years went by the pastoral drove all other forms of drama out of the field. By the second half of the sixteenth century, it was the most important theatrical type, along with eclogues and bucolic poems, which were also very much in vogue.[27] While Beccari's *Sacrifizio* marked the beginning of the new species, critics agree that Tasso's *Aminta* (1573) represents its purest expression. The *Aminta* had many imitators but its primacy has never been challenged. Its simplicity and out-pouring lyricism have been preferred to the more elaborate artifice of its only rival, the *Pastor Fido*.

It has been claimed that had Petrarch excelled in epic rather than lyric poetry, Ariosto and Tasso would have nonetheless been his humble followers because sixteenth-century poets did not stray far from the traces of Petrarch.[28] It is clear, however,

---

their loves is met by obstacles, which are gradually removed in the course of the play. Satyrs, magic slaves and rustic scenes are part of the play.

[24]The music for the *Sacrifizio* was rediscovered by Arnaldo Bonaventura and published for the first time by Angelo Solerti in his "Precedenti del melodrama" in *Rivista Musicale Italiana*, vol. X, (1903), pp. 217-20. The third scene from the third act for solo and a chorus of four voices is given and the *canzone* for four voices concludes the piece. The solo part was sung by Alfonso's brother, who accompanied himself on the lyre. Solerti presents it as one of the earliest attempts known in the monodic style. The solo is repeated three times without change in three successive strophes, while the choral responses are different each time. "Egli mi osserva," says Solerti, "che la musica delle tre strofe del sacerdote e uguale, mentre invece quella della risposte del coro e sempre differente. Non esiste alcuna indicazione di accompagnamento ma la nota posta in principio ove e detto che M. Andrea adopero la lira, farrebbe ritenere che egli si accompagnasse. Ad ogni modo questa parte ha molta importanza come saggio di stile monodico gia nella prima pastorale." p. 216.

[25]For the general imortance of Ferrara in the history of the theater, see Angelo Solerti, *Ferrara e la corte Estense nella seconda meta del secolo XVI*, Citta de Castello: S. Lape Tipografo, 1891.

[26]Lord, *op. cit.*, p. 60.

[27]See Angelo Ingegneri, *Della Poesia rappresentativa e del modo di rappresentare le favole sceniche*, Ferrara: V. Baldini, 1598, pp. 7-9.

[28]For a discussion of "Petrarchism" in the sixteenth century, see Giuseppe Toffanin, *Il Cinquecento*, Milan: 1935, ch. III.

that Italian literature of the Renaissance moved steadily in the direction of lyricism rather than drama for less arbitrary reasons. Economic, political and religious circumstances combined with national characteristics to affect the development of literature, leading to an ever-increasing emphasis on lyricism.

The *Aminta* represents the pastoral in its purest expression. Not being weighted down by an elaborate apparatus of shepherdom, it was free to concentrate with greater force on feelings. The feelings, too, were reduced to an essential simplicity. In Tasso's poetic world, love reigns supreme. Love is the soul of his world and its fullest expression. Hence, "Lost is all that time not spent in loving."[29]

While the *Aminta* has long been considered the purest and strongest poetry of the Italian Renaissance, in fact poetry here is "on the point of expiring." The narrative is almost completely foregone, while emotions find vent in song. It speaks the language of music. Indeed, because of the musical feeling that emanates from his poetry, Tasso has often been viewed as a poet-musician. This musical feeling is partially created by the sheer sound of his poetry, but probably more by the particular way in which he describes emotions. His descriptions are mostly vague, more concerned with setting up an atmosphere than achieving exactitude. This is the way of musical description, which is indefinite by nature. As Spitzer says about Petrarch, "Airy as is this environment, it is 'full'[pieno] of substance, however imponderable. This person-encompassing air may give new enjoyment to the inner sense, to sight and smell and hearing. By this step we have attained a musical air [musica ora /=aura as Tasso will say], or airy music—both of them achievements of the Christian mind, perhaps flavored by Tasso with a touch of revived pantheism, which tends to deify the human being."[30]

Pirrotta, in his usually insightful way, stresses the relation-

[29]Aminta loves Silvia. Silvia does not return his love. The whole play revolves around the conversion of Silvia to the world of love. Daphne, trying to persuade Silvia, says: "Mayhaps if thou but once didst taste the thousandth part of that bliss which a heart beloved finds in love requited, thou wouldst repentant sighing say, 'Lost is all that time not spent in loving. Alas, my lost youth, how many widowed nights, how many lonely days have I consumed in vain which I could have employed in that engagement which most repeated is most sweet.' Change, change thy thoughts, mad child that thou art, for late repentance naught avails." Lord, *op. cit.*, pp. 113-14. Part of the first scene of the first act, this little speech sets the tone for the entire play.
[30]Spitzer, *op. cit.*, p. 62.

ship between the pastoral aura and the aria, calling attention to the fact that the *stile rappresentativo* has been mistakenly thought of in terms of the later recitative "as mere non-aria." The aria as "an indefinite quality and aesthetic goal," claims Pirrotta, was important in the formation of the *stile rappresentativo*. For men and women, shepherds and nymphs were not only happier in the Arcadian world, they were

> also endowed with a spontaneous feeling for beauty and a natural gift for artistic expression, poetry, and music. The nostalgic dream of a utopia of perfect happiness thus becomes the aesthetic vision of an idealized world, the imitation of which leads not to crude realism but to a more refined, and also more malleable, *vraisemblance*. Gods and demigods are not too often present in the pastoral; yet they are always around the corner, and whenever they decide to intervene among the humans, their sudden appearance produces awe but no surprise . . . There is no breach of *vraisemblance* in the fact that the gods are exquisite singers; indeed, to all the characters of the pastoral landscape, the gift is given to express themselves in verse and in a language that has a harmony surpassing that of ordinary speech![31]

It is known that Tasso loved music and that many of his friends were musicians. Since music, according to Tasso, constitutes the soul of poetry, he was primarily concerned with music that was expressive of poetry.[32] His association with Gesualdo

---

[31]Pirrotta, "Early Opera and Aria," *op. cit.*, pp. 72, 81. He goes on to show how some of these ideas were clearly expressed by Guarini in his defense of his pastoral play and that they were "in the air," particularly in Florence. "One result of the strong influence exerted by the theories of pastoral poetry on the early *stile rappresentativo* and opera," says Pirrotta, "was a lack of a clear distinction between enhanced speech and song . . . embracing, as it does, the full range of nuances from the most prosaic and matter-of-fact utterances to the most lyrical and even florid outbursts." p. 82.

[32]In Tasso's dialogue on Tuscan poetry, Orsina Cavaletta, one of the discussants, abruptly turns the conversation to music at one point, saying: "Se 'l mio parere e degno d' alcuna stima, non lasciamo la musica, ch' e la dolcezza e quasi l'anima de la poesia, come poco inanzi accennaste di voler fare." In the ensuing conversation, it is taken for granted that music is "the soul of poetry." The question with which they concern themselves is simply what kind of music is preferable "qual piace a' giovani lascivi fra' conviti e fra' balli de la saltatrici, o pur quello ch' a gli uomini gravi e a le donne suol convenire?" See "La cavalette overo de la poesia Tuscana" in Torquato Tasso, *Dialoghi, edizione critica a cura di Ezio Raimonchi*, Florence: G.C. Sansoni, Editore, 1958, vol. II, pp. 665-8.

and Marenzio is significant, therefore, because of their role in fashioning music to interpret emotions. Yet of even greater significance is Tasso's personal relationship with Laura Guidiccioni, Emilio de' Cavalieri and Ottavio Rinuccini, who took an active part in the creation of Florentine opera.

Laura Guidiccioni collaborated with Cavalieri in 1590 on the *Satiro* and on the *Disperazione di Fileno*. It has been assumed that these works were written in recitative style. The assumption is based on Cavalieri's own testament, in which he claims to have revived ancient music that stirs up "divers passions."[33] Unfortunately, the works are not extant and Cavalieri's claims cannot be verified.

Shortly before the *Satiro* and the *Disperazione* were presented at court, Laura Guidiccioni and Cavalieri worked on the production of Tasso's *Aminta*, which was produced with music. *Aminta* no doubt influenced Guidiccioni's and Cavalieri's own works, and Rinuccini, who was an ardent disciple of Tasso, was the first to adapt pastoral drama to the musical stage.

It is difficult to say, however, whether in 1509 pastoral opera was emerging from the pastoral with music, or whether the pastoral had become opera.[34] Whatever the case, the Italian negation of medieval asceticism, mysticism and chivalry found its fullest expression in the lyrical drama, the goal toward which the Italian spirit had been steadily advancing throughout the Renaissance. However, the intermediary stations on the roads to the goal were many.

Sacra Rappresentazione: Pageant and Passion

The secularizing spirit of the late Renaissance was evident even earlier, in the development of religious drama. A precursor of the pastoral drama, its origins—and perhaps the origin of all Italian drama—lay in the *laude*, the religious popular poetry of the late Middle Ages. The *laude* were recited and sung by societies, some of whom were ascetic in their orientation and others not. Their songs were lifted from the popular tunes of the day,

---

[33]See Rolland, *op. cit.*, p. 66, note 1, whose discussion is based on Angelo Solerti, *Laura Guidiccioni Lucchesini ed Emilio de' Cavalieri*, 1902.
[34]See Rolland, *op. cit.*, p. 68.

and the mundane subjects with which these dealt were replaced by religious poetry.[35]

Mixing the sacred with the profane did not betray irreverence in this case, nor a lack of concern for the religious significance of the *laude*. One cannot speak of the music as being ill-matched to the content, since no attempt was made to match the two. Instead, the *laude*, as a whole, betrays that same disregard for intellectual consistency and the Italian love for music *per se*.[36] Of course, the Italians have never been pious in a primarily contemplative sense. Their religious feelings seem to lack restraint, and are themselves sensuous and erotic. The spirit of a prayer addressed to God is not markedly different from the spirit conveyed in a confession of love to one's beloved.

Thus, the origin of the *sacra rappresentazione*, and for that matter of Italian theater as a whole, can be traced to the religious practices of the *laudesi*.[37] The dramatic potential of the *laude* was revealed as early as Jacopone da Todi (d. 1306), the greatest and most famous of *laude* writers. Among Jacopone's many poems, is found the earliest example of a *lauda* assuming the form of a dialogue.[38]

In the two centuries that followed Jacopone's early example, an increasing number of *laude* assumed a dramatic form and were called *devozione*.[39] The sole purpose, however, of these *devozione* was to express in dialogue the substance of a Scriptural narrative, with no theatrical effect intended. Though the evolution of the *devozione* has not been established conclusively, its relationship with the *sacra rappresentazione* is apparent. It is believed that the *sacra rappresentazione* evolved from the *devozione* within the precincts of the confraternities, to which members of

---

[35]"The same music would not have been applicable to various texts if it had been expressive of the words. It was, actually, neutral, and this is strikingly illustrated by the use of the same music for the *lauda, Jesu, Jesu* and for the *canto carnascialesco, Visin, visin*." Reese, *op. cit., p.* 167. *Also see* Fernando Liuzzi, *La lauda e i primordi della melodia italiana*, Rome: 1935.

[36]Though they were affected radically during the temporary fall of the Medici and the rule of Savonarola, it is of interest to note in this connection that some of the well-known melodies of the *canti carnascialeschi* were newly fitted with sacred and penitential words. See Reese, *ibid.*, p. 170.

[37]See Alessandro D'Ancona, *Origini del teatro italiano*, Turin: 1891, vol. I, ch. X.

[38]The dialogue is between Mary and Christ upon the Cross, followed by the lamentation of the Virgin over her dead Son. The whole poem is reproduced in Symonds, *op. cit.*, p. 37.

[39]See D'Ancona, *op. cit.*, vol. I, ch. XIII.

the best Florentine families belonged. These companies were wealthy and delighted in the display of their wealth.[40] D'Ancona believes that the *sacra rappresentazione* was a hybrid combining the *devozione* and the pageants that formed prolusions to the yearly feast of St. John, the patron saint of Florence. The feast of St. John gave place to stately processions that the Florentines spent months preparing. Different religious subjects were represented on chariots which were part of the procession. After the march, the occupants of each chariot gave a play in an open square in the town. In these plays, which were primarily pantomimes with little dialogue, music played a major part.[41]

The *sacra rappresentazione* represented the highest point in the development of religious drama in Italy. It was an art form primarily of Florence and the Tuscan cities (a significant fact for the future role of Florence in the history of opera). The *maggi*, the rural counterpart of the *sacre rappresentazioni*, were also to be found in Tuscany.[42] There is abundant testimony, however, from fifteenth century chroniclers that in all parts of Italy, sacred and profane shows formed a prominent feature of municipal festivals to welcome distinguished foreigners, celebrate the election of magistrates and the like.[43] Yet it appears that Florence had a monopoly on such shows, and that its artists were employed for the preparation of pageants in other cities. Without sparing expense, poets, painters, architects and musicians were all employed to produce lavish spectacles with calculated theatrical effects.[44] The greatest artists of the Renaissance contributed their

---

[40]Symonds, *op. cit.*, pp. 48-51.

[41]See D'Ancona, *op. cit.*, vol. I, ch. XVI.

[42]See D'Ancona, *op. cit.*, vol. II, Supplement.

[43]See Jakob Burckhardt, "Society and Festivals," in *The Civilization of the Renaissance in Italy*, trans. S.G.C. Middlemore, London: G. Allen & Unwin, Ltd., 1928, Part V.

[44]An adequate notion of the scenic apparatus of the *rappresentazioni* may be gathered from the stage directions to *S. Uliva*. The presentation of *S. Uliva* extended over two days and was interrupted at intervals by dumb shows and lyrical interludes connected to the story only by slight threads. For a detailed description of the performance of the play and for an analysis of the play from a dramaturgical point of view, see D'Ancona, *La rappresentazione di Santa Uliva*, Pisa: Fratelli Nistri, 1863, pp. vii-xlii.

Ancona lends aditional support to some of the points made earlier. On p. xxiv of the same work, he remarks: "Sotto la penna degli autori italiani, le Leggende miracolose il piu delle volte, spogliandosi della loro indole sopranaturale, diventano miete piu che Novelle da raccontarsi fra le brigate per intrattenerle nella narazione di fatti straordinari e di avventurose vicende. Potrei

efforts to these plays.[45] The ingenuity of the stage machinery and the careful design of the scenery are all the more apparent in contrast to the childish simplicity of the plays themselves, a result primarily of their unbending religious and didactic approach. The complexity of humanity and a true knowledge of the world were obscured by the repeated presentations of virtue and wickedness by saints and tyrants, regardless of the specific content dealt with in the play.[46] *Novelle* transformed into religious fables displayed no less monastic piety than did the dramatized legends of saints.[47]

As a rule, the drama followed the tale of the legend without artistic structure or plot. The authors simply versified prose they

---

citare qui molti esempi di queste trasformazioni, per le quali si potrebbe arguire che la cultura generale si trovasse allora fra noi in una condizione piu inoltrata, e che certe classi del popol nostro, nel complesso almeno, fossero percio meno creduli che in altre parti d'Europa."

[45]Even Brunelleschi, whom Vasari considered a genius "sent us by heaven to revive architecture which for hundreds of years had been all but lost," (p. 89) partook in the preparation of pageants and the like. For a description of Brunellischi's realization of Paradise for the pageant prepared for the festival of the Annunciation, see Giorgio Vasari, *Lives of the Artists*, New York: Simon and Schuster, 1946, pp. 83-4.

[46]"Determinata, come a dire, l'incorniciatura del Dramma, secondo le norme castanti di un' Arte tradizionale, la materia non aveva altra diversita dall' un caso all' altro, se non quella dei nomi e di alcuni avvenimenti di minore importanza. Religioso era il fine, devota l'impressione da produsi negli animi, leggendarie le fonti, i personaggi rivestiti di sacro carattere; la tela dei fatti sempre identica. Si cominciava per lo piu della conversione del protagonista: poi si trovara lui a contrasto con un regalo pagano. Imperatore o Profetto, Re o Proconsolo, e passando pel martirio, si chiudeva colla glorificazione dell'anima, accolta in cielo. Anche i personaggi secondari sano quasi sempre i medisimi: accanto al Principe sta un Siniscalco; le volonta e i decreti di quello sono annunziati per mezzo di un Banditore; i Cavallari e gli Angeli recano ai piu lontani paesi, o dal cielo alla terra, gli ordini dei Re di quaggiu o del Sovrano al mondo; la Passione non ha luogo senza l'accompagnata obbligata dei Birri, del Cavaliere, del Manigoldo.

Di siffatta semplicita, anzi monotonia, a la struttura di una Rappresentazione, e si puo dire che i caratteri sopra accennati si trovino in tutte, o almeno ciascuna ne abbia questo o quello. L'identità della composizione trae seco anche quella di certe formole e frasi. Ogni Banditore di dichiara pronto a far l'uffizio suo, e fatto che l'abbia, chiede vino o danari; ogni Siniscalco inchinando il Re fa proteste devote della sua obbedienza; ogni Ambasciatore, esposta la sua commissione, torna addietro a dire di aver fatto l'obbligo proprio; i Birri bisticciano fra loro, il Cavaliero le sgrida, il Manigoldo costantemente svillaneggia la sua vittima: sono formole fisse, sacramentali: di lievemente varia dizione." D'Ancona, *Origini, op. cit.*, vol. II, pp. 132-3.

[47]See for example *del Re Superbo* in D'Ancona's *Sacre Rappresentazione. op. cit.*, vol. III.

found ready at hand. Rarely did they aim at development of character; the same fixed personages appear again and again. The authors of these *sacre rappresentazioni* were often lesser literary figures or anonymous, though some were well known, such as Belcari and Castellano Castelani, not to speak of Lorenzo de' Medici—who also contributed a drama to the body of *sacre rappresentazioni*.[48] In combining childish naiveté with theatrical ingenuity and magnificence of stage, the *sacra rappresentazione* is another manifestation of the desire to please the senses without particular regard for the contemplative qualities and cohesion of the play as a whole.

In the desire to please the senses, music was given its full share. Music, along with scenery and costumes, was an attraction on which the success of the play depended. It is the more interesting in view of the fact that in all of Christian religious drama the pains and tortures of martyrs are but momentary, as momentary as the torments of lovers in later opera, for redemption lurks around the corner. While "ultimate bliss" is a given, the momentary still requires elaboration. From an oft-cited remark made by Vincenzo Borghini (an early sixteenth-century chronicler), there is reason to believe that the *rappresentazioni* not only employed music, but that in their early development were sung throughout. According to Borghini this practice was changed at the turn of the fifteenth century in favor of the spoken word with music freely interpolated in the text.[49] While the surviving texts of *rappresentazioni* do not imply the continuous use of music, they indicate that music played an important role in these religious representations. Instrumental as well as vocal

[48]Isaac's name has been mentioned in connection with the music written for Lorenzo's *rappresentazione, San Giovanni e Paolo,* see André Pirro, "Leo X and Music," *Musical Quarterly,* vo. XXI, 1935, p. 1; also Federico Ghisi, "Le Musiche di Isaac per il San Giovanni e Paolo di Lorenzo il Magnifico," *La Rassegna Musicale,* vol. XVI, 1943. However, Reese raises some questions based on the fact that Lorenzo's play dates from 1471 whereas Isaac entered Lorenzo's service only ca. 1484. The composition of Isaac's *battaglia* (DTO XVI[1], 1909, p. 221) may have been interpolated in later performances. See Reese, *op. cit.,* p. 172, note III.

[49]D'Ancona, *Origini,* vol. I, p. 332. In this connection Rolland wisely observes that "there is some irony in the fact that a dramatic improvement at the beginning of the sixteenth century should result in suppressing music, while at the end of the same century another improvement brought music back again. Thus the perpetual see-saw of artistic evolution goes on—Corsi e Ricorsi," Rolland, *op. cit.,* p. 325.

music was employed, and the action of the plays was occasionally interrupted by interludes in which dances were performed.[50] The references to musical interpolations in the surviving texts are chiefly in the form of stage directions.[51]

The consistent use of freely composed music with popular appeal, regardless of the function it was intended to serve, is one of the significant differences between the *sacra rappresentazione* and its Northern counterparts. The latter resorted more often to the chant and sacred polphony as important musical vehicles.[52] This essential difference marked a point of departure for all lyrical presentations prior to the invention of the dramatic recitative, from which they proceeded to move into a musical world of their own.

The basic difference between the *rappresentazione* and the mysteries of France, Germany and England arose out of the different development of religious drama in these countries in the late Middle Ages as compared to its development in Italy. From the tenth to the thirteenth centuries, when liturgical drama achieved its primary devolopment, it was an essentially universal phenomenon. It grew out of religious ceremonies, from the trope to the introit for Easter and Christmas, written in the form of dialogues.[53] Since these dialogues were sung, music was retained in the scenes which grew up around them. For the most part, the earliest liturgical dramas were sung throughout.[54]

At first the plays were composed by clerics and performed within the precincts of the Church.[55] Gradually, as both playwrights and audience felt the desire to enlarge the scope of these

[50]D'Ancona, *Sacre Rappresentazioni, op. cit.,* vol. II. p. 132 *(Rappresentazione di Santa Margherita).*
[51]*Ibid.,* p. 237 *(Rappresentazione di San Giovanni e Paulo).*
[52]For a discussion on the use of plainsong in sacred plays, see André Pirro, *Histoire de la musique de la fin du XIV siècle à la fin du XVI,* Paris: 1940, p. 124.
[53]See Karl Young, *The Drama of the Medieval Church,* Oxford: 1933, vol. I, pp. 201-22, for discussion of the earliest stage of the liturgical drama. Also see W.L. Smolden, "Liturgical Drama," in *The New Oxford History of Music,* vol. II, London: 1954, pp. 175-219.
[54]Gustave Reese, *op. cit.,* pp. 193-7. The earliest performances consisted merely of unaccompanied monody. There is evidence, however, that musical instruments were used in the larger works. See Smolden, *op. cit.,* p. 177, W.L. Smolden, "The Music of the Medieval Church Drama," *The Musical Quarterly,* vol. XLVIII, No. 4 (1962), pp. 476-497, and Edmond de Coussemaker, *Drames liturgiques du moyen age,* Paris: 1861, pp. 50, 59, 60.
[55]Smolden, "Liturgical Drama," *op. cit.,* p. 175.

performances, they were transferred from religious to secular auspices. This change was accompanied by substitution of local color, the partial introduction of the vernacular and a general enrichment of content, comic elements and "worldly appeal." Such transitional plays were ultimately succeeded by religious plays in the vernacular, often of several days duration and covering the whole gamut of religious history. As the influence and control of the Church thus diminished from the fourteenth century on, prominent national differences became apparent.[56]

A comparison of the history of the religious dramas in France, Germany and England reveals parallels at every point: Latin gave way early to the vernacular; the text grew in scope as the music diminished in importance; and some concern for the drama as literature became evident.[57] These tendencies found fullest expression in the mysteries of these three countries, where the function of the music finally became merely incidental.

Developments in Italy were different, however. Here, Latin persisted beyond the Middle Ages as the language of religious drama. Very few examples of early vernacular religious drama from Italy have been found, in contrast to the large number from the other countries. By the time the vernacular had completely replaced Latin elsewhere, Latin plays continued to develop independently in Italy, alongside the rising vernacular. Nor did the text undergo the same kinds of extensions and elaborations as in northern drama; altogether, there was less literary concern. Compared to the other countries, the emphasis in Italy was increasingly placed, instead, on embellishing the production.[58]

Relative to the development in France, Germany and England, then, the Italian emphasis on the "grand production" became even more apparent. Creizenach's remark in this connection is especially noteworthy: "Die Neigung zur Ausdehnung und Abrundung des liturgischen Dramas, ist jedoch nicht mehr bemerkbar. Um so deutlicher zeigt sich eine andere Tendenz, die auch weiterhin in der Geschichte des italienischen

---

[56]For a summary of the stages of this development, see Young, *op. cit.*, vol. II, pp. 397-426.

[57]For a full discussion of the religious drama in the late middle ages, see Wilhelm Creizenach, *Geschichte des neuren Dramas*, Halle: 1893, vol. I, pp. 162-358.

[58]Creizenach, *op. cit.*, pp. 298-305.

Theatres von Bedeutung wurde, die Tendenz nämlich, das Hauptgewicht nicht auf das gesprochene Wort, sondern auf die glanzende Ausstattung zur verlegen . . . "[59]

Returning to the *sacra rappresentazione* which was performed in Italian, it is important to remember that it cannot simply be seen in historical sequence, nor in its direct bearing on the establishment of opera, although, as has been shown, it probably had such bearing. Rather, it is here maintained that what can be learned from the *rappresentazione* is of a more latent nature. When compared to the development of religious drama elsewhere, the *sacra rappresentazione* is revealed as symptomatic of the southern genius that gave rise to opera.

The *sacra rappresentazione* lacked dramatic declamation, a recitative modeled on the speaking voice, nor did music play an important part in the articulation of the story. It has earned its position as forerunner of opera primarily because of the materials it employed; but no less important was the spirit it conveyed. Like many of the Italian operas of later centuries, the *sacra rappresentazione* did not try to resolve the incongruity presented by the aesthetic refinements characteristic of the sensuous aspects of the play, and the essentially crude and unpolished qualities characteristic of its intellectual content. Nor did it attempt to integrate all its elements into an organic whole. Instead, the story served as a vehicle for display—in which perfections and imperfections are balanced—that delighted the senses and amused the soul, while it could not fail to be understood because of its childish simplicity. In the attempts to secularize the *sacra rappresentazione* that took place prior to the revival of classical comedy, D'Ancona saw the germ of a vernacular farce.[60] The playwrights of the Renaissance preferred Plautus and Terence to indigenous growth, yet they did not succeed altogether in depriving the Italians of a national theater; although the *sacra rappresentazione* did not lead directly to the production of a national Italian theatre, it anticipated the spirit of the new medium just as it portrayed and captured the Italian imagination.

[59]*Ibid.*, p. 301.
[60]See D'Ancona, *Origini, op. cit.*, vol. II, ch. XLI.

Roman Theater

The progress from the sensational to the sensuous and lyric in Italian literature and drama has another strand, the theater, which should be interlaced here. More than any other literary genre, the drama was dominated by the rules laid down by the ancients and revived and codified by the academies.[61] Interest in the past, and in the cultural—if not imperial—continuity of Roman glory, was reinforced by the Humanists who revived the style of ancient language and rhetoric. "Abicumque est parlata lingua Romana ibi est imperium Romanum" was one of their phrases.[62] Patronage for classical scholarship was not lacking, and the courts saw in works of eloquence an added source of luster. Poliziano, for example, not only a great poet but the outstanding classical scholar of the second half of the fifteenth century, was in the employ of the Medicis. The writings of the ancients, both Greek and Roman, grew steadily in importance.

Tragedy was hardly able to free itself from the fetters of academic rules. At first, based on Aristotle's dramatic theories, it followed the examples set by the great Greek dramatists.[63] However, imitation of the Greeks was superseded by the Latin model, more specifically by Seneca, its only representative whose works were still extant.[64] According to Giraldi, leading

[61]A considerable impetus was given to the study of Greek by the conclave that came over to Italy in 1438-1439 in connection with the negotiations for a reunion of the Greek and Roman churches. Though the hopes of healing the schism between East and West failed, the coming of the group, among whom were some notable Greek scholars, left its mark. The rebirth of Platonism has been attributed to the influence of these Greek scholars. See Nikolaus Pevsner, *Academies of Art Past and Present*, London: Combridge University Press, 1940, ch. I.

[62]A statement made by Lorenzo Valla in the preface to his thesaurus of Latin phrases, cited, among others, by Jefferson Butler Fletcher, *Literature of the Italian Renaissance*, New York: 1934, p. 7.

[63]Trissino was a man of great erudition who devoted himself to the study of ancient writers seeking to establish canons for the regulation of correct Italian composition. Although it lacked imagination and vitality, his *Sofonisba* was hailed as a triumph of skill by the learned audience to whom the author appealed. Some of the foremost writers of the time were among his imitators (Giovanni Rucellai, Sperone Sperone, and Luigi Alamanni). "Dieses eine Drama, das einen Stil begrundete," says Gregor, "fürte eine ganze Reihe von Klassischen Tragödien herauf, die keineswegs auf Italien beschränkt blieben; ihr Einfluss reicht von Saint Gelais bis auf Corneille, in Deutschland bis auf Lohenstein und Geibel." Joseph Gregor, *Weltgeschichte des Theaters*, Zurich: Phaidon-verlag, 1933, p. 184.

protagonist of the revival of Roman Theatre, Seneca had improved the form of Greek drama.[65] Giraldi himself tried to imitate Seneca in his writing, thus hoping to provide a fresh impulse to tragedy. All efforts were made to involve the audience in the goings-on on stage. In his *Discorso ovvero lettera al compore delle Commedie e delle Tragedie,* Giraldi states clearly that the construction of the play is "solo per servire agli spettatori, e farle riuscir piu grate in iscena e conformaci piu con l'uso dei nostri tempi."[66]

The naturalness of the Greeks did not meet the taste of the time. Seneca's tragedies, on the other hand, not only came closer to the Italian spirit of the day,[67] but were applauded, no doubt, by perennial national taste. While the predominance of the rhetorical element in Seneca's tragedies met with the approval of the rhetoricians,[68] the sensational character of the plays appealed to the audience at large, which had experienced its own share of horrors. Roman drama in antiquity underwent a process of secularization in the course of its development, and as a whole was less intimately connected with the national religion than was Greek drama.[69] Historic subjects, enhanced by magnificent spectacles, constituted a major part of its development.[70] Affect was a significant factor in Roman drama almost from the outset. Compared to Greek drama, Latin plays provided allure

[64]The forms of Greek and Roman tragedy are essentially alike, except that in the Roman tragedy, the part of the chorus is reduced and the plays were eventually divided into five acts. Though the types of characters are also the same, there is a marked difference in their speech. The dialogue in Roman tragedy is more rhetorical and solemn, "compensating for its lack of deeper feeling by exaggerated imagery." See Karl Mantzius, *A History of Theatrical Art*, trans. Louis von Cossel, New York: 1937, vol. I, pp. 209-19.

[65]*Ibid.*, p. 240, note 17.

[66]Quoted in Heinz Kindermann, *Theatergeschichte Europas*, Salzburg: 1959. For an analysis of Giraldi's tragedies see Kennard, *op. cit.*, pp. 140-44.

[67]As a result of his thorough investigation of sixteenth-century literature, Symonds reached the conclusion that Humanism and all its consequences were a revival of Latin culture, "only slightly tinctured with the simpler and purer influences of the Greeks." See Symonds, *op. cit.*, pp. 243, Note 20.

[68]Seneca's plays were doubtless intended for recitation, whether or not they were designed for the stage. See the discussion of Seneca's plays under "Drama" in the *Encyclopaedia Britannica*, 11th edition. Also see W. Beare, *The Roman Stage*, Cambridge: Harvard University Press, 1951, pp. 224-25.

[69]Margarete Bieber, *The History of the Greek and Roman Theatre*, Princeton: Princeton University Press, 1939, chs. I, II, XI, XV.

[70]See Beare, *op. cit.*, pp. 29-34. Also see the discussion of Naevius' plays in Kindermann, *op. cit.*, vol. I, pp. 147-49.

more for the senses than for the intellect.[71] However, this lack of profundity and its somewhat superfluous external polish, were no more considered defects in the Italian Renaissance than in Nero's Rome. The Rome of Nero, like that of the Italian Renaissance, was a cosmopolitan city. Its philosophy of life, its social patterns and its religious tone were not markedly different from those of urban centers of the later period. The temper of the age of Nero was materialistic, and there was no more room for philosophy in the commercial world outlook of the Roman middle class than there was in that of the pleasure-seeking society of the Italian Renaissance.[72]

Though the preoccupation of the Italian Renaissance with imitation of the classics was at the expense of the growth of an indigenous drama more representative of the nation, the theater nonetheless reflected the spirit of the time and, to a certain degree, the aesthetic predilections of the nation. Drama, like the rest of the literature of the time, exhibited the subordination of substance to expression, emphasizing instead a direct appeal to sensibility.

It should be mentioned, however, that despite the fantastic display and the lurid plots of cinquecento tragedies, the plays are decorously dull and tame. The dramatic essence of the plays—the clash between characters, the insurmountable circumstances and the "fall" of the great—is rarely actually witnessed; it is mostly heard tell of. Moreover, the spectator is not admitted to the intimacies of the great, i.e., the principal charac-

---

[71]The Roman theater was constrained more and more to incorporate elements that would lure the audience, in order to compete with the sensations and spectacle provided by the mimes, which constituted a greater source of attraction for the Roman public. See *ibid.*, pp. 154-5. On this point, see also Beare, *op. cit.*, p. 61, and Schatz has the following to say: "Mehr als Rhetor denn als Dichter tritt Seneca an seine griechischen Muster heran, und dramatische Bewegung steht ihm erst in zweiter Linie. Er muss starke Töne anschlagen, um die abgestumpften Nerven seines Publikums zu erregen. Der am meisten in die Augen springende Grundzug dieser Stücke ist daher das Masslose, das Forcierte, das Pathetische, Alle Gefühle sind hoch gespannt wie die Reden, alle Leidenschaft gesteigert bis zum Exzess. Der Schmerz rast in Körperlichen und seelischen Qualen, dem Toben der Rache liegt raffiniert bewusste Bosheit zugrunde. Das Pathos wird zum Übermass gesteigert, und die mythischen Gestalten werden Träger und Beispiele überspannter Affekte . . . " Martin Schatz, *Geschichte der Römischen Literatur*, München, H. Beck's Verlagsbuchhandlung, 1959, vol. II, p. 466.

[72]For historical and social background of Seneca's plays, see Clarence W. Mendell, *Our Seneca*, New Haven: Yale University Press, 1941, ch. II.

ters. He sees and hears them converse mostly with anonymous and insignificant nurses, messengers and counselors.[73] It is often left to the final messenger to make up, in part, for the overall dullness of the play by particularizing in his report every atrocity and horror excluded from the scene itself and, if necessary, by exhibiting the head or limbs of the slain. Indeed, cinquecento tragedies present the curious spectacle of a strong-nerved, sensation-loving people being short-changed on what they actually received from the stage.

Though strong-nerved and sensation-loving, the Italians do not support soulless brutality. They surrender readily to emotions more refined, tender or ardent. Even in their acts of violence the emotional factor overrides the intellectual. Violence is committed in the heat of passion, rather than calculated in cold blood. Like all their other acts, the Italians' violence results primarily from a fundamental involvement with the values and aspirations of mankind. People and situations are hardly ever treated in a detached manner and, as a result, cannot be objectified. The process of objectification entails the potential for dehumanized violence on a mass scale, the kind of violence that is basically alien to the Italians. The act of violence most acceptable to the Italians, in life and theater alike, is that which results from the passion of love.

The career of Roman comedy followed a somewhat different path than tragedy. Though the process was slow, comedy was able to deviate gradually from its classic models and more closely reflect contemporary life and new social conditions. Altogether, comedy is more bound by time and place than tragedy. One may say, perhaps, that tragedy is more philosophical and comedy more sociological by nature. Thus the fact that comedy was freer than tragedy to deviate from set models is not accidental. Eventually, it had to do so in order to survive. It should be pointed out, however, that when they adapted comedies of Plautus and Terence, the playwrights were aware of the correspondence between certain dramatic intrigues presented in these plays and the intrigues in the life of Italian society. Il Lasca, who fought against adaptations in favor of translation and origi-

---

[73]This holds equally true for the pastorals. But since the objective of the pastoral is to create a lyrical mood rather than dramatic tension, the dramatic "flaw" of the tragedies is absent in the pastorals.

nal plays, complains in the prologue to his *Gelosia*, of the stereotyped plots about lost relatives; of the hodgepodge of old and
new ideas, settings and manners; and about the impotent de-
pendence on the classics.[74]

Free rehandling of Latin originals grew from close or slighty
varied tranlations and gradually opened the way for comedies
that acknowledged little or no convention at all. The process of
freeing comedy from translation and imitation began almost immediately after the first staging of Plautus' *Menaechmi* in 1486,
which was ordered by Duke Ercole of Ferrara, a great admirer of
Plautus and Terence, and largely responsible for their dissemination.[75]

Though the process of transforming comedy began very
early, it took decades to throw off completely the literary prescriptions of the ancients. The transition from Latin to Italian
comedy was primarily effected by Ariosto, Machiavelli and
Aretino. Ariosto was one of the earliest to free himself from strict

[74]"All the comedies which have been exhibited in Florence since the Siege, end
in discoveries of lost relatives. This has become so irksome to the audience that,
when they hear in the argument how at the taking of this city or the sack of
that, children have been lost or kidnapped, they know only too well what is
coming . . . Authors of such comedies jumble up the new and the old, antique
and modern together making a hodgepodge and confusion, without rhyme or
reason, head or tail. They lay their scenes in modern cities and depict the manners of today, but foist in obsolete costumes and habits of remote antiquity.
Then they excuse themselves by saying: Plautus did thus and this was Menan-
der's way and Terence's, never perceiving that in Florence, Pisa and Lucca
people do not live as they used to do in Rome and Athens. For heaven's sake
let these fellows take to translation, if they have no vein of invention, but leave
off cobbling and spoiling, the property of others and their own." Quoted in
Symonds, *op. cit.*, p. 239.
[75]"Plautus und Terenz waren Ercoles besondere Lieblinge. Oft mussten
zeitgenössische Dramatiker zurückstehen, wenn es am theaterfreudigen Hof
von Ferrara um Plautus und Terenz Aufführungen ging. Und Ercole begnügte
sich nicht mit den Vorstellungen am eigenem Hof, sondern brachte sein Ensemble auch zu Gastspielen an andere Höfe, etwa an den seines Schwieger-
sohnes Ludovico Moro, nur um, fast mit einer Art von Künstlerischem
Sindungs-bewusstsein, die theatralische Botschaft der wiedergewonnenen
antike möglichst vielen Empfanglichen zu schenke. So galt diese Hofbühne
Ercoles bei den Zeitgenossen mit Recht auch als die hohe Schule für die
Schauspieler, die von da an die fremden Höfe, in aller Herren Landerzogen.
Man darf auch vorwegnehmend sagen, dass Ariost sein damals modernen
Renaissance-Dramen nicht hatte so theaternähe entwerfen können, wäre er
nicht schon in seiner Jugend am Hof von Ferrara durch viele Aufführungen mit
dem Komödienwerk von Plautus und Terenze vertraut geworden." Kinder-
mann, *op. cit.*, pp. 39-40. See also D'Ancona, *Origini, op. cit.*, vol. II. pp. 236-43.

imitations: yet writing for the amusement of a court, he did not stray very far from the conventions he knew would satisfy his audience. Ariosto's actual achievement in his comedies is less important, however, than the path he forged to new possibilities. Once the way was opened, many followed. Machiavelli's *Mandragola* served as an important step in this development. Its cynicism and immorality were meant to mirror the corruption of the Italian society. By the time Aretino contributed his share (1520-1536), conventions were hardly acknowledged. Local dialects found their way into comedy in attempts to depict local scenes. Finally, the *commedia dell'arte*, with its improvisational character, stood as a marked contrast to the stiff imitation with which comedy began.[76]

It is noteworthy that in both comedy and tragedy, the elements of love and romance increased in prominence during the course of the sixteenth century, and found their fullest expression in the literature of the seventeenth century. Comedy abounded in young lovers who deceived their parents or guardians, and in young wives unhappily married to old, cold and jealous husbands, but the sorrows and frustrations of the lovers were more sincerely emphasized and seriously treated.[77] Defying middle-class morality, comedy supported bourgeois sentimentality.

[76]The *commedia dell'arte* was a professional dramatic art. Since only the indispensable course of the play was outlined in advance (the so-called "scenario") and the dialogue, jokes, outbursts of feelings, etc. were all left to the actor, it required not only professional proficiency but long experience in the theater. Yet although it was improvised theater, a certain tradition could not help but be formed. From the stock characters a number of stock plays were created and the same set phrases were used on occasions in which the situations were similar. Also, the same actors nearly always performed the same kind of parts. A Harlequin, A Pantalone or a Dottore seldom played anything but that one part during his whole life. However, the "lazzi"—the superfluities suggested to the actor on the spur of the moment, which had no connection with the subject of the play—were always left to the actor's own genius. It is the latter that added freshness and contemporaneity to the plays. The plays themselves were essentially based on intrigues and comic situations borrowed from the contemporary written comedy, which in turn descended from Plautus and Terence. For detailed discussion of the above, see Karl Mantzius, *op. cit.*, pp. 211-318. Also see Vito Pandolfi, *La commedia dell' arte*, Florence: 1957, vol. I, pp. 23-5. For illustrations see Lucien Dubech, *Histoire Générale Illustrée Du Théâtre*, Paris: 1931, vol. II, pp. 247-60. Note the stylized gestures of the actors, p. 258.
[77]See Marvin T. Herrick, *Italian Comedy in the Renaissance*, Urbana: 1960, pp. 112-64. Adaptations and imitations of ancient drama continued in the second half of the century, but more and more use was made of material drawn from *novelle* and romances.

Similarly, tragedy incorporates the element of love even when it is not an integral part of the plot. In the historical trage-dies, accuracy was often sacrificed in favor of complicated ro-mance. On the whole, tragedy, like comedy, moves from an at-mosphere of royal beings towards an outlook characteristic of the middle class.[78] The latter finds expression in tragicomedies, which are generally more sentimental and always end happily.[79] The lyricism of Tasso's style and the spirit of his golden age, the lawfulness of all that pleases, gradually invaded all literary genres, culminating in a "sensuality exhaled in tenderness, vo-luptuousness, gallantries and sweetness."[80] Even the Jesuits, in-terested as they were in regaining lost souls for the Church, eventually introduced shepherds and lovers into their tragedies in an attempt to satisfy public taste.[81]

It should be stressed again and again that tragedy in the Greek sense was alien to the Italians. Altogether, the re-enactment on a public stage of private anguish, divorced from reason and justice, is not universal. Even in the West, where it has become part of a dramatic tradition, this tradition is not marked by an ordinary continuity, but punctuated by occasions. "Out of the surrounding darkness," says Steiner, "energies meet to create constellations of intense radiance and rather brief life." Without unduly pondering over this enigmatic statement,

---

[78]See Kennard, *op, cit.*, pp. 198-212.

[79]See Herrick, *op. cit.*, pp. 165-209.

[80]De Sanctis, *op. cit.*, vol. II, p. 703.

[81]Overlooking the "lesser evil" for the sake of the "higher truth," the Jesuits saw in the theater a popular stage for the pronouncement of their doctrines. In his discussion of the use of the theater by Jesuits, Flemming says, "Das in allen Perioden sich gleichbleibende Hertz des Jesuitendramas ist seine Tendenz. Galt es zunächst die Massen aufzurütteln und anzuziehen, so hiess es weiter, sie festzuhalten. Allen Kreisen sollten die Grundwahrheiten der katholischen weltanschauung eingeprägt werden. Man wusste, dass stets auf den Mens-chen das Mitangeschaute am nachhaltigsten wirkt, ja, für die breiten Massen stets wohl das eigentlich Überzeugende bleiben wird. Darum könnte von allen Dichtungsgattungen nur das Drama als Vehikel der Mission in Betracht kom-men, aber eben nie als Selbstzweck, als Kunstwerk, sondern günstigstenfalls als Kunstgewerbe, nämlich als wirksames Theaterstück. Im Gegensatz zu der Überschätzung des Wortes und des Verstandes bei den protestantischen Ten-denzdramatikern liess der Orden alle nur erreichbaren Mittel der sinnenhaften Veranschaulichung spielen: Kleiderpomp, Maschinen, Feuerwerk, Musik, Ge-sang, Tanz und nicht zuletzt viele und reiche Dekorationen. Solch ein Un-terordnen des Wortes bringt ohne Zweifel grosse Gefahren, und man ist ihnen nicht immer entgangen." Willi Flemming, *Geschichte des Jesuitentheaters*, Berlin: 1923, p. 1.

we may agree with Steiner that Periclean Athens, Elizabethan England, seventeenth-century Spain, France between 1630-1690 and other occasions represent "such high moments."[82] However, tampering with hidden forces, blind fates, punishments "in excess of guilts," etc. did not appeal to the Italians, nor was their imagination fired by the idea that man's claim to dignity lies in the very excess of his suffering.[83] Instead, the search for the lawfulness of all that pleases turns its back on the Greek vision of man and substitutes common-sense realism for realistic mystery; it creates, above all, an aura of legitimation at once more fantastic and less formal than Greek tragedy.

In a way, the development discussed above is but another manifestation of the importance attached to love during this period. Love played a great role, for example, in the conversations of the cultivated classes and polite society. The many dialogues and treatises on love in the course of the sixteenth century contributed to the spread of the custom of discussing love and, moreover, made such discussions fashionable.[84] Along with eloquent discourses on spiritual love—influenced by the general revival of Platonism—questions such as "how to choose the best lover" (old, young, rich, poor, handsome and well-dressed, or no lover at all) are asked and answered with painstaking care. Nor were problems such as "how to induce love and maintain its fervor" overlooked.[85]

The importance attached to love grew in part out of a general recognition and legitimation of individual feelings brought about by the Renaissance. Individualism, the logical continuation of the general emphasis placed on Man, was bound to assert itself not only in theory but also in practice. As has often been noted, recognition of man as an individual--a unique composite of thoughts and feelings--placed new emphasis on the sensual, expressive and lyrical elements in art. This change was

[82]See George Steiner, *The Death of Tragedy*, London: Faber and Faber, 1963, p. 107.
[83]See Steiner's attempt at a definition of Greek tragedy, *ibid.*, ch. 1.
[84]See Baldesar Castiglione, *op. cit.*, Book IV, chaps. 51-70. For an extensive discussion on love in the sixteenth century and for a detailed analysis of some of the dialogues and treatises written on the subject, see Lorenzo Savino, "Di alcuni trattati e trattatisti d'amore italiani della prima meta del secolo XVI," in *Studi di litteratura italiana*, Naples: 1912-1914, vols. IX, X.
[85]See Thomas Fredrick Crane, *Italian Social Customs of the Sixteenth Century*, New York: 1920, chapt. III, pp. 98-158.

most apparent in Italy, where it gained the support of a nation whose character was already in sympathy with the new development.[86]

Stylistically speaking, lyricism is the quality expressive of the feelings of the artist as an individual. Lyric poetry reflects the soul of the poet more directly than does epic poetry, which is concerned with outward incidents and events. The feelings expressed in an epic poem are those of a group, a people, a nation or an intellectual faction, not of the individual.

However, a lyric poem is not simply the expression of an individual baring his emotions for all to see. Regardless of the specifics of a lyric poem, it may possess a universal quality allowing others to identify with the feelings expressed. Although the reader's or listener's emotions may be part of a different world than the poet's, the reader is able to project his own feelings onto those expressed in the poem, provided the latter are in essence familiar to him. At its best, lyricism is able to express basic emotions shared by mankind ranging from love to hate, but leaving room, nevertheless, for the specific nuances with which they are experienced by particular individuals. This can be achieved only where specific ideas and descriptive details are employed for the sole purpose of creating an atmosphere, or desired mood, and not because of the significance they possess in themselves. It is this concern with *specifying mood*—the irony

---

[86]"In his definition of the Renaissance, Burckhardt combines the idea of individualism with that of sensualism, the idea of the self-determination of the personality with the emphasis on the protest against medieval asceticism, the glorification of nature with the proclamation of the gospel of the joy of life and the 'emancipation of the flesh.' Out of this association of ideas there arises, partly under the influence of Heine's romantic immoralism and as an anticipation of Neitzsche's amoral hero-worship, the well-known picture of the Renaissance as an era of unscrupulous brutes and epicures—a picture the libertine features of which are, perhaps, not directly related to the liberal conception of the Renaissance, but which would be inconceivable without the liberal trend and individualistic approach of the nineteenth century. The discomfort with the world of middle-class morality and the revolt against it produced the exuberant paganism which tried to find a substitute for pleasures beyond its grasp by depicting the excesses of the Renaissance . . .

"The characteristics of the individualistic liberal and of the sensualistic conception of the Renaissance apply only in part to the actual Renaissance, and almost as much as they apply to it, they also apply to the late Middle Ages. The frontier here seems to be more geographical and national than purely historical. In the problematical cases—as for instance in that of Pisanello or the van Eycks—as a rule, one will assign southern phenomena to the Renaissance and northern

of trying to state a common feeling uniquely—that links the character of the Italian genre to the powers of music.

As in the *sacra rappresentazione* and the pastoral, music was not only implicit in the theater but explicit as well. Indeed, the classic themes of the Latin plays, and their imitations and translations, were ornamented by occasional musical pieces for solo, duet, chorus or instruments. These were used to punctuate the plays in the prologue and between acts and they came to be called *intermedi*. They were linked allegorically to the subject of the play, says Il Lasca, but, unfortunately, it is not clear just how this was done.[87]

Again we turn to Pirrotta for illumination. To begin with, Pirrotta stresses the fact that those characters within the plays—primarily in comedy—who sang and danced did so in situations in which dance and song were accepted in daily life.[88] The legitimation to engage in song and dance did not come from within the play but from without. The *intermedi*, on the other hand, functioned to divide the plays into acts and, with the help of music and gesture, to create diversion from the spoken parts. This development did not take place all at once. At first, the *intermedi* were those "open parts" in which the sound of music could be heard coming from an invisible source, while nothing happened on the stage. The division into acts was thus made more clearly. However, some visible *intermedi*, came to prevail

---

phenomena to the Middle Ages. The spacious representations of Italian art, with their freely moving figures and the spatial unity of their settings, seem to be Renaissance in character, whilst the impression made by the confined apaces of Old Netherlandish painting, with its timid, somewhat awkward figures, its laboriously assembled accessories and its delicate miniature technique, is wholly medieval . . . the individual character of races and notions has different significance in the different epochs of history. In the Middle Ages it was hardly of any importance at all; in that age the great collective of Christendom has an incomparably higher degree of reality than the separate national individualities. But at the end of the Middle Ages the place of the universal western feudal system and of international chivalry, of the universal Church and its uniform culture is taken by the nationally and civically patriotic middle class with its economic and social forms subject to local conditions . . . The national and racial elements now come more strongly into the foreground of the picture as differentiating factors and the Renaissance appears to be the particular form in which the Italian national spirit emancipates itself from universal European culture." Hauser, *op. cit.*, vol. I, pp. 269-72.

[87]Grout, *op. cit.*, p. 30. Also see Pirrotta, *op. cit.*, pp. 189-200, 209.
[88]Pirrotta, *ibid.*, pp. 92-3.

somewhat later.[89] In the early stages, at the turn of the fifteenth century, the term *moresca* was almost synonymous with *intermedi*. The *moresche*, we are told, were important more for their novel presentation than for their subjects. Using elaborate costumes and gesture, they seem to have stressed the visual; they abounded in representative dances and the action in them was largely mimed.[90] The nature of their music is not altogether clear. It is apparent, however, that the instruments used were mostly for beating rhythm. The drummer, often the only visible instrument on the scene, was accompanied by other instruments that were not seen.[91] When singing was used, solo voices were preferred to polyphony.[92] The true *intermedi* were either dances or instrumental music at this stage.[93]

The reason so little is known about specific musical compositions related to theater, suggests Pirrotta, resides in the fact that there was a division of labor between the dance experts and the musicians. The former would compose or choose the music for the choreographic parts, while the latter would choose the vocal music for the theatrical actions. This, believes Pirotta, explains in part the lack of descriptions and documentation concerning the adaptation and employment of music. The majority of comedies published in the sixteenth century also rarely mention the *intermedi*, which were executed between the acts, or the music inserted during the acts. The growing formalism, suggests Pirrotta, aimed at maintaining contrast between the main action and its formal frame and the *intermedi*. The lack of references to music, in both formal as well as "realistic function," was determined by practical considerations. Although the *intermedi* were, in a way, a "necessity" for the performances of comedies, they were not "prescribed": they were left to the executors to choose in accordance with their needs. This may have been the case also with regard to those insertions of musical elements that were an added ornament to the texts; they, too, were left to the responsibility of the executors. These conjectures seem to be confirmed by the tendency of the theater in the sixteenth century to develop on two levels, that of "literary activ-

[89] *Ibid.*, pp. 54-5.
[90] *Ibid.*, pp. 59-62.
[91] *Ibid.*, p. 61.
[92] *Ibid.*, p. 56.
[93] *Ibid.*, p. 82.

ity" and that of "practical activity." The latter was largely dominated by the desire to amuse and please. It does not mean that
the authors of comedies were not concerned with giving pleasure to their audience, but that they expended the larger part of
their energies on plots, structure, dialogue, etc., knowing they
had little control over the rest. Looked at from this point of view,
Pirrotta adds, the text of the comedy was only an outline to be
integrated during the performance. The absence of music, in
other words, did not mean literal absence, even if documentation is scarce.[94]

Machiavelli was apparently the first author to have conceived a series of *intermedi* for his comedy the *Mandragola*. Pirrotta tends to believe that he followed a Florentine practice
whereby playing or singing was introduced at the end of each
part of a play. The novelty, here, was primarily of a musical
nature. The single singer accompanied by a lyre was replaced by
madrigalesque polyphony executed by a group. In addition, the
music between the acts was executed by the same group of singers, creating a kind of unification. The sung madrigals became,
in fact, the main part of the *intermedi* by the middle of the sixteenth century.[95] At this point, it is the "un-natural" way of singing that has to be explained.

The theater in the Renaissance started following Aristotelian unities before the doctrine had been reformulated in theoretical writings. The unity of place and action came naturally to a
theater which used a fixed stage. The need to add the element of
time was keenly felt by an audience that had already experienced representations of classical tragedy in which the chorus,
commenting on every action, remained a constant on the scene.
The chorus established continuity in the time of the performance, limiting the length of the action to the length of a solar
day. However, even a solar day had to be compressed. It called
for an artificial perspective of time, says Pirrotta, similar to the
scenic one. While the intermissions between the acts allowed for
jumps in the time of action, it was the intervention of the *intermedi*, commanding full attention to themselves, which compressed the waiting-time between the acts. The acts no longer
appear as interrupted because the jumps no longer seem so

[94]*Ibid.*, pp. 96-9.
[95]*Ibid.*, pp. 146-7.

abrupt. It is the problem of temporal continuity, suggests Pirrotta, that Machiavelli sought to solve in his *Mandragola*, and the madrigal literature includes compositions clearly meant to serve as *intermedi* for comedies.[96] Outside of Florence, people still indulged in *intermedi-moresche*, but the Florentine *intermedi* acquired, in due time, a classical composure comparable to that of the chorus in tragedy. The Florentine *intermedi* were really choirs commenting, as it were, on the action, bestowing a solemn sense of celebration on the performance. Belonging to "a world outside the world and outside time," they made the employment of song more plausible![97]

Pirrotta never loses sight of the fact that conventions also have a history and need to be explained. This is all the more admirable, inasmuch as it is the antecedents of opera with which he is ultimately concerned. He tries at all stages to uncover the circumstances and constellations that make the "un-natural" seem "natural", i.e., to explain how a convention can pass unchallenged. This last phrase has a quasi-tautological ring, at least in the world of language. Agreement, however, is not automatically implied in the history of conventions, or for that matter, in their various applications. It is the process of establishing rules and the striving for their acceptance that helps to explain the very nature of particular conventions.

Up to this point, the *intermedi* had certain attributes and functions. They were integrally related to the plays to which they were attached, though they were not part of the plays themselves. This situation began to change as the analogy between *intermedi* and the tragic choirs, the true custodians of unity, eroded. Unwittingly, the observance of the unity of time broke the unity of the frame when the same characters who appeared at the end of scenes also commented on the development of the main action. The characters and themes of the *intermedi* no longer bore a relationship to each other or to the main action. The sober madrigalesque choruses were now replaced by a greater variety and richness of color. In this search for variety, along with enlarged choirs, the single voice accompanied by instruments was re-introduced, renewing the ancient Humanistic tradition.[98]

[96]*Ibid.*, pp. 148-165.
[97]*Ibid.*, p. 172.
[98]*Ibid.*, pp. 175-185.

Because of the relative silence about the *intermedi*, there is a tendency to associate them with a special, rather exceptional, type of performance connected with the celebration of specific court events. Unlike the others, these are described in detail, revealing their ostentatious and splendorous character. Shows of this kind, we are told, were more frequently used and advertised by the Florentine court, though they were offered by various other courts as well. Music in these *intermedi*, though rich and various, was subordinate to the plastic and pictorial images; it was only one of the elements which contributed to their "marvel."[99] In these *intermedi*, which were less conditioned by the actions of the plays than by the dictates of the scenography, music was primarily able to influence the way in which they were performed rather than the subjects with which they dealt. Dialogues between chorus and soloist and between chorus and chorus began to take a prominent part.

The basso-continuo made inroads into the various dialogues, thereby anticipating its use in the concerted style. Accompanied monody forms a link between the Florentine Camerata and the activity of an earlier Neapolitan group, which Pirrotta calls to our attention. He reminds us, however, that accompanied monody was no more an invention of the Neapolitan group than it was of the Florentines, for it harks back to the Humanist ideals of the fifteenth century.[100]

Enumerating some of the best-known *intermedi* and the ceremonial occasions on which they were performed, Grout tells us that perhaps the most famous *intermedi* were those for Bargagli's comedy *La pellegrina*, performed at Florence in May of 1589 as part of the festivities attending the wedding of the Grand Duke Ferdinand de'Medici and Christine of Lorraine. Noting that there is some confusion in the source documents about details of the composers, it is clear that members of the Camerata and their friends were well represented. As Grout summarizes it,

> The six intermedi were planned by Count Giovanni Bardi; some of the texts were by Ottavio Rinuccini, and the music was by several different composers, including Luca Marenzio, Emilio de-'Cavalieri, and Cristofano Malvezzi. Forty-one of the most celebrated musicians of the time took part in the performance. There

[99] *Ibid.*, pp. 200-207.
[100] *Ibid.*, pp. 215-24.

were five- and six-part madrigals, double and triple choruses, and a final madrigal calling for several different vocal ensembles in a total of thirty parts, each part sung by two voices. These songs were accompanied by various groups of instruments, which also played a number of 'sinfonie.' The orchestra included organs, and other instruments, used in different combinations for each number. The style of orchestration is like that in Monteverdi's *Orfeo*. Three of the six solos are in ordinary madrigal style with the lower voices played on instruments. The others exemplify the florid solo style of the sixteenth century, the voice ornamenting a melodic line which is given simultaneously in unornamented form in the accompaniment.[101]

With Symonds, Grout concludes that the scale of the *intermedi* was such—not only on this one occasion—that audiences must surely have been distracted from the play. The dances and pageants, together with music, may have overwhelmed the drama.[102]

Music and the Dramatic Arts

It seems obvious, even from this quick review, how the dramatic arts of Italy reached out for an alliance with music. Thus, an aesthetic examination of the literature of the Italian Renaissance is important, not because it was able at one point of its development to incorporate music as an integral part of its expression, but more important, because it conveys with clarity the Italian spirit of the time, which directly affected the development of all the arts. It contains some of the elements of choice that modern social scientists might refer to as a "social code."[103]

Before attempting to summarize the major elements of this "code," it seems important to recall that, despite the popularity of dramatic forms—both religious and secular—and the inclination of the culture to dramatize, great drama in the English sense did not develop in Italy. Symonds tries to explain this in a variety of ways, and though sometimes confused, his argument that the absence of a unifying national purpose or self-image in terms

[101]*Ibid.*, Grout, *op. cit.*, p. 31.
[102]*Ibid.*, Grout quoting Symonds.
[103]See footnote 10.

of which heroes can emerge, seems persuasive.[104] Drama in Italy never freed itself from spectacle and celebration, whether of court or Church, and if these gave impetus to the other arts, they did not seem to create the kind of free stage of writers, players and audience from which great drama arises.

The locale for these performances was not fixed; even courts had no permanent stages. Stages were erected, as a rule, for specific occasions only. It was not until the middle of the sixteenth century that theaters began to form a part of the palatial residence of princes.[105] It is important to remember that in general lavish displays were not put on to attract the masses. They were produced primarily for the consumption of nobles and dignitaries, by popes and princes who expressed their rivalry through the luxury of their fetes. Though these displays have rightly been attributed to the lack of political unity in Renaissance Italy, it is no less clear that moderation was not paramount in the aesthetic outlook of the Italian upper class.

The contribution of the Renaissance to closing the gap between the classes should, however, not be overlooked. The middle and upper classes moved toward each other, as has been noted, exchanging tastes and ultimately joining together to pursue mutual interests. From the early Renaissance, the Italian upper class was an urban class, affected by the culture of the city while contributing to its facilities. The development of art in Italy was dictated in part by this factor, which was most consequential indeed for the development of opera, with respect to which the aristocracy cultivated essentially middle-class tastes.[106]

In fact, most of the dramatic forms examined here may be considered, collectively, as variant forms of art that aim at a popular appeal. Although theatrical spectacles were performed in private by pious confraternities, and erudite academies, or on state occasions in princely halls, they reflect the free flow of cultural influences among the various social and cultural classes.[107]

---

[104]Symonds, *op. cit.*, p. 248.

[105]*Ibid.*, p. 249. Also see D'Ancona, *op. cit.*, vol. II, sec. XXIX.

[106]However, as mentioned before, the aesthetic outlook of the Italian aristocracy was not markedly different from that of the middle class. Opera, costly as it is, could not have gotten off the ground without the financial and moral support of the aristocracy. See "Die Oper" in Hans Engel, *Musik und Gesellschaft, Bausteine zu einer Musiksoziologie*, Berlin: Max Hesses Verlag, 1960, pp. 17-53.

[107]It is a well known fact that even carnivals and other celebrations that primarily catered to the masses were encouraged by the upper classes, who seem to

The latter is directly related to the fact that sensibility prevails over intellectuality in all social and cultural strata of Italian society, facilitating the cultural exchange among them.[108] Works of art which result from such an exchange characteristically derive their strength, magnitude and intensity from the uncultivated masses, and their refinement from the aristocratic classes.[109]

In this cultural context, certain salient features emerge, suggesting that the literary and dramatic arts share many features. They say something about Italian national character. They hint, and more, at the ease with which words married music in sixteenth century Italy.

First, there is the emphasis on form. Form—in the sense of elegance, manners, grace, organization (but *simple* organization)—is transposable to many types of content. The *novelle* could serve sacred stories as well as profane ones. The music of the streets could be adapted to the *laude* without causing offense.

---

have enjoyed participating in these festivities themselves. Savonarola's accusation that Lorenzo encouraged the celebration of carnivals for the sole purpose of keeping his populace from thinking about political liberty was not well founded. Lorenzo's contribution to the *canti carnascialeschi* was most genuine indeed (see Ghisi, *I canti carnascialeschi nelle fonti musicale del XV e XVI secolo*, Firenze-Roma: L.S. Olschki, 1937, p. 2, 46). His interest in popular lyrics in general was most sincere. Like Poliziano and Luigi Pulci, he contributed largely to the reunification of the two currents in Italian literature—the plebian and the cultivated—by giving refined form to popular lyrics of diverse kinds. The poets of the later quattrocento who were subject to proletarian influences contributed largely to the cultivation of secular popular music of the time. For their share in the development of secular music and the part it played in their lives, see Rubsamen, op, cit., pp. 20-23.

[108]"It has been well said that Italian Poetry exhibits a continual reciprocity of exchange between the cultivated classes and the proletariat. In this respect the literature of the Italians corresponds to their fine art. Taken together with painting, sculpture, and music, it offers a more complete embodiment of the national spirit than can be shown by any other modern race . . . The close rapport which thus connects the taste and instincts of the proletariat with the culture of the aristocracy, is rooted in peculiar conditions of Italian society. Traditions of a very ancient civilization, derived without apparent rupture from the Roman age, have penetrated and refined the whole nation. From the highest to the lowest, the Italians are born with sensibility to beauty. This people and its poets live in sympathy so vital that, though their mutual good understanding may have been suspended for short intervals, it has never been broken . . . " Symonds, *op. cit.*, p. 7.

[109]This is most apparent in the history of the dance, where leaping gestures invariably turn into gliding motions in their cultural transformation from crude folk dances to refined dances of the middle and upper classes. See Curt Sachs, *World History of the Dance*, New York: Norton & Company, 1937.

172

Consistent use of freely composed music that had popular appeal, regardless of the function which it was intended to serve, is one of the significant differences between the *sacra rappresentazione* and its Northern counterparts. This is not wholly because of form, or even simplicity of form. There is also similarity of content in the various forms. Emotion, particularly love and adoration, are ubiquitous—now secular, now profane. Perhaps this should better be called "mood" than content. The words aim to set a mood, to create an ambiance rather than to deliver a complex message. Hence the emphasis on the brushstroke portrait of characters in the *novelle*, the familiar figures of the pastorals, the simple motives and actions that propel the characters, the relative absence of dramatic conflict. And hence the ease with which music could be mobilized to give explicit expression to mood.

Pageantry or display, rather than drama, might better describe the theatrical representation. The aim was arousal of emotion rather than intellectual effort. The easy realism of the *novella* and the escapism of the idyll are two sides of this coin. The sensationalism of the Roman theater plays the same role. It is in this sense of direct emotional involvement that the baroque, too, may be said to have experienced an "eclipse of distance," compared with the perspective and discipline that preceded it.

Throughout, the brutal yields to the lyrical, not only in form but in content. And lyricism is a leveller; sacred and secular emotions are not clearly differentiated, nor are pagan and Christian imagery. The *novella* serves the sacred; the sacred serves the pageant, and so on.

Three movements have been sketched here. The one leads from the idyll to the pastoral drama, reaching its high points in the *Arcadia* and the *Aminta*. Music accompanied the *Aminta* in the telling of the lyrical story, and the two media embraced. The other leads from the *laude* and the *devozione*, with some influence from the *novella*, to the *sacra rappresentazione*, which unites the magic of music, stage mechanics, pageantry and color with the simple sketch and immediate action of the *novelle* to produce a "music drama" under religious auspices.

The theater falls between the two. Modeled after the Roman theater, it partook of the theatrical and the sensational and, ironically, shares some of the spirit of the *sacra rappresentazione*. Its increased attention to the subject of love led it, on the other hand, to embrace lyrical motifs and some of the mood of the pastoral.

Again, here are the twins of the Renaissance—the pagan and Christian—converging. The curious combination of intellectual simplicity, sensational action and emotional subtlety describes all. Music found it easy to join them. Unlike the Camerata, who were disturbed by the disjunction between words and music, the wedding of music to drama in Italy benefitted from a tolerance for disjunction and disparity. Italians freely linked words and music that were not made especially "for each other." The lack of concern for consistency often resulted in the combination of opposites, such as dramatic tension with lyrical placidity, frivolity with lyrical fervor; but drama cries out for music, and "vocal music," as Spitzer says, "is the music of the human heart."

As always, Spitzer says it all in a long sentence. Arguing with Grove's attribution of the origins of opera to the revival of Greek drama, he insists on adding Vossler's stress on "the medieval drama (which was also, and necessarily, a Musikdrama, given the medieval conception of 'musica mundana') and, more especially, of the Italian mystery (*sacra rappresentazione* or *lauda*), which came to be fused with ancient pastoral poetry, as revived by the humanists at the court of the Medici in the fifteenth century."[110]

And so we have the picture of an Italian concerned with patent form, with lyricism, with emotion, and unconcerned with complex intellection, complicated structures or separation of sacred and secular—bursting into song. Addison and Steele, says Spitzer, cannot understand this, being men of the Enlightenment. They are probably joined by "the masses of most countries," thinks Spitzer, "who can no longer easily imagine [as, however, the Italian peasant still can do, who, when he sings, sings always an aria] a level of existence on which man spends his life in song."[111]

Whatever one says about the "death of tragedy" or, for that

---

[110]Spitzer, *op. cit.*, p. 120.

[111]*Ibid.*, p. 124. Palisca has masterfully shown how Galilei's reaction to polyphony, for example, was primarily due to his devotion to the homophonic idiom of Italian popular music. For Galilei, vocal monody was an "affirmation of the continuity of the Italian tradition." See Palisca, "Galilei and Links . . . ," pp. 359-60.

matter, "the birth of tragedy," it is amply clear that melodra-matization attended this "rebirth," effecting changes in the very conception and essence of tragedy. It is the concept of life as a "show", "the world as a theater," which attained the highest degree of artistic manifestation in the baroque. And within baroque theater, it was the music drama that offered the most suitable stage for the fulfillment of this concept.[112] In "the world as theater," human passions and the conflicts among them override all other concerns. These became the essence of dramatic opera, and the fact that "the mover of all the intrigues and struggles which drove men to their violent actions was the god Amor"[113] only strengthened these passions. The passions that govern the heroes of Italian operas "ravage the human soul like demons," says Schrade, and it is this demonic nature of human passions, he insists, that make action appear "as though it were guided by a fateful force." "If anything played the role of Fate in the baroque opera," he continues, "it was not Providence, not Moira, but man himself under the sway of the demon of his passion."[114] While the distaste for irrevocable catastrophes, discussed earlier, prevented the rebirth of tragedy in the Greek sense, all forces combined to herald tragic episodes in a way which put the highest premium on the manner and adequacy of their display.

[112]See Leo Schrade, *Tragedy in the Art of Music*, Cambridge: Harvard University Press, 1964, pp. 59-60.
[113]*Ibid.*, p. 64.
[114]*Ibid.*, p. 72.

Plate 13. Saul and David. A seventeenth century engraving by Co-
chin depicting David soothing Saul (I Samuel, XIX).

176

Chapter Seven
Exhaustion of the Paradigm

In an effort to reinterpret the emergence of opera in Italy around 1600, this book has tried to retell the story of the melodramatization of 150 years of social and cultural history. Practical experiments on the relationship between words and music characterized the period; underlying these experiments was a belief in the persuasive powers of music and in the value of defining their nature and limits. Definitions in aesthetics seem to serve a role similar to that of theories in science, i.e., to achieve structure and organization. They are used or discarded according to their ability to provide "unity to laws and observations which are contained in science" and frameworks within which "cognitive progress can be made in the study of the arts."[1] Opera was one major result—perhaps unwitting—of this period of experimentation; and the history of opera may be reviewed as a continuing effort to work out the "metaphysical paradigm" according to which music has the power to relate people to one another emotionally, in much the same way that a group of scientists share the belief that "heat is the kinetic energy of the constituent parts of the body." Artistic work, like scientific work, is guided by paradigms, by a "series of related assumptions—theoretical, methodological and empirical—which are generally accepted by those working in a particular area,"[2] as the doings of the Camerata serve to illustrate.

Reviewing the Argument: Origins

Each of the preceding chapters has detailed one of the ways in which music and words reached out for each other in the late

---

[1]Lee Lewis K. Zerby, "A Reconsideration of the Role of Theory in Aesthetics— A Reply to Morris Weitz," *The Journal of Aesthetics and Art Criticism*, 1957, No. 16, pp. 253-5.
[2]See ch. 1, footnote 1.

Renaissance and early baroque. Recall the neoplatonists and their belief in the magic of musical incantations: they believed that humans could tune themselves to cosmic influences by the proper use of music and other astrological aids; they believed in the salubrious influence of the proper combination of music and words on body and soul; they believed in the communicative powers of music. So did the Aristotelians; extending the bond of "natural sympathy" between poet and audience to include music, they meditated on the means of "inducing in others the passions one feels" or "moving the affections of the soul in others."

Literature and theater have been shown, in their several forms, to be inclined toward the sweep of lyricism, and disinclined to either the complexities of verbal analysis of character or the professed pursuits of bona fide drama. Their followers found pleasure in spectacle, realism and, most of all, in the romantic pastures of Arcadia. Music was interwoven into each of the dramatic forms of the period. Freely composed music, however, led to the facile transfer of both musical forms and of compositions from one context to the other: from street to stage, from secular to sacred and vice-versa. Music's theme was universal rather than specific, its message was mood, "stimmung," rather than detail. It epitomized the literature of love, both sacred and profane, ideal and real.

The aesthetic principles reflected in the development of Italian literature in the Renaissance were likewise reflected in Italian music during the same period. Music, like literature, was steadily moving in the direction of lyricism. Perfection was sought less and less in purity of outline, musical magic depended more and more on a direct appeal to sensibility. The growing concern with expression eventually culminated in the establishment of monody. Steadily moving towards the individual utterance of the solo voice, Italian music parted company with that of Northern Europe, which towards the end of the sixteenth century already revealed a more serious concern with instrumental polyphony, foreshadowing its future development.

In Italy, the development of monody reflected the persistent concern of the entire period with antiquity and, specifically in the case of music, with theorizing about how music must have been employed to animate the ancient texts. It continued the belief that the ancients had uncovered the secret of harnessing music effectively to heighten the expressive and persuasive powers of rhetoric.

On the Limits of Words and Music: Extending the Argument

Ostensibly, two different and seemingly contradictory trends were at work during this period. The one emphasized the predominance of words, and the need for music to be closely attuned to the words. The other saw music as "free," autonomous, unfettered by the specific message of a particular poem, play or pageant, but adaptable to any or all.

Without minimizing these differences, since the latter ultimately triumphed over the former with the development of opera, it can be shown that they were reconcilable, at least in part. Similar music could serve both sacred and secular, ideal and real ends, because some of the underlying themes remained the same. If the theme of the words was adoration, music associated with such a theme could serve to express it regardless of the context in which it arose, provided that tradition, convention and style were attuned to one accord. Indeed, only an art that "marshalled all the refined idioms of musical rhetoric into the rigor of a ceremonious style was capable of rising above the ambiguities of emotional expression . . . the composer relied so completely on the perfect mechanism of the stylish vocabulary that he needed no extraneous indication of the passion he wished to reveal, though on occasion he took recourse to a special instruction to designate the shades he fancied. An unequivocal rhetoric strengthened his steadfast belief in the powers of music to demonstrate human passions in terms at once effective and infallible."[3]

The contradiction noted here links up more profoundly with the persistent argument between the "absolutists" and the "referentialists" over the question of meaning in music. Aestheticians have called the two major schools of thought "autonomous" and "heteronomous," respectively. The one group—the referentialists—argue that "music also communicates meanings

---

[3]Schrade, *op. cit.*, p. 68.

which in some way refer to the extramusical world of concepts, actions, emotional state, and character." The other group—the absolutists, who hold an autonomous theory—insist that the message of music resides exclusively within the composition itself.[4] The latter position reiterates that music is the art, *par excellence*, in which separation between form and content is not easily made, if indeed it can be made at all. Whatever the aesthetic theory—whether it defines the essence of music in terms of "sound and motion" as does Hanslick[5] or, according to Langer's more recent theory, as a symbol of time[6]—as long as music remains expressive of musical ideas only, the concepts of form and content overlap. It is apparent that "form" in these theories does not pertain to a set of prescriptions, but is an abstract concept, used in the sense of something "formed" by the interaction among the elements of the art. For this reason, some aestheticians add to the word "form" a modifier, e.g. "significant form" (Bell and Fry), "expressive form" (Langer) or "aesthetic form" (Parker).

At this point, it is worth at least mentioning that the debate between "referentialists" and "absolutists" in music is closely linked with the debate between the "intentionalists" and the "intentional fallacists" in literature and the plastic arts.[7] The symbolic nature of each of the different arts, however, places constraints on the definitions, and the use of terms such as "reference" and "intention." These in turn, may modify the understanding of a concept such as "meaning." It is relatively easier to reconcile "absolutist" and "referentialist" positions in music than those of "intentional fallacists" and "intentionalists" in the plastic arts. In music, moreover, such a reconciliation does not

[4]See Meyer, *op. cit*, ch. 1.
[5]Hanslick, *op. cit.*, p. 48.
[6]Langer, *Feeling and Form, op. cit.*, ch. VII.
[7]The debate centers on whether external factors—social, intellectual, historical, etc.—are relevant to comprehending and evaluating works of art. The "intentionalists" argue that what the artist "intended" depends on "all the causal influences on him"; hence their relevance to his work. The "intentional fallacists" argue that such external factors are not relevant, and that the work of art speaks for itself. See William K. Wimsatt and Monroe C. Beardsley, "The Intentional Fallacy," in *Problems in Aesthetics*, Morris Weitz, ed., New York: The MacMillan Company, 1959, pp. 275-88. Also see Erwin Panofsky, "On Intentions," and Henry David Aiken, "The Aesthetic Relevance of Artists' Intentions," in *Problems in Aesthetics, ibid.*, pp. 288-95 and pp. 295-305.

necessarily rule out either position, though it is easier to handle the "intentionalist" than the "intentional fallacist."

Not only are the positions of the "referentialists" and the "absolutists" reconcilable but, as Meyer points out, their proponents ought to have recognized that they share a problem to which neither has a very good answer; namely, how meaning (whether intrinsic or extrinsic) comes to be attributed to music at all. How, in other words, do specific emotional or cognitive reactions come to attach themselves either to "an abstract, non-referential succession of tones" or to "the musical symbolisms depicting concepts, emotions and moral qualities"?[8] Replying to Hanslick, Meyer argues that "all significant responses to music, the affective and aesthetic as well as the designative and connotative, vary with our experience and impressibility. The response to style is [also] a learned response . . . there is a causal nexus [between music and referential experience], as is evidenced not only by the practice of composers within a given style but also by the responses of listeners who have learned to understand the style."[9]

There is no use debating whether music is an autonomous art; it is. Hence distinctions between form and content are not very useful, though one can talk usefully about "complex" and "simple" musical structures or even about essentially intellectual, as compared to predominantly sensual, music. When music is talked about as a means of representing emotions, it is not meant in a Schopenhauerian sense, (i.e., music as the embodiment of emotions reflecting the 'universalia ante rem') but rather in the sense that music can be used to serve an expressive function. Emotions can be bestowed on music through its association with concrete, conceptual ideas expressed in words. Once such associations are established, music is then perceived as conveying emotions.

Indeed, the issue is quite reconcilable. Music takes meaning, in its narrow sense, from a text; words can say what the music is about. The words, in turn, are enhanced by the music. Having given the music a label—i.e., the words having told us what the music is about—the music can often say more than the words.

[8]Meyer, *op. cit.*, p. 4.
[9]*Ibid.*, pp. 270-71.

This is what Goodman's approach suggests. Music, unlike words, can say something uniquely and unambiguously—once you have announced the subject. Fernando's statement of love for Dorabella in *Cosi fan tutte* is unique: it does not have the multiple layers of meaning contained in the metaphor "Un' aura amorosa." As has already been noted, music is a notational system and is therefore capable of making specific that which is ambiguous or "dense" in the symbolic system called language. Language provides the cue or the label; music provides the specificity. Goodman is not concerned simply with the "languages of art"; he is concerned with symbols and symbol systems, and the ways in which they function in man's perceptions, actions, arts and sciences—in short, in the "creation and comprehension of our worlds."[10] In analyzing the attributes of the symbol systems intrinsic to the various arts, he is, in a sense, following Lessing, who tried to demarcate the arts, claiming that their natures limit the subject matter that each can handle effectively.[11]

Opera is forever an experimental world in which music is called upon to do what words cannot do, to say what words can not say. But, paradoxically, it is dependent on words at least to announce the subject. It is no coincidence that the preoccupation with musical "affections" came as a high point following the experimentation and theorizing about the powers of music. Stereotyped musical "figures," or *loci topici*, depicting both emotional states and punctuation marks were specified and codified in the late baroque. The *locus notationis*, proposed by Mattheson, dealt with abstract figures of musical organization such as imitation, inversion, repetition, etc., while the *locus descriptionis* referred to extra-musical ideas.[12]

Aware of some of the pitfalls of using music as an index, theorists of the affections warned that the composition must be introduced with a clear musical statement of the subject and that only one affection must be treated throughout.[13] Whether one holds that all humans understand these messages because there is one "common man," or that affections are meanings shared by agreement and socialization of both composer and listener,

[10]Goodman, *Languages of Art, op. cit.,* p. 265.
[11]See ch. 11.
[12]See Bukofzer, *op. cit.,* pp. 388-90.
[13]*Ibid.,* p. 389.

there is clear indication here of the mutuality of labeling by means of words and elaboration and specification by means of music.

The Paradox of the Camerata

If members of the Camerata were asked to take a stand in the debate between referentialists and absolutists, they would probably tend to favor the former. At least they would insist that music must serve the meaning of the words and must not wander off on its own. The proper alliance between words and music was considered one in which music underlined speech and heightened its underlying meaning.

The Camerata wanted to enhance the words, and to restrain and discipline music. They wanted to put a stop to the use of music simply to please the ear. In working out their part of the paradigm however, their zeal to achieve the proper use of music almost led to its emasculation. To be sure, Cavalieri's *Rappresentazione*, Gagliano's *Dafne* and Caccini's and Peri's *Euridice*, especially the latter, include some interesting musical sections, but one can not easily overlook those other parts which, intoned monotonously and punctuated by cadences, made each sentence sound like the end of a long sermon. The monodic recitatives broke the flow of the music. As Grout remarks "The foremost opera theorist of the early seventeenth century, G.B. Doni, still argued for this reason that the ideal dramatic work was one in which music alternated with spoken dialogue and strongly advocated the use of choruses and arias to vary the monotony of the recitative".[14]

"No distinct style of monody," summarizes Palisca, "emerged during the years of its life. It spoke for, and to some degree achieved, a style of song imitative of impassioned speech, a kind of melody that could stand alone to project a text with characteristic affective means, pitched to the contours of the speaking voice and measured to the cadence of a state of mind, harmonized by simple chords that seconded the melody

---

[14]Grout, *op. cit.*, p. 59.

and were faithful to its restricted means. It was a style intermedi-
ate between sung poetic recitation and the monodic performance of polyphony from which it grew, and dramatic recitative
toward which it was moving."[15]

Paradoxically, however, the orthodoxy of the Camerata led
to the birth of the idea of beautiful singing. Caccini, the musician, devoted his practical efforts—theory notwithstanding—to
the art of beautiful singing. Monteverdi and Gluck, each building on the doctrines of the Camerata in his own way, nevertheless applied their considerable musical talents to their *Orpheus.*
Aided by the "powers of music," they delved into the depth of
human nature, uncovering human passions.

Indeed, as has often been noted, the Camerata played a
curiously paradoxical role, achieving the opposite of what they
set out to do as often as they achieved their aims. They wanted
music not simply to "delight the ears," and as a result, the idea
of beautiful singing emerged. They wanted to revive classic
forms of "musical rhetoric," and opera was the result. They
wanted to restore the "powers of music" by disciplining music,
and music took center-stage in the lyric theater instead.

Yet, situated as they were in Florence, heir to the Renaissance and godfather to the baroque, the Camerata can legiti-
mately be credited with ushering in opera. It is not altogether
their "fault," of course, but rather the coincidence of their particular aims and the cultural setting in which they were situated.
In fact, there was another group in France working on the same
paradigm at virtually the same time, and arriving at almost the
same solution—yet they deserve far less "credit" than the Camerata so far as the development of opera is concerned. This was,
of course, Baif's well-known academy, about which Walker says
that they tried "to create a new kind of song which should unite
powerfully effect-producing music with poetry of profound religious or philosophical meaning . . . to revive the emotional or
ethical effects of ancient music . . . This leads up to a demand for
the reformation of French poetry and music on the model of
antiquity. Poet and musician are to be identical or close collabo-
rators. The music is to be monodic, and the poetry either *vers
mesurés à l'antique,* as in Baif's academy, or rhymed verse written

---

[15]See Palisca, " . . . A Reappraisal," *op. cit.,* p. 234.

specially for music. Such song will produce 'un veritable revisse-ment d'âme'."[16] Others of the French Renaissance academies fit this description, and some even had practical musicians who tried to implement the program. But these efforts did not find expression in the lyric stage. Science too, knows many examples of the simultaneous working out of parallel discoveries—what Merton calls "multiples."[17]

In retrospect, it would seem that only the Florentines must have tried faithfully to obey the principle esteemed as authenti-cally Greek; namely, to have music reign over the drama in its entirety. It does not matter whether this principle was a reality in ancient Greece, "for only by translating the concept literally into the terms of actual art did the modern music drama, the opera, come to be set upon its irresistible course."[18] As we have seen, monody as a solo song, the revisions in the relationship between words and music or, for that matter, the dramatic monologue, had their precedents. The claim to the "merit of perpetuity" that can be conferred upon the Camerata is closely linked to their "having supplied a complete translation."[19] This "translation" allotted to human nature, and to the passions of man, their most direct mode of expression. And it is, after all, human nature, not the condition of man, which was central to the new concept of "the world as theatre."

Opera Is Italian

It is important to reiterate that opera arose from the con-junction in Italy of the urban bourgeois court and the idea of individualism; from the literary and dramatic forms that re-flected the search for classic models, together with the traditions of Church and theater; from the Italian taste for sensuality and elegance, together with the spirit of doing or "operating" on the world.

The contrast between the musical styles of Italy and the Northern countries points this up even more vividly. In the for-

[16]Walker, *Spiritual and Demonic Magic, op. cit.,* pp. 119-21.
[17]Merton, *op. cit.*
[18]Schrade, *op. cit.,* p. 54.
[19]*Ibid.,* pp. 54-55.

mation of the baroque style, Italy contributed the major share towards the development of vocal monody, and England to the development of an abstract instrumental style, which spread from England to the Netherlands, and from there to other European countries.

The explanation for the differences between the South and North must be sought in the deliberate quality characterizing the latter's expression and the spontaneous quality characterizing the former. The Northern feeling for organization and for things organic bestows an intellectual quality on the manifestations of its genius. Gothic architecture, Netherlandish church music and the German fugue all demonstrate equally a powerful feeling for organization. Italian art, on the other hand, was less intellectual and less concerned with organization *per se*, displaying an increasing aversion to hidden detail and driving steadily towards the effects created by grand and patent relationships. This tendency, though most clearly expressed in architecture, found its way into Italian music and even affected the music composed by Netherlanders who settled in Italy.[20]

Euphony was never sacrificed to structure in the musical art of Italy; simplicity and homophony were always native to Italian music, whereas individuality of melodic lines within a polyphonic complex seemed foreign to it. The polyphonic technique, to be sure, was brought at times to unsurpassd heights, as is evident in the works of Palestrina, yet it was inevitably encroached upon by a native preference for homophony and solistic music. To be sure, the concerted style, which grew in conjunction with the music drama, was a new musical idea to experiment with but, more than that, it was a solution to a problem: namely, how to present passions in conflict.

In Italy, moreover, secular or religious music could divorce itself more readily than anywhere else from the function it served in the theater or Church. Music used in conjunction with poetry and various stage presentations was free of the pressure to become an inseparable part of either.[21] Intellectual consistency, or for that matter, intellectuality in general, gave way to visual and aural harmony of works of art. Beauty was perceived sensually rather than intellectually . Lacking the need to assert

---

[20]See G. Reese, *Music in the Renaissance, op. cit.*, chs. VI, VIII.
[21]See ch. VI.

itself intellectually, the artistic spirit of the Italians displayed the expressiveness that is latent in Italian art at all times. The combination of some Renaissance ideas and aesthetic predilections led toward the individual utterance of the solo voice.

It is important to remember, however, that the "objectivity" that Renaissance composers retained even in their subtle tonal organizations and bold chromatic harmonies was replaced by a more personal feeling in other countries as well. Expressiveness and affect pervade all of baroque music. The purpose of music was now to "move human affections," and composers everywhere enlisted their creative powers towards the realization of this professed purpose. "On these very grounds," we are told by Schrade, "modern times which start with the baroque, and old music, which ends with Palestrina, part company forever."[22] Of no less interest is the following assertion from Schrade:

> For the sake of the *ariosi spectacoli*, a term which ambiguously moves between 'airy' spectacles and spectacles of 'arias,' the composers, beginning with Monteverdi himself, strained all their efforts to build up musical rhetoric expressive of passions, and carried the *stile concertante*, the style of competitive implements, to its widest range and to perfection. Now, the arias of passionate emotions—of jealousy, wrath, . . . love . . . lament . . . misery and pain . . . —were all subject to the standards of style, with the structure and figurative materials establishing the scope of expression. And when the arias followed each other, driven by Amor, the mover of action, they came in succession as image followed image, truly ariosi spectacoli, and the whole was nothing less than a war of antagonistic forces, with the stile concertante being the most faithful interpreter of conflicting passion . . . [23]

Nonetheless, Italy was, not only an early contributor to this development, but a major contributor for, as we have seen, the Italians were in basic sympathy with its tenets. The concept of music as a formulation of expressive ideas grew indirectly from the belief in the union of musical theory and practice, attributed to the Greeks by the Humanists. Historically, it led at first to the subjection of musical practice to the precepts of "musical sci-

[22]Schrade, *op. cit.*, p. 99.
[23]*Ibid.*, pp. 67-68.

Plate 14. Monteverdi. A Diviner of the ''powers of music''.

ence" before it emerged with precepts of its own. The belief in the correspondence between the "harmony of soul" or "the pleasing of the soul" and the similar harmony in "sounding numbers" underwent a transformation so that a distinction was eventually made between objective acoustic truths and subjective determinations. The former were relegated to *bona fide* science, the latter to the experimentations of musicians.[24] The Italians contributed to each and every stage of this transformation and to the actual experimentations, which in turn gave rise to new conceptual formulations. Indeed, aesthetic theory, in general, gained a position paralleling that of theory in science in the early part of the seventeenth century, for both sprang from the veneration of empiricism. Opera was one of the main results of these theories; moreover, it also constituted a forum in which they continued to be tested.

The Dissemination of Opera

In fact, opera did not leave Italian soil until after a great deal of experimentation had taken place. In Florence, it was largely limited to the working out of the recitative over a figured bass. Wedded to the text, punctuated by cadences after each sentence, recitative was bound by rigidities and lack of either musical organization, individuality of characterization or genuine musical inspiration. Courtly weddings were its major locus.

In 1607 in Mantua, Monteverdi proved that more could be done within the same paradigm. As a composer of the first rank, he could not forgo musical organization for the monotony of the orthodox *stile rappresentativo*. His was the first real opera. Spinning the fabric of the music drama, he employed an enlarged orchestra, certain instruments for certain situations, tremoli, pizzicati, syncopations, recitatives in the arioso style, and many other elements, including "innovations," like the *concitato*, for example. Indeed, he enlisted his powers as a musician to create dramatic tension, by a "musical rhetoric" expressive of passions.

[24]See ch. IV; also see Palisca, "Scientific Empiricism in Musical Thought," *op. cit.*, pp. 92-3.

189

Opera moved from Florence and Mantua to Rome, in the decade 1620-30. Though the "holiness" of some of the cardinals was questionable, notice had to be taken of the clergy in the audience, and religious themes were often emphasized. There was increased differentiation between recitative and aria altogether, further musical differentiation, generous use of the chorus, and the beginnings of an introduction of comic elements.

Of all the Italian cities, it was Venice in which opera flourished most, even though it came to Venice only towards the middle of the century. Here, performances were largely financed from the sale of tickets. Opera became institutionalized, a source of financial speculation for Venetian noblemen and of permanent employment for musicians. Operas were now performed throughout a season rather than for special festivals, and a great number of people were thus able to see them. With the increase in the number of public musical institutions in Venice, opera contributed to the steady growth of a musically informed public.

Differentiation of aria and recitative was now fully developed, and virtuosity of singing together with lavish stage designs were the distinguishing marks. The operas composed in Venice over a period of years numbered in the hundreds, and Monteverdi once again was a pioneer in ushering in the *bel canto* style. There was a decline in the use of chorus, a rise in the importance of instrumental interludes, and buffa elements took a greater part. The boom in Venetian opera was such that it, in turn, contributed to an increase in the number of composers writing operas, some of whom began to spread out to other parts of Europe.[25] By then, however, opera had already spread to many other cities in Italy.

Opera was transplanted to other countries thereafter, and was influenced everywhere by native traditions and predilections, but for any place, or at any time, it cannot be said that opera—as a generic medium—was anything but Italian. In France, there was more serious drama on the lyric stage, in keeping with the greater achievements of French drama. Ballet and chorus were more central features; scenery and grand design were also important. There was more instrumental music, but the arias were simpler and often had a dance-like quality.

Just as opera in France was influenced by the other French

---

[25]About Italian opera in Germany and Austria see Grout, *op. cit.*, pp. 105-115.

arts, so in English opera the declamatory, rhythmic elements of the masque had a share. In Germany, opera was mostly in the hands of the Venetian composers except for the short period when indigenous opera flourished in Hamburg around 1700-though even then, composers wrote mostly in the Italian style.

The development of opera in Naples in the early eighteenth century set an international style that traveled round the world. More melodic, with *da capo* arias, employing simple harmonies, down-playing the role of orchestra and practically eliminating the chorus, Neapolitan opera was a seesaw of action and reflection, drawing on historical subjects and trying to integrate the whole within its dramatic organization.[26]

Obviously, this is not the place to discuss in detail either the dissemination of opera or national differences that arose in its development. The point is that opera didn't leave Italy until it was fully developed, and that even later the world continued to look to Italy for developments such as the international style, which came to be known as Neapolitan. Of course, there were important moments in France in the seventeenth and eighteenth century and in Germany and England in the nineteenth century, but as for the peculiar marriage of words, music and theater that is opera—and the shared understanding that it implies among composers, librettists, performers and audiences—the fact is inescapable that the medium is Italian. Its transplantation elsewhere, despite the creative adaptations it underwent, Wagner not excepted, (though his use of "labels" force music to mean something beyond itself), was accompanied by the full set of formal and informal understandings surrounding its institutionalization in Italy. These were part not only of the development and dissemination of opera, but also of the development of critical thought and the refinement of aesthetic theory.

Exhaustion of the Paradigm

Indeed, one of the reasons for the declining popularity of opera in the world may be related to the rigidity with which

[26]On the reform in dramatic organization see Andrea Della Corte, "Appunti sull' estetica musicale di Pietro Metastasio", *Rivista musicale italiana*, 1921, pp. 94-119.

certain social and cultural trimmings have clung to opera. The rich baroque setting of the opera house, the class-stratified architecture of the hall and the trappings of wealth and class displayed by its audience are no longer as attractive, perhaps, as they once were. The democratization of opera, moreover, may not have been successful because of the inability of common people in other cultures to accept the convention of actors telling each other how they feel in song. The acceptance of the "world" created on the stage fares best, as we have seen, when there is nothing to remind the audience that it is partner to an illusion. Opera was not always successful in meeting this challenge.[27] Even if one does not accept Spitzer's theory of the demusicalization of the modern world, it is easy enough to agree that there are but few groups who take the singing of a melodrama seriously.

From an aesthetic point of view, there may be a better reason for the decline of opera. From the days of the Camerata up to the high point of the theory of affections in the late baroque, opera was a medium of individual expression and shared meaning. Whether the shared meaning was innate or learned—the question discussed earlier in this chapter—is of little import here. What matters is that the effort to communicate ideas and emotions through the interaction of words and music in the opera was successful. The nineteenth century, however, departed from this shared set of meanings: there was no longer one music, but many musics. The Romantics cared less about moving others than about expressing themselves. The hypothesis that music can underline the meaning of a text if the text provides the reference to the music gave way, gradually, to the idea that the mere hint of a label is enough and that affections can be clearly articulated by the music alone. This is possible, but only where uniformity of aesthetics prevails. While the period of affections was still rooted in the idea of shared meanings, the Romantic period not only paid less heed to communication, but also tended to disengage the music from the text. In a sense, Wagner deliberately invented his own language, his own world of symbolisms, which he addressed to those who wished to understand—but not others.

Altogether, the nineteenth century preferred to think of

[27]See chs. II, VI.

music as indefinite, mysterious, magical. Except for the group of "classicists," music was now written by "free association," relating to its most elemental aspect, its sound, with reduced attention to shared forms and discipline.[28] Opera declined in importance—despite the "business" of grand opera, the "success" of verismo opera, the "popularity" of Verdi and the inherited repertoire—though music and poetry, together and in combination, was of central importance.[29] The sense of continuous striving and cumulation that characterized the idea of progress—in the arts as in the sciences—through the eighteenth century gave way to a relativism no longer devoted to human solidarity and improvement, having lost faith in both. Music is no longer the main articulator in most of contemporary opera, its place usurped by staging, lighting and other dramatic techniques of the theater; music has become part of the dramatic shell in to which the story is fitted.

From Numerology to Statistics

An interesting idea about the contemporary state of opera emerges from another quarter. While it views the problem of ossification of opera from a statistical point of view, it recalls—at least by free association—the early concern of music theorists with numbers.

Numbers, proportions, and numerical relationships figured large in cosmologies and theories about order in the universe. While their relationship to music was rooted in physical reality, relating music to conceptions of "order" outside the musical sphere reflected symbolic and hermeneutic concerns. Interestingly, the "scientific" past of music was partially known and experimented with in cosmological world views. This scientific component, as we have seen, found its way later into *bona fide* physics as part of acoustical inquiries. Freed from such inquiries about sound phenomena, aesthetic theory was able to address

[28]See Alfred Einstein, *Music in the Romantic Era*, New York: Norton & Company, 1947, pp. 3-44.
[29]The Romantics attached importance to music in the nineteenth century precisely because it was viewed as "indefinite" and "mysterious." The reasons, thus, for the centrality of a particular art in a given time or place are no less telling than the centrality itself. For a discussion of the of music in the nineteenth century and the relationship between words and music, see *ibid.*, ch. III.

Plate 15. Pythagoras. Iamblichus, *In Nicomachi Geraseni arithmeticam introductionem*, Samuel Tennulius, ed. (Arnhem, 1668). Pythagoras (in the center) holds an open scroll with the word "numbers" on it. Aristoxenus (in the lower left) plays a bass viol insisting, as it were, that the ear, not the intellect, should determine the consonance of intervals.

itself more systematically to questions about the nature of music *qua* music.

Ever since Pythagoras, music has been a science expressed in numbers, or more exactly, a science that deals with relationships between whole numbers expressed as ratios. (The musical notes are an expression of numbers in sound, and their ratios are judged as consonant or not.) Since music belongs both to the world of pure concept and to the world of sense perception, it can be judged by either the intellect or the ear. The debate between the Pythagoreans and the Aristoxenians, between music conceived as numbers and music perceived aurally, is a matter of emphasis. As such, it occupies an honorable place in the history of music in the West. More often than not, musical theory paid tribute to the quantitative basis of music, while musical practice looked to its perception by the senses. It is the mathematical basis for musical harmony, however—the realization that music was regulated, as it were, by divine reason—that made it possible for music to become the metaphor, par excellence, for the "comprehensiveness" and "consonance" of the natural order. In itself it represented that universal force that "organizes contraries" and "generates unity."[30] This use of music as metaphor traversed the whole gamut, from the music of the universe, through the world-soul as a composite of numerical ratios, to the individual soul which is concordant with it. From here, it is a direct road to musical therapy; in fact Pythagoras himself engaged in musical therapy.[31] The systematic approach to musical "operations" served as bridge between "beliefs" concerning music and a "science" of its efficacy. However, efficacy could be observed only by the senses in the final analysis. Musical practice was, naturally, boosted thereby, for sense perception was always integral to it. If musical operations had import similar to

---

[30]The diapason, for example, cannot be divided into equal parts, yet its extremes are made consonant in the harmonic mean. Furthermore, the diapason is comprised of a fourth and a fifth regardless of whether 8 or 9 is used as the mean -

$$2:3 \qquad 2:3$$
$$6:8:12; \quad 6:9:12.$$
$$3:4 \qquad 3:4$$

For a detailed discussion see S.K. Heninger, Jr., *Touches of Sweet Harmony: Pythagorean Cosmology and Renaissance Poetics*, San Marino, CA: The Huntington Library, 1974, pp. 91-104.

[31]*See* Peter Gorman, *Pythagoras: A Life*, London: Routledge & Kegan Paul, 1979,

that of magic, it was because, like magic, they occupied a place between religion and science. Indeed, modern musical aesthetic theory is inconceivable without divining (in the double sense) the powers of music.

But "unspirited" numbers in their modern use work wonders; they possess the power to describe, if not to explain, some of the trends in the occurrence of phenomena one happens to be interested in. Indeed, what happened to opera? How did it dwindle to that familiar standard repertory? While opera began humbly from a few productions in celebration of very special occasions, it developed in the course of fifty years into a major institution of entertainment comparable to the films of today. In Venice alone, in the second half of the seventeenth century, new operas were required each season for its many opera houses. Moreover, wherever opera flourished it reflected the spiritual life of the place and was an integral part of it. Where are all those operas, and why did opera lose its centrality to the point of virtually disappearing?

In his brilliant analysis of "survival theory in culture," McPhee attributes the current repertoire of any medium not only to problems of production and demand but to problems of selection, or more specifically, to the logic of selection. Thus, in his analysis of the poor survival rate of good television programs, he postulates that the difference between high culture and mass culture lies in the screening logic applied to their items. He argues that "single screening"—where all items compete for a single season, and an entirely new group of items compete for the following season, as in hit songs—is the rule of the game for mass culture, while repetitive screening is the rule for high culture. McPhee goes on to prove, mathematically, that the best policy in single screening entails screening for incompetence, i.e., identifying and rejecting the worst. On the other hand, the best policy for repetitive screening is to refine the selection over and over again, always looking for what is best.[32]

Since culture in this analysis represents, in a way, "all messages absorbed," the repetitive system, one may argue, is essential for cumulation. In order to make room for new works, however, some good works—survivors of repetitive

---

[32]William N. McPhee, "Survival Theory in Culture," in his *Formal Theories of Mass Behavior*, Glencoe: The Free Press, 1963, pp. 26-73.

screenings—must move out of the competition. Shakespeare and Beethoven are no longer put through the sieve; they are a fixed part of the accumulation. With "purification," of course, what remains upon successive screenings is better able to survive. Discovery or rediscovery of great works in history is a correction in a repetitive system, a correction impossible, by definition, in a single screening system.

Opera, one may further argue, had less chance for repetitive screening. If Mozart's operas survived, it was not least because Mozart survived in his other works, although the centrality of his operas is not disputed. *Fidelio* "rides" on Beethoven's coattails. And scholars are "searching" for operas by Schütz and others who "might have" written operas because they "could have," as suggested by what did survive.

If older opera was treated somewhat like Broadway plays and did not get a proper chance for survival in a proper repetitive system, operas of the nineteenth century, with the reduction of new input, are held in such reverence that the repertory has little room to encourage fresh creations. While the "classic logic" according to McPhee is to avoid losing the best, it is crucial to the argument that the input not be limited by an arbitrary ceiling as to size.[33] The reservoir from which choices are made has to be constantly replenished. In other words, a small unvaried repertory is self-defeating in a repetitive screening system.[34]

McPhee shows, mathematically again, how size and quality are negatively correlated in a single system and positively correlated in a repetitive one. One should therefore decrease the regularity of performance of any one item in the repertory as the repertory increases in size.

Considering what was said before, however, it does not pay to improve input as long as one maintains the logic of transient "hits." With all due respect to the wonderful attempts to encourage the writing of new operas by securing for them a production of one season, such attempts must necessarily fail both the composition and the institution, for they fail to change the repertory in any substantial way, nor do they affect a revival of interest in opera. It should be remembered, on the other hand, that survival itself does not necessarily mean a work is better; it

---

[33]*Ibid.*, pp. 39-54.
[34]*Ibid.*, pp. 54-9.

is largely determined by the rules of the game, which themselves are an end result and not a starting point. The screening process, perhaps, can be corrected by better policy. But the policy, in turn, depends not on the statistics of decision making, but on the factors that determine the decision making policy, and perhaps, also on the elements which explain the attractions of audiences. The latter raises the question of why entertainment comes to be associated with familiarity, a question to which we have no answer. As for the question what would affect the revival of interest in opera altogether, the answer does not belong, it seems, to the manifest wonders of mathematics, but to its hidden magical realm.

With these speculations about the survival rate of operatic composition and the fate of opera as an institution, we come full circle. All we have attempted to do is to show how the struggle for definition of the nature of music proceeded, even if it has waned. And the answer which we have suggested is in the nature of a paradox: Music is the most articulate of media but cannot say what it is articulate about. This book has tried to make some part of this paradox articulate.

Bibliography

Abrams, M.H., *Natural Supernaturalism*, New York: Norton and Company, 1971.

Ambros, W.A., *Geschichte der Musik*, Vol. III Reprografischer Nachdruk, Leipzig, 1891.

_____. *The Boundaries of Music and Poetry*, J. H. Cornell, trans., New York: G. Schirmer, 1893.

Aristoxenus, from the "Harmonic Elements" in *Source Readings in Music History*, Oliver Strunk, ed., New York: Norton, 1950.

Aron, Pietro, *Lucidario in musica*, (1545), Oppinione XV, 2nd Book.

Austin, William W., ed., *New Looks at Italian Opera, Essays in Honor of Donald J. Grout*, Ithaca: Cornell University Press, 1968.

Basalla, George, ed., *The Rise of Modern Science: External and Internal Factors*, Lexington: 1968.

Baum, Rainer C., "Authority and Identity: The Case for Evolutionary Invariants," *Sociological Inquiry*, 1975.

Beare, W., *The Roman Stage*, Cambridge: Harvard University Press, 1951.

Bekker, Paul, *The Changing Opera*, Arthur Mendel, trans., New York: Norton and Company, 1935.

Bell, Daniel, *The Cultural Contradictions of Capitalism*, New York: Basic Books, 1976.

Betolotti, Antonio, *Musici alla corte dei Gonzaga in Mantova del secolo XV al XVIII*, Milan, 1890.

Biagi, Guido, *Men and Manners of Old Florence*, London, Fisher Unwin, 1909.

Bee, Oskar, *Die Oper*, Berlin, S. Fischer Verlag, 1913.

Bianconi, Lorenzo and Walker, Thomas, "Production, Consumption and Political Function of 17th Century Opera," a paper read at the 12th Congress of IMS, 1977.

Bieber, Margarete, *The History of the Greek and Roman Theatre*, Princeton: Princeton University Press, 1939.

Boas, Marie, *The Scientific Renaissance, 1450-1630*, London: 1962.

Bonaventura, Arnaldo, *Saggio storico sul teatro musicale italiano*, Livorno, 1913.

Booth, Cecily, *Cosimo I, Duke of Florence*, London: Cambridge University Press, 1921.

Bukofzer, Manfred J., *Music in the Baroque Era*, New York: Norton and Company, 1947.

Burckhardt, Jakob, "Society and Festivals," in *The Civilization of the Renaissance in Italy*, S.G.C. Middlemore, trans., London, G. Allen & Unwin, Ltd., 1928.

Calmus, Georgy, "Drei satirisch-kritische Aufsätze von Addison über die italienische Oper in England (London, 1710)," *Sammelbände der Internationalen Musikgesellschaft*, vol. IX.

Canal, Pietro, "Della musica in Mantua. Notizietratte principalmente dall' Archivio Gonzaga," *Memorie del R. Instituto Veneto di Scienze, Lettere ed Arti*, vol. XXI, 1879.

Castelnuovo-Tedesco, Mario, "Problems of a Song-Writer," *Musical Quarterly*, vol. XXX, 1944.

Child, Harold, "Some Thoughts on Opera Libretto," *Music and Letters*, vol. 11, 1921.

Clagett, Marshall, ed., *Critical Problems in the History of Science*, Madison: 1968.

Clay, Felix, "The Origin of the Aesthetic Emotion," *Sammelbände der Internationalen Musikgeselleschaft*, vol. IX.

Cohen, Dalia and Katz, Ruth, "Quantitative Analysis of Monophonic Music: Towards a More Precise Definition of Style," *Orbis Musicae*, vol. 11, 1973-1975.

_____. "Remarks Concerning the Use of the Melograph in Ethnomusicological Studies," *Yuval*, vol. I, 1968.

Collison-Morley, Lucy, *Italy After the Renaissance*, London: George Routledge & Sons, 1930.

Corte, Andrea Della, "Appunti sull' estetica musicale di Pietro Metastasio," *Rivista musicale italiana*, 1921.

Coser, Lewis, *Men of Ideas*, New York: Free Press, 1965.

Coussemaker, Edmond de, *Drames liturgiques du moyen âge*, Paris, 1961.

Crane, Diana, *Invisible Colleges: Diffusion of Knowledge in Scientific Communities*, Chicago & London: The University of Chicago Press, 1972.

Crane, Thomas Fredrick, *Italian Social Customs of the Sixteenth Century*, New York, 1920.

Creizenach, Wilhelm, *Geschichte des neuren Dramas*, vol. I, Halle, 1983.

D'Ancona, Allessandro, *La rappresentazione di Santa Uliva*, Pisa: Fratelli Nistri, 1863.

_____. *Origini del teatro italiano*, 2 vols., 2 eds., Torino, 1891.

_____. *Sacra Rappresentazione dei secoli XIV, XV, e XVI*, 3 vols., Florence: 1872.

Danto, Arthur, C., *Analytical Philosophy of History*, Cambridge, 1965.

Davidson, Robert, "Über die Entstehung des Kapitalismus," *Forschungen zur Geschichte von Florenz*, vol. IV, Berlin, Siegfried Mittler, 1908.

Dent, Edward J., "A Best-Seller in Opera," *Music and Letters*, vol. XXII, 1941.

Dilla, Geraldine P., "Music-Drama: An Art Form in Four Dimensions," *Musical Quarterly*, vol. X, 1924.

Dolce, Lodovico, *L'Arentino ovvero dialogo Della Pittura*, (1557), Milan: Daelli e comp., 1863.

Doren, Alfred, *Entwicklung und Organisation der Florentiner Zünfte in 13 und 14 Jahrhundert*, Leipzig: Duncker e. Humblot, 1897.

Dubech, Lucien, *Histoire Générale Illustrée Du Théâtre*, vol. II, Paris: 1931.

Duffy Bella, *The Tuscan Republics*, London: Fisher Unwin, 1903.

Eaton, Ralph M., "Music or Poetry," *Musical Quarterly*, IX, 1923.

Ehrenhaus, Martin, *Die Operndichtung der deutschen Romantik*, doctoral dissertation, University of Breslau, 1911.

Ehricks, Alfred, *Giulio Caccini*, Leipzig: Hesse & Becker, 1908.

Einstein, Alfred, "Galilei and the Instructive Duo," *Music and Letters*, vol. XVIII, 1937.

_____. "Die mehrstimmige weltliche Musik von 1450-1600," in *Handbuch der Musikgeschichte*, Guido Adler, ed., Berlin, 1930.

_____. *Music in the Romantic Era*, New York: Norton, 1947.

_____. *The Italian Madrigal*, vol. I, Princeton, 1949.

_____. "The Mortality of Opera," *Music and Letters*, vol. XXII, 1941.

Eisenstadt, S. N., "Post-Traditional Societies and the Continuity and Reconstruction of Tradition," *Daedalus*, 1973.

Elison, Louis G., "Atrocities and Humor of Opera," *Musical Quarterly*, vol. VI, 1920.

Engel, Hans, *Musik und Gesellschaft, Bausteine zu einer Musiksoziologie*, Berlin: Max Hesses Verlag, 1960.

Fano, Fabio, ed., *La Camerata Fiorentina: Vicenzo Galilei*, vol. IV, *Instituzioni e monumenti dell'arte musicale italiana*, Milan, 1934.

Flemming, Willi, *Geschichte des Jesuitentheaters*, Berlin, 1923.

Fletcher, Jefferson Butler, *Literature of the Italian Renaissance*, New York, 1934.

Fortune, Nigel, "Italian Secular Monody From 1600-1635," in *Musical Quarterly*, vol. XXXIX, 1953.

Franklin, Rev. Mr. trans., *The Dramatic Works of M. de Voltaire*, vol. XXI, Dublin: R. Marchbank, 1772.

Gatti, Guido M., "Gabriele D'Annunzio and the Italian Opera Composers," *Musical Quarterly*, vol. X, 1924.

Ghisi, Federico, *I canti carnascialeschi nelle fonti musicale del XV e XVI secolo*, Firenze-Roma: L. S. Olschki, 1937.

_____. "Le Musiche di Isaac per il San Giovanni e Paolo di Lorenzo il Magnifico," *La Rassegna Musicale*, vol. XVI, 1943.

Goldschmidt, Hugo, *Die italienische Gesangmethode des XVII, Jahrhunderts und ihre Bedeutung für die Gegenwart*, Breslau: S. Schottlaender, 1892.

_____. "Die Reform der Italienischen Oper des 18 Jahrhunderts," *III Kongress der internationalen Musikgesellschaft*, 1909.

Gombrich, E. H., "The Renaissance Conception of Artistic Progress and its Consequences," in *Norm & Form*, London & New York: Phaidon Press, 1966.

_____. *The Story of Art*, London: Phaidon Press, 1950.

Goodman, Nelson, *Languages of Art*, New York: Bobbs-Merrill Company, 1968.

_____. "The Status of Style," *Critical Inquiry*, vol. I, 1975.

Gorman, Peter, *Pythagoras: A Life*, London: Routledge & Kegan Paul, 1979.

Gregor, Joseph, *Weltgeschichte des Theaters*, Zurich: Phaidon-Verlag, 1933.

Grout, Donald Jay, *A Short History of Opera*, New York: Columbia University Press, 1947.

Hanning, Barbara, *Of Poetry and Music's Power, Humanism and the Creation of Opera*, UMI Research Press, an imprint of University Microfilms International, Ann Arbor, Michigan, 1980.

Hanslick, Edward, *The Beautiful in Music* (1854), Gustav Cohen, trans., New York: The Liberal Arts Press, 1957.

Hathaway, Baxter, *The Age of Criticism: The Late Renaissance in Italy*, Ithaca: Cornell University Press, 1962.

Hauser, Arnold, *The Social History of Art*, London: Routledge & Kegan Paul, 1951.

Henderson, Isobel, "Ancient Greek Music," *The New Oxford History of Music*, vol. I, London, Oxford University Press, 1957.

Heninger, S. K Jr., *Touches of Sweet Harmony: Pythagorean Cosmology and Renaissance Poetics*, San Marino: The Huntington Library, 1974.

Herrick, Marvin T., *Italian Comedy in the Renaissance*, Urbana: 1960.

Heseltine, Philip, "The Scope of Opera," *Music and Letters*, vol. I, 1920.

Huth, Hans, *Künstler und Werkstatt der Spätgotik*, Augsburg: Filser verlag, 1923.

Ingegneri, Angelo, *Della Poesia rappresentative e del modo di rappresentare le favole sceniche*, Ferrara: V. Baldini, 1598.

Katz, Ruth, "The Egalitarian Waltz," *Comparative Studies in Society and History*, vol. XV, 1973.

Kennard, Joseph Spencer, *The Italian Theatre*, vol. I, New York: William Edwin Rudge, 1932.

Koenigsberger, H. G., "Music and Religion in Modern European History," in *The Diversity of History: Essays in Honour of Sir Herbert Butterfield*, H. Elliot and H. G. Koenigsberger, eds. Ithaca: Cornell University Press, 1970.

Kristeller, Paul Oskar, *Renaissance Thought: The Classic, Scholastic, and Humanist Strains*, New York: Harper & Brothers, 1961.

Kroeber, A. L., *Style and Civilization*, Berkeley: University of California Press, 1963.

Kroyer, Theodor, "Zwischen Renaissance und Barock," *Jahrbuch der Musikbibliotek Peters*, vol. XXXIV, 1927.

Kuhn, Thomas S., The Structure of Scientific Revolutions, second ed., Chicago: The University of Chicago Press, 1970.

Langer, Susanne K., *Feeling and Form*, New York: Charles Scribner's Sons, 1953.

_____. "The Art Symbol and the Symbol in Art," in *Problems of Art*, New York: Charles Scribner's Sons, 1957.

Lessing, Gotthold Ephraim, *Laocoön: An Essay Upon the Limits of Painting and Poetry*, Ellen Fothinham, trans., New York: The Noonday Press, 1957.

Liuzzi, Fernando, *La lauda e i primordi della melodia italiana*, Rome, 1935.

Loesser, Arthur, *Men, Women and Pianos*, New York: Simon & Schuster, 1954.

Loft, Abram, *Musicians' Guild and Union: A Consideration of the*

Evolution of Protective Organization Among Musicians, unpublished Ph.D. dissertation, Department of Music, Columbia University, 1950.

Malraux, André, *The Voices of Silence*, Stuart Gilbert, trans., New York: Doubleday and Company, 1953.

Mantzius, Karl, *A History of Theatrical Art*, vol. I, Louis von Cossel, trans., New York: 1937.

Martin, David, *The Religious and the Secular: Studies in Secularization*, London: Routledge & Kegan Paul, 1969.

Mattheson, Johann, *Der Volkommene Capellmeister*, Hamburg: Christian Herald, 1739.

Matthews, Brander, "The Conventions of the Music-Drama," *Musical Quarterly*, vol. V, 1919.

McPhee, William N., "Survival Theory in Culture," *Formal Theories of Mass Behavior*, Glencoe: The Free Press, 1963.

Mendell, Clarence W., *Our Seneca*, New Haven: Yale University Press, 1941.

Merton, Robert K., *The Sociology of Science*, Chicago: The University of Chicago Press, 1973.

Meyer, Leonard B., *Emotion and Meaning in Music*, Chicago: The University of Chicago Press, 1956.

Mueller, John H., "Baroque—Is it Datum, Hypothesis, or Tautology?" *The Journal of Aesthetics and Art Criticism*, vol. XII, 1954.

Mulkay, M. K., *The Social Process in Innovation*, London: The Anchor Press, 1972.

Nisbet, Robert A., *Social Change and History: Aspects of the Western Theory of Development*, New York & London: Oxford University Press, 1969.

Oliver, A. R., *The Encyclopaedists as Critics of Music*, chapter V, "Instrumental Music," New York: Columbia University Press, 1947.

Orenstein, Martha, *The Role of Scientific Societies in the Seventeenth Century*, New York: 1975.

Palisca, Claude V., "Girolamo Mei, Mentor to the Florentine Camerata," *Musical Quarterly*, vol. XL, 1954.

_____. *Mei's Letters on Ancient and Modern Music to Vincinzo and Giovanni Bardi*, Rome: American Institute of Musicology, 1960.

_____. "Musical Asides in the Diplomatic Correspondence of Emilio de' Cavalieri," *Musical Quarterly*, vol. XLIX, no. 3,

1963.

_____. "Scientific Empiricism in Musical Thought," in *Seventeenth Century Science and the Arts*, Hedley Howell Rhys, ed., Princeton, N.J.: Princeton University Press, 1961.

_____. *The Beginnings of Baroque Music: Its Roots in Sixteenth Century Theory and Polemics*, unpublished Ph.D. dissertation, Department of Music, Harvard University, 1953.

_____. "The Camerata Fiorentina: A Reappraisal," *Studi musicali* I, 1972.

_____. "Vincenzo Galilei and Some Links Between 'Pseudo-Monody' and Monody," *The Musical Quarterly*, vol. XLVI, 1960.

_____. "Vincenzo Galilei's Counterpoint Treatise: A Code for the Seconda Pratica," *Journal of the American Musicological Society*, vol. IX, 1956.

Pandolfi, Vito, *La commedia dell' arte*, Florence, 1957, vol. I.

Panofsky, Erwin, "Artist, Scientist, Genius: Notes on the 'Renaissance-Dämmerung'," in *The Renaissance: Six Essays*, New York: Harper & Row, 1962.

Pater, Walter, "The School of Giorgione," in *The Renaissance*, New York: Modern Library.

Peri, Jacopo, "Dedicatoria e prefazione a L'Euridice," in Solerti, *Le origini* . . . .

Pevsner, Nikolaus, *Academies of Art Past and Present*, London: Cambridge University Press, 1940.

Pirro, André, *Histoire de la musique de la fin du XIV siècle à la fin du XVI*, Paris, 1940.

_____. "Leo X and Music," *Musical Quarterly*, vol. XXI, 1935.

Pirrotta, Nino, "Early Opera and Aria," in *New Looks at Italian Opera, Essays in Honor of Donald J. Grout*, William W. Austin, ed., Ithaca: Cornell University Press, 1968.

_____. *Li due Orfei: da Poliziano a Monteverdi*, Torino: Einaudi, 1969.

_____. "Temperaments and Tendencies in the Florentine Camerata," *Musical Quarterly*, vol. XL, 1954.

Price, D. J. de S., and Beaver, D., "Collaboration in an Invisible College," *American Psychologist*, vol. XXI, 1966.

Prunieres, Henry, *L'opéra Italien en France Avant Lulli*, Paris: Champion, 1913.

_____. "The Italian Cantata of the XVII Century," *Music and Letters*, 1926.

Reese, Gustave, *Music in the Middle Ages*, New York: Norton, 1940.

———. *Music in the Renaissance*, New York: Norton, 1954.

Richards, Gertrude, ed., *From Florentine Merchants in the Age of the Medici, Letters and Documents from the Selfridge Collection of Medici Manuscripts*, Cambridge: Harvard University Press, 1932.

Rickman, H. P., ed., *Meaning in History: W. Dilthey's Thoughts on History and Society*, London: Allen & Unwin, 1961.

Robb, Nesca, A., *Neoplatonism of the Italian Renaissance*, London: George Allen & Unwin, 1935.

Rolland, Romain, *Some Musicians of Former Days*, Mary Blaiklock, trans., New York, 1915.

Rosenberg, B., and Fliegel, N. E., *The Vanguard Artist*, Chicago: Quadrangle Books, 1965.

Rossi, Vittorio, *Il Quatrocento*, Milan, 1938.

Rubsamen, Walter, *Literary Sources of Secular Music in Italy (ca. 1500)*, Berkeley, 1943.

Sachs, Curt, *The Commonwealth of Art: Styles in the Fine Arts, Music and Dance*, New York: Norton, 1946.

———. *World History of the Dance*, New York: Norton, 1937.

St. Evremond, *Oeuvres*, III.

Sanctis, Francesco de, *History of Italian Literature*, vol. I, Jean Reford, trans., New York, 1931.

Sapori, Armando, *La crisi delle compagnie mercantili dei Bardi e dei Peruzzi*, Florence: S. Olscheki, 1926.

Sayino, Lorenzo, "Di alcuni trattati e trattatisti d'amore italiani della prima meta del secolo XVI," in *Studi di litteratura italiana*, vols. IX, X, Naples, 1912-1914.

Schatz, Martin, *Geschichte der Römischen Literatur*, vol. II, München: H. Beck's Verlagsbuchhandlung, 1959.

Schopenhauer, Arthur, *The World as Will and Idea*.

Schrade, Leo, *Monteverdi*, New York: Norton, 1950.

———. *Tragedy in the Art of Music*, Cambridge, Harvard University Press, 1964.

Sear, H. G., "Operatic Mortality," *Music and Letters*, vol. XXI, 1935.

Smolden, W. L., "Liturgical Drama," in *New Oxford History of Music*, vol. II, London, 1954.

———. "The Music of the Medieval Church Drama," *Musical Quarterly*, vol. XLVIII, no. 4, 1961.

Solerti, Angelo, *Ferrara e la corte Estense nella seconda meta del secolo XVI*, Citta di Castello: S. Lape Tipografo, 1891.

_____. *Laura Guidiccioni Lucchesini ed Emilio de' Cavalieri*, 1902.

_____. *Le origini del melodrama*, Torino: 1903.

_____. "Precendenti del melodrama," *Rivista musicale italiana*, vol. X, 1903.

_____. "Un viaggio in Francia di Giulio Caccini," *Rivista musicale italiana*, 1903.

Sondheimer, R. J., *Die Theorie der Symphonie*, Leipzig: Breitkopf und Härtel, 1925.

Sonneck, Oscar George, "A Description of Alessandro Striggio and Francesco Corteccia's Intermedi Psyche and Amor, 1565," *Miscellaneous Studies in the History of Music*, New York: 1921.

Spitzer, Leo, Classical and Christian Ideas of World Harmony, Baltimore: The Johns Hopkins Press.

Steiner, George, *The Death of Tragedy*, London: Faber and Faber, 1963.

Stern Randolph, "Meaning-Levels in the Theme of Historical Decline," *History and Theory: Studies in the Philosophy of History*, vol. XIV, 1975.

Strunk, Oliver, *Source Readings in Music History*, New York: Norton 1950.

Symonds, J.A., *Renaissance in Italy*, New York: Modern Library, 1925

Sypher, Wylie, *Four Stages of Renaissance Style*, New York: Doubleday and Company, 1955.

Tasso, Torquato, *Dialoghi, idizione critica a cura di Ezio Raimonchi*, vol. 11, Florence: G. C. Sansoni, Editore, 1958.

Toffanin, Guiseppe, *Il Cinquecento*, Milan, 1935.

Tommasini, Vincenzo, "Del drama lirico," *Rivista Musicale Italiana*. vol. XXXIX, 1932.

Trinkaus, Charles, *In Our Image and Likeness*, Chicago: The University of Chicago Press, 1970.

Valentin, Erich, "Dichtung und Oper: eine Untersuchung des Stilproblems der Oper," Archiv für Musik-forschung, vol. III, 1938.

Vasari, Giorgio, *Lives of the Artists*, New York: Simon and Schuster, 1946.

Walker, D. P., "Musical Humanism," *Music Review*, vol. 11, 1941.

_____. *Spiritual and Demonic Magic from Ficino to Campanella*, London: 1958.

_____. *Studies in Musical Science in the Late Renaissance*, London: 1978.

Walsh, W. H., "The Causation of Ideas," *History & Theory*, 1975, vol. XIV.

Weinberg, Bernard, *A History of Literary Criticism in the Italian Renaissance*, Chicago: University of Chicago Press, 1961.

Weinryb, Elazar, "The Justification of a Causal Thesis: An Analysis of the Controversies over the Theses of Pirenne, Turner, and Weber," *History & Theory*, vol. IV, 1966.

Weisstein, Ulrich, ed., *The Essence of Opera*, Glencoe: The Free Press, 1964.

White, Harrison C. & White, Cynthia A., *Canvases and Careers: Institutional Change in the French Painting World*, New York & London: John Wiley & Sons, 1965.

Whitfield, J. H., *A Short History of Italian Literature*, New York: Penguin Books, 1960.

Wimsatt, William K. and Beardsley, Monroe C., "The Intentional Fallacy," in *Problems in Aesthetics*, Morris Weitz, ed., New York: The Macmillan Company, 1959.

Yates, Frances A., *Giordano Bruno and the Hermetic Tradition*, New York: Vantage Books, 1969.

_____. *The French Academies of the Sixteenth Century*, London: Warburg Institute University of London, 1947.

Young, Karl, *The Drama of the Medieval Church*, vol. I, Oxford: 1933.

Index